ORGANIZATIONAL LIFE
ON TELEVISION

PEOPLE, COMMUNICATION, ORGANIZATION

LEE THAYER, Series Editor
University of Wisconsin, Parkside

Associate Editors

Charles Conrad
University of North Carolina, Chapel Hill

Gerald M. Goldhaber
State University of New York, Buffalo

W. Charles Redding
Purdue University

Organization ⟷ Communication: Emerging Perspectives I, edited by Lee Thayer

Organization ⟷ Communication: Emerging Perspectives II, edited by Lee Thayer

Communication and Power in Organization: Discourse, Ideology, and Domination, by Dennis K. Mumby

Studying Human Communication: Evaluating Method and Data, edited by Nancy J. Wyatt and Gerald M. Phillips

Organizational Life on Television, by Leah R. Vande Berg and Nick Trujillo

ORGANIZATIONAL LIFE
ON TELEVISION

LEAH R. VANDE BERG

and

NICK TRUJILLO

49-073

ABLEX PUBLISHING CORPORATION
NORWOOD, NEW JERSEY

Library of Congress Cataloging-in-Publication Data

Vande Berg, Leah R. (Ekdom)
  Organizational life on television.

  Bibliography: p.
  Includes index.
  1. Organizational behavior in television
—United States. I. O'Donnell-Trujillo, Nick.
II. Title.
PN1992.8.O72V36 1988   791.45'09'09355   88-7558
ISBN 0-89391-489-4 (cloth); 0-89391-567-X (ppk)

Ablex Publishing Corporation
355 Chestnut Street
Norwood, New Jersey 07648

Contents

Preface

The idea for this book has its roots in a conversation between two authors a few years ago. One author, an assistant professor of radio, television, and film at Northwestern University, was undertaking a critical study of a television program about a hospital (*St. Elsewhere*) which she believed epitomized television's "caring companies." The other author, an assistant professor of organizational communication at Purdue University, was conducting an ethnographic study at a hospital which had just developed a new corporate philosophy—a philosophy based on the value of "caring." The authors were surprised to discover that while they were conducting research in somewhat different academic areas and with different kinds of data bases, their methods and their findings were remarkably similar. That realization provided the impetus to explore collaboratively how organizations are presented on prime time television drama. And so, a few years later, the expression "We should write a book together" was brought to completion.

This book, like any book (especially a research-oriented book), is in some ways already outdated by the time it hits the market. In some of the chapters in this book, for example, we have analyzed sample weeks of television which were videotaped in 1986 and 1987. Not surprisingly, then, some of the shows we have analyzed are no longer even running on prime time television (e.g., *Hill Street Blues* and *St. Elsewhere*) while others have changed significantly since we examined them (e.g., *Cheers*). Interestingly, however, some of these programs no longer on prime time can now be seen as reruns in syndication (e.g., *Hill Street Blues* and *St. Elsewhere*) so in that sense we believe our analyses remain timely. But more importantly, we are less concerned with the idiosyncracies of the particular programs analyzed in this book and more interested in the broader values and patterns exhibited by prime time television dramas. These broader values and patterns do not change much over time and, thus, we believe our analyses remain relevant in an historical context as well. After all, as Gregory Bateson (and other scholars) have noted, the more things change, the more they stay the same.

Of course, a book is never truly the sole product of the authors. There are a number of people who have helped us along the way. Our mentors at Iowa (especially Sam Becker and Bruce Gronbeck) and Utah (especially Mike Pacanowsky and Mary Strine), both past and present, have inspired us to do our best work. Our colleagues at Northwestern, Purdue, Michigan State and, most recently, Southern Methodist universities all influenced our thinking on this book. Of course, our families (Morry, Norma, Kevin & Deb Vande Berg and Claudia & Bill Trujillo) have provided additional support. So, too, have Rory and Wrigley and our many academic and nonacademic friends whose reflections, opinions, pithy judgments and constructive critiques helped immensely. Indeed, we are grateful to many people who directly and indirectly moved us toward this project, including especially our colleagues from the summer 1986 ICA/SCA Alta, Utah, Conference on Interpretive Approaches to Organizational Communication.

Leah R. (Ekdom) Vande Berg and Nick Trujillo

Chapter 1

Television and Organizational Life

You can't eat for eight hours a day nor drink for eight hours a day nor make love for eight hours a day — all you can do for eight hours is work. (William Faulkner, cited in Terkel, 1975, p. xi)

By 1976, almost every American home had television, and that fall the average television household had a set on almost seven hours a day. (Comstock, Chaffee, Katzman, McCombs, & Roberts, 1978, p. 1)

Working in organizations and watching television are two of the most pervasive activities in America. We spend more time working than doing any other activity — with the possible exception of sleeping — and when we are not working, we are often watching television. In fact, watching television ranks third as a primary activity of American adults — right behind working and sleeping (Comstock, Chaffee, Katzman, McCombs, & Roberts, 1978; Csikszentmihalyi & Kubey, 1981). Somewhat ironically, many of the television news and entertainment programs we watch when we are not in our own organizations center on the lives of people who belong to other organizations (real or fictional). Quite simply, our work organizations and our television sets have become primary instruments for providing information, for structuring our time, for giving us grist for conversation and criticism, and for helping us identify with the social world in which we live.

The relationship between organizations and the medium of television is a powerful and complex one in contemporary society. Representatives from work organizations, especially the more visible representatives from "big business," have begun to pay closer attention to the needs and preferences of the public whose attention and dollars they hope to attract (see, for example Simons & Califano, 1979). Quite naturally, they have become dependent on television and other media to reach these varied audiences. So, too, the medium of television increasingly has been studied and understood in the context of the television industry, itself a network of organizations with varied consumers and constituencies (see, for example, Cantor, 1980; Gitlin, 1983; Turow, 1984a & 1984b). Despite the apparent interdependence of the medium of television and the world of work, however, the relationship between these two institutions has often been described as an adversarial one (see Aronoff, 1979; Sethi, 1977). Representatives of big business and of the television industry have blamed each other for a variety of social problems while outside critics have attacked them both. In short, the relationship between television and organizational life is a complex one that deserves special attention by communication scholars.

In this book, we focus on one special aspect of the relationship between television and organizational life — how organizational life is portrayed on the medium of prime time television drama. "Organizational life" is a broad term which we use to describe the occupations, industries, activities, and values as experienced by organizational members. By "prime time television drama" we mean those comedic or dramatic programs considered fictional in nature which are produced directly for network television and which are first broadcast during the evening hours when the greatest number of people are watching television (8 p.m. to 11 p.m. EST).

We direct our attention to portrayals of organizational life on prime time television drama for several reasons. First, prime time television drama is one of the most popular forms of entertainment in history. It is viewed by millions of national and international audience members across all age, racial, and socioeconomic groups (Cantor, 1980). Second, while the presentation of organizations — especially "business" organizations — on television *news* programs has generated much scholarly attention, its portrayal on prime time television *dramas* has been understudied. Although the topic has generated attention in scattered studies and essays, no one book addresses this topic in any detail. This is surprising given the fact that organizational life has become a more integral part of dramatic programming in recent years. As Sklar (1980) suggested, "The frequent appearance on prime time network television of people who work, indeed, of people in the workplace, contrasts sharply with the good old days, when we used to argue fiercely about precisely what Ozzie Nelson of *The Adventures of Ozzie and Harriet*, did for a living" (p. 19). Finally, and most importantly, we believe that prime time television drama is a far more subtle and potentially more powerful vehicle for displaying organizational life than television news and information programs. In entertainment programs, audiences watch their favorite actors *as organizational members performing organizational activities* in comedic and dramatic contexts. In news and information programs, such organizational performances are typically reported or narrated by anchors, and viewers do not actually watch organizational members enact those performances. With prime time television dramas, however, viewers watch characters perform episodes of information processing, interpersonal networking, decision making, and politicking and other types of organizational action. To the extent that television reflects and reaffirms organizational reality, these portrayals of organizational life on television drama may play a very important role in shaping our understanding and expectations of organizational America.

In the remainder of this chapter, we develop the context of this book in more detail. First, we discuss television as a mass medium of society, focusing specifically on how television reflects and shapes the organizational reality of viewing audiences. Second, we turn our attention to the organizational realities of network television since these realities influence the processes by which the contents of television programs are produced and distributed. Third, we discuss a few key studies which have examined aspects of organizational life in television entertainment programming. Fourth, we review approaches for studying organizational life on prime time television that informed this project. Finally, we provide an overview of the book, offering a brief summary of each chapter.

TELEVISION AND ORGANIZATIONAL REALITY

The relationship between television and social (and organizational) reality is, of course, dependent upon the ontological and epistemological assumptions of those who describe the relationship. Two broad positions have dominated scholarly understandings of this relationship; both are relevant to our examination of organizational life on television. The first position is that television *reflects* reality; this position is often endorsed by professional journalists who assert that television does (or should) accurately "report" the literal *facts* of the social world and also by scholars of media culture who, from different perspectives, argue that television metaphorically "displays" the social *values* of society. The second general position is that television *shapes* reality; this position is advocated by social scientists — who argue that television has "effects" on society — as well as by critical scholars — who argue that television "(re)affirms" the dominant ideologies of society. Because these various positions have relevance for the study of television's portrayal of organizational life, we turn first to a review of the general assumptions underlying both positions, then to critiques of these positions, and finally to the position we adopt in this book.

Television Reflects (Organizational) Reality

Those who have adopted a classical journalistic position have argued that television "reports" (or should report) the *facts* of social reality; they typically have rested their arguments on a notion of "objectivity," defined either in terms of accuracy and neutrality or fairness and balance. Although such a notion of objectivity has been subject to extensive criticism, especially in the academic world, this position still attracts many adherents. Professional journalists and media executives are especially fond of using such canons of objectivity to protect their authority and autonomy, to justify their coverage of the world on nightly newscasts, and to argue the importance of a "free press" in American society.[1] Such a position, then, suggests that television reflects the social facts of organizational life.

Not surprisingly, this position — that television and other mass media report social facts — has been widely challenged on a number of theoretical and practical grounds. As Theodore Glasser (1985) pointed out, this perspective with its emphasis on empirical objectivity presupposes "a belief in the separation of facts and values, a belief in the existence of a reality" (p. 58), a presupposition which has been critiqued by a number of scholars. Some critics have asserted that the idea of detached objectivity is simply untenable (Epstein, 1973; Phillips, 1977; Tuchman, 1978). These critics have argued that even though the camera "never blinks," television

---

[1] As an aside, an interesting variant of the journalistic position that televsion can accurately and objectively report reality is that television can metaphorically report reality. For example, Epstein (1973, pp. 21–23) has recounted the story of a government investigation which disclosed that CBS had created rather than accurately reported the "reality" of their 1968 documentary entitled *Hunger in America*. In the documentary's opening scene, the narrator tells the viewing audience that hospitalized babies are dying of starvation while the video shows a hospitalized baby. However, as the investigation revealed, that particular dying baby in the opening scene was the premature infant of a school teacher who had been in a car accident and was not dying of poverty-induced hunger. In defending this apparent misrepresentation to its critics, CBS advanced the argument that the media *metaphorically* mirrors reality. Indeed, Richard Salant, president of CBS News at the time, responded to congressional criticims by saying, "In that area and at that time and in that hospital, babies were dying of malnutrition."

images are not without structural bias since the camera only presents events as mediated by human operators who select the events to capture (and the manner in which to capture them) and by producers who select which events to air (and how to air them) on the nightly news. Other critics have argued that television and other media offer a highly political and partisan view of social reality, a view that is right-wing conservative, left-wing liberal, and everything in between, depending upon the critic (see, for example, Aronson, 1972; Cirino, 1971; Efron, 1971; and Keeley, 1971). We agree with the general arguments of these critics and, thus, believe that television cannot neutrally report the social facts of American organizations.

A variant of this position holds that television "reflects" (not "reports") reality, a position that we and many scholars of media culture support. From this position, television does not reflect objectively the manifest facts of social and organizational reality but rather reflects metaphorically the symbolic contents of social and organizational reality. Thus, although television cannot provide an entirely accurate or comprehensive mirror of manifest social reality, television does reflect the myths, values, and beliefs of American culture, including those related to American organizations (see Comstock, 1978; Comstock et al., 1978; Fiske, 1984; Fiske & Hartley, 1978; Gerbner, 1977; Goethals, 1981; Gronbeck, 1983; Hartley, 1982; Newcomb, 1974, 1982a). From this position, all television programs — including commercials, news stories, and prime time comedies and dramas — are cultural productions which reflect the multiple realities of the culture in which they are produced and distributed.

The position that television *reflects* the social world has led many, including business representatives and scholarly researchers alike, to pay attention to the manner in which television has portrayed organizations and organizational activities. The motivation of business representatives (e.g., Mobil Oil) to monitor the images of big business on television has been grounded largely in the classical journalistic assumption that because television *news* coverage is framed in an ethic of accuracy and fairness, *negative* news coverage of business activities will be regarded by viewers as an undistorted reflection of all businesses. Some of these same representatives also have expressed concern about negative portrayals on *prime time television drama* because they have assumed that viewers interpret television drama as an accurate mirror of organizational America. For some viewers, the distinction is admittedly blurry. During the years when *Marcus Welby, M.D.* aired weekly, for example, thousands of viewers wrote to actor Robert Young asking the "doctor" for medical advice (see Real, 1977). Indeed, Young's ethos as a doctor no doubt contributed to his appearance in television commercials endorsing a particular brand of pain-killing medicine.

Television Shapes (Organizational) Reality

Another position endorsed by many researchers and critics of television is that television *shapes* social reality for viewing audiences. On the one hand, a diverse group of social scientists (Comstock, 1978; Gerbner, 1972, 1977; Gerbner, Gross, Jackson-Beeck, Jeffries-Fox, & Signorielli, 1978; McCain, Chilberg, & Wakshlag, 1977; Rubin, 1983) have studied empirically the influence of television on society from different vantage points. Some of these researchers have studied the "effects" of television on viewers and have argued that television shapes the actions and attitudes of viewers and may even cause certain prosocial or antisocial behaviors in viewers, though the causes of such effects have remained cloudy (see Phillips & Hensley, 1984; and Vidmar & Rokeach, 1974). Other researchers have argued that television influences audiences not by causing changes in attitudes or behaviors but by generating public agendas — or, stated another way, television does not tell us what to think but does tell us what to think *about* (see Benton & Frazier, 1976; McCombs & Shaw, 1972; McLeod, Durall, Ziemke, & Bybee, 1977; Weaver, McCombs, & Spellman, 1975). Still other researchers have argued that television does not have effects on viewers but rather is used *by* viewers to satisfy certain needs and gratifications such as information, relaxation, and conversation (see Katz & Gurevitch, 1976; Robinson, 1972; Rosengren, Wenner, & Palmgreen, 1985). For all their differences, however, these researchers generally agree, as Elisabeth Noelle-Neumann (1983) summarized, "that the mass media have a decisive effect on people's conceptions of reality" (p. 157).

A second set of scholars who are more critically inclined have argued that television shapes social reality by reproducing and reaffirming the dominant ideologies of the culture of which it is a part. Indeed, many critics of television and other mass media (Becker, 1984; Garnham, 1983; Gitlin, 1983; Tuchman, 1978, 1983) have argued that the American media frame their news and entertainment programs in ways that support the dominant values of American capitalism and, in so doing, perpetuate the socioeconomic hierarchy of American society. Thus, these critics have suggested that television shapes social reality by reaffirming and reproducing the dominant (and often oppressive) ideologies of the culture. From this perspective, then, the mass media "naturalize" current social, economic, and organizational roles and attitudes such that possibilities for change are stilted if not excluded from the common view. Some of these critics, however, also have pointed out that the mass media can (indeed, must) serve an emancipatory role in the culture by deconstructing these dominant roles and attitudes and by liberating viewing audiences.

The Authors' Position

To a certain extent, we agree with both of the above sets of researchers regarding television's ability to shape organizational reality. First, we agree that prime time television drama *reflects* organizational reality, though not with the neutrality that the classical journalistic position asserts. In a very limited way, television does reflect the social *facts* of organizational life inasmuch as prime time organizations (e.g., the St. Gregory Hotel on *Hotel* and St. Eligius Hospital on *St. Elsewhere*), positions (e.g., hotel manager and bellhop, nurse and doctor), and actions (e.g., checking in hotel guests, diagnosing hospital patients) do represent the types of organizations, positions, and actions actually found in American society. Nevertheless, prime time television is "unrealistic" insofar as it overrepresents and underrepresents certain aspects of organizational life and grossly exaggerates and stereotypes other aspects. On the other hand, however, we believe that prime time television does reflect organizational life more accurately in its presentation of many social *values* of organizational America. In sum, we believe that although the social facts of organizational life are highly distorted on prime time, the social values of organizational and American life are reasonably represented on prime time.

Second, and more importantly, we believe that prime time television drama *shapes* organizational reality. Our particular position is perhaps best summarized by saying that we agree with those who argue that television is an important socializing agent which teaches audiences about social and organizational life (Comstock, 1978; Gerbner, 1977). Thus, we agree generally with Gerbner (1972) who argued that while dramatic television does not accurately represent the social world, it does teach us collective lessons about the social world, especially about social values. Janis (1980) has concurred, suggesting that television acts as a socializing agent by providing models or "scripts" of (organizational) action in society.

At the very least, then, television enables individuals to observe vicariously aspects of organizational life that they might not otherwise observe, as is the case with dramatic portrayals which feature organizational settings relatively unfamiliar to viewing audiences. Indeed, Greenberg (1980) has suggested, for example, that prime time portrayals of law enforcement provide some viewers with their first experiences with the criminal justice system. At most, then, television provides explicit models or "scripts" of appropriate and inappropriate organizational performances. In so doing, television (as a product and process of mainstream organizations) ultimately reaffirms dominant organizational ideologies in America.

We note, however, that television drama shapes the organizational realities of viewing audiences only insofar as these audiences participate in the construction of meanings as they watch prime time enactments of organizational life. We regard audiences not merely as passive receptors of television presentations but rather as active participants who do share in creating the meaning of television performances. As many scholars have observed (Goffman, 1959; Gronbeck, 1984b; Turner, 1977), one required performance of an audience *qua audience* is the willingness to suspend disbelief in the factual reality of the performance they are watching. In other words, audiences are audiences precisely because they temporarily ignore their knowledge that a television drama is not "real" but is staged for their benefit. Thus, even though we as audience members knew that the actor James Brolin was not the *Hotel* manager Peter McDermott, we were willing to "see" Brolin as McDermott if his performances as McDermott were relatively believable and if these performances fit our expectations regarding what a hotel manager does for a living. In this way, prime time television shapes our expectations of organizational life — not by providing the factual presentations of organizational life but rather by presenting plausible organizational performances which help us develop our expectations about organizational members and organizational life.

The tension between viewers' willingness and unwillingness to suspend belief in what they are watching on television helps us understand how audiences can learn about "real" organizations by watching fictional presentations of organizations which they themselves label as "unrealistic." Indeed, to call a prime time organizational performance "unrealistic" is to judge that performance against other real or fictional performances in the same category and to evaluate it as having less plausibility or verisimilitude than these other performances. It is precisely by comparing and evaluating these organizational performances that we develop a better understanding of "good" and "bad" performances and, thereby, shape our expectations about organizational life.

We believe that television, as a part of the broader social reality, cannot be studied apart from that social reality. More specifically, network television is a part of the broader reality of organizational America and thus our study of television drama should not proceed without first acknowledging the organizational realities of the television industry. In the next section of this chapter, we examine these organizational realities of network television, paying particular attention to the constraints that the television industry places on the development and distribution of prime time television drama.

THE ORGANIZATIONAL REALITIES OF NETWORK TELEVISION

As Cantor (1980) has argued, "the content of television drama represents a negotiated struggle and exchange among a number of participants: the three major networks, the Hollywood program suppliers and their creative people, the United States government (especially the Federal Communications Commission and Congress), social critics, and citizen groups" (p. 117). Indeed, television networks, like other mass media organizations, are themselves organizations with complex structures and pressures. As commercial businesses, television networks tend to pay close attention to such "bottom-line" activities as keeping production costs down and selling audiences to advertisers for the highest prices. As organizational systems in society, they tend to pay close attention to such environmental concerns as governmental regulations and public advocacy groups. In order to function as effective organizations themselves, then, television networks must deal with a number of constraints which affect the development and distribution of programs. Here we briefly consider three such constraints: (a) audience constraints, (b) political constraints, and (c) societal constraints. As will be seen, each of these constraints has an impact on the content of television drama and thus on the way in which these programs portray organizational life.

Audience Constraints of Network Television

The business factor of network television which has attracted the most attention is no doubt the audience. Network television, after all, sells its products — its news and entertainment programs—to this audience, and then sells this audience — as a mass of consumers—to advertisers. Brown (1972) put it succinctly: "Programs come into being to deliver . . . an audience to advertisers" (pp. 49–50). Networks make profits when they can charge substantially higher rates to advertisers who wish to sponsor programs which attract the largest audiences (i.e., programs which capture the highest Nielsen and/or Arbitron ratings). As Comstock (1980) summarized, "[S]ize of audience, modified somewhat by its predilection for consumption, is the determinant of profits" (p. 22).

Each network thus makes programming decisions about prime time television drama with the constant goal of reaching and keeping the largest audience. In effect, each network attempts to "win the night" in the audience ratings by setting up a schedule to maximize audience "flow" from one show to next. At 8:00 p.m., for example, shows are typically designed to lure both children and parents since it is assumed that the children are still awake and watching television at that hour. After 9:00 pm, however, shows are designed to be more "adult" since the children are assumed to have fallen asleep or to have abdicated control of the television set to their parents (Turow, 1984a). In sum, prime time television drama is designed to maximize the viewing audience and, in so doing, maximize the network profit.

The audience's "predilection for consumption," as Comstock (1980) called it, is quite important when advertisers and networks consider the audience. Indeed, the mere quantity of the viewing audience, although critical, is qualified by the demography of that viewing audience. The most attractive target audience historically has been regarded as 18- to 49-year-old individuals since this large group is presumed to have more discretionary income and more control over that income than other age groups. However, in the last several years, television advertisers (and thus television networks) have become more selective in the type of audience they wish to attract, paying particular attention to audience demographics such as gender and level of income as well as age. In fact, advertisers now examine the particular demographics of their own consumers and then select television programs with audiences who match these demographics. Thus, frequently programs like St. Elsewhere (NBC) and Hill Street Blues (NBC), which had lower ratings than many other programs, have been renewed because their audiences consisted primarily of young adult professionals who were assumed to have substantial discretionary income and whom advertisers were willing to pay more to reach (see Feuer, Kerr, & Vahimagi, 1984; Gitlin, 1983; Turow, 1984a).

Not surprisingly then, the audience has an important impact on the content of prime time television drama. Quite simply, the content of prime time programs must appeal generally to a wide audience, including viewers with preferred demographic characteristics. Thus, programs typically feature characters who reflect or attract this audience and feature more "action" (since such action is presumed to stimulate the audience's attention to the program and the advertisements). As Turow (1984a) quipped: "An 8:00 pm family adventure show must therefore have a child for the youngsters in the house to like, a good-looking male lead for women to ogle, and at least one pretty woman in tight (though not terribly revealing) clothes for male encouragement" (p. 63). As a result, many have argued that audience constraints of prime time programming have led to a relative homogeneity of content (Comstock, 1980), a general lack of innovation and creativity of content (Cantor, 1980), and a general avoidance of controversial content (Turow, 1984a).

Political Constraints of Network Television

In his book *Inside Prime Time*, Todd Gitlin (1983) has suggested that a prime time program becomes a reality only when a chain of political "ifs" are accomplished: only "*if* a producer gets on the inside track; *if* he or she has strong ideas and fights for them intelligently; *if* they appear to be at least somewhat compatible with the network's conventional wisdom about what a show ought to be at a particular moment; *if* the producer is willing to give ground here and there; *if* he or she is protected by a powerhouse production company that the network is loathe to kick around; *if* the network has the right niche for the show; *if* the project catches the eye of the right executive at the right time, and doesn't get lost in the shuffle when the guardian executive changes job" (p. 273). In other words, the *political* constraints — in particular, the politics of production — play a vital role in the development and distribution of prime time drama.

As many have argued, even though a massive interdependent group of people are involved in the production and distribution of prime time drama, a very select few determine what programs will be created and broadcast. Cantor (1980), for example, argued that even though the networks are dependent on production companies for producing a program, network executives exert a great deal of control over the production process. The networks, after all, finance the development of stories, scripts, and pilots and they decide what to broadcast, when to broadcast, and whether to continue to broadcast a program. Thus, the so-called "creative types" (producers, directors, and writers) who actually produce the content of prime time television "do not necessarily express their own values, but rather the values of those in control of the bureaucratic structures" (Cantor, 1980, p. 17). This point has been echoed by James Brooks, one of the original writer-producers for MTM. Brooks noted that as the small mom-and-pop MTM company of the early 1970s grew into a 300-person major independent production house and began producing more network series, "a subtle shift from creative people to business people" occurred in decision-making control (Kerr, 1984, p. 94).

Not surprisingly, the primary concern of those who make the television decisions is whether the show will appeal to a large enough audience to make profits and sell products. As a result, the small group of network decision makers turn to another small group of production companies with proven track records in producing popular programs (Gitlin, 1983). One result, critics have charged, is that these political constraints of prime time television often encourage the same safe, bland, and homogenized content that the audience constraints of prime time television encourage.

Societal Constraints of Network Television

It is very difficult to assess the influence that society has on the network television industry. Market researchers, for example, have tended to argue that audiences have considerable power over network television because their viewing patterns ultimately determine the content of television programs. Critical researchers, especially Marxist scholars, have taken the opposite position and have argued that audiences are powerless with regard to the media content inasmuch as the media elite and not "the public" control the technology of television (as well as the production and distribution of programming). Nonetheless, some public advocacy groups have enjoyed relative success in influencing the content of prime time programming.

Some pressure groups have been very active regarding the content of prime time television programs. Several groups, such as Action for Children's Television and the Parent-Teachers Association, who have objected to the content (e.g., the sex and violence) of television drama, have directed their pressure through governmental and regulatory agencies with relative success, at least throughout the 1960s and early 1970s. Indeed, Cantor (1980) has suggested that pressure from the above groups protesting violent content on television played a significant role in the shift in television programming from the action/adventure drama to the situation comedy in the 1970s. However, as Turow (1984b) observed, while advocacy groups who have pressured networks through governmental groups have influenced some changes in television content, that change has not always been what the pressure groups had in mind (e.g., less violent action/ adventure shows but more sexual content in situation comedies).

Other pressure groups, such as the National Gay Task Force, have also enjoyed some success in their efforts to change prime time television content by pressuring the networks themselves. Indeed, according to Montgomery (1981), the National Gay Task Force was one of the most effective and more organized special interest groups to lobby the television industry because they directed their efforts at the networks themselves — or, more precisely, because they directed constant and immediate feedback to the network broadcast standards departments which set the policies for the treatment of controversial programming.

Thus, the influence of pressure groups has had important, if uncertain and sporadic, impacts on network television content. These pressure groups, and there are many, represent highly vocal, visible, and political audience members who have attempted to change some of television's most entrenched practices and, in the process, some shared cultural myths and values. Such changes do not come easy. Indeed, as Turow (1984b) and others have summarized, television networks have generally provided noncontroversial representations of American culture despite the variety of demands and relative successes of some pressure groups.

In summary, the organizational realities of network television, including audience, political, and societal constraints, have a substantial impact on the content of prime time television drama. Of particular concern in this book is how these and other constraints affect the portrayal of organizational life on prime time television drama. What types of portrayals of organizations might attract the largest audiences? What types of portrayals of organizations might be produced given the organizational constraints of network television? And what kinds of portrayals of organizational life might be produced given the potential and actual pressure from advocacy groups, especially advocates of big business? In short, have the networks portrayed organizational life in a homogeneous, bland, and/or safe manner, as might be suggested by these constraints?

This book provides some answers to these and other questions about the portrayal of organizational life on prime time television drama. However, before we proceed with our analyses and discussions, we first review a few key studies of those who have considered the questions regarding the portrayal of "business" and "labor" on prime time television.

ORGANIZATIONAL LIFE ON TELEVISION: IMAGES OF LABOR AND BUSINESS ON PRIME TIME

As noted earlier, the portrayal of organizational life on prime time television drama is especially important because of the popularity and subtlety of the dramatic medium and because portrayals of organizations on American prime time programs have increased in recent years.[2] Despite the increasingly important role that organizational life has played on prime time television, however, there has been very little research on its portrayal on prime time television drama, with the notable exception of a group of studies which have examined the types of occupations presented on television (to be reviewed in Chapter 2) and a few key studies on the image of labor and business. Here we briefly consider these key studies on the images of labor and business on prime time.[3]

---

[2] This, however, apparently is not the case on Canadian-produced television programming. According to Gale and Wexler (1983, "Business generally does not have a very visible entertainment of 'play' presence on [Canadian-produced] television, but rather is firmly connected to information and serious [i.e., public affairs] television" (p. 23). Specifically, in their two-phase study of the depiction of private enterprise on Canadian-produced television programming on three channels (CBC, CTB, Global TV) for one week, they found that 90% of the business mentions occurred during public affairs programming. Using as their measure any verbal or visual appearance of private enterprise (including verbal or visual references to business-in-general, specific firms, industries, or business people), these researchers concluded that light entertainment, children's programming, educational, religious, advice, sports and documentary programming altogether accounted for less than 10% of the television time and items devoted to business.

[3] The portrayal of business in news and entertainment programs has been widely discussed and studied. Many scholars (e.g., Aronoff, 1979; Sethi, 1977; Simons & Califano, 1979) suggest that there exists a divisive schism between business and the news media. Some business leaders complain that the news media is simply anti-business whereas others argue that the news media is uninformed — even "primitive" in its knowledge and understanding about business and economics (Efron, 1979). *Television* news in particular has been castigated for its portrayal of business because

Machinist Union's Media Monitoring Project

In 1979, the Machinist Union, led by international president William Winpisinger, launched a multiphased project to monitor the images of unions on television news and entertainment programs. The first phase of this program involved an analysis of prime time programs including 53 series, 24 television movies, and 24 television specials. Coders for the Media Monitoring Project judged each program character on several dimensions including: (a) *character type* (major, minor, background), (b) *unionized occupation* (occupation associated with a recognized union or guild), and (c) *labor/nonlabor role* (unionized or nonunionized position). Monitors then evaluated all characters as to the frequency with which they displayed 22 personality traits (including friendliness, intelligence, seriousness, etc.). Rollings (1983) summarized the main findings of the first phase of the project: (a) "Unions are almost invisible on television," (b) "television depicts unions as violent, degrading, and obstructive," (c) "occupational

---

it is a "headline medium" (i.e., broadcast news is too brief to adequately cover business) and because it is an "entertainment medium" (i.e., news stories are designed to reach and appeal to large audiences and thus sensationalize and dramatize conflict-oriented stories in which business is often presented in a villainous light). Research by media scholars has generally supported these claims that television news presents a pretty negative and shallow image of business (see, for example, Bennett, 1981; Dominick, 1981; Dreier, 1982; Feldman & Aronoff, 1980).

Of course, media proponents have corresponding responses to these complaints and some complaints of their own. Most media proponents dismiss business complaints of anti-business bias and uniformed coverage of business news as unfounded. As Sethi (1977) has suggested, "what business people call 'bias,' media people often describe as oversensitivity to adverse news" (p. 242). Such adverse news might include, for example, reports of oil spills, lowered sales, recalled car models, etc. Media proponents also argue that business itself contributes to any inadequate coverage because business executives are generally unavailable to reporters, a point made by Lawrence (1979) who suggested that "many chief executives believe it is beneath them to talk to reporters" (p. 84).

Finally, other critics argue that the schism between business and the news media is a myth since the news media is "too soft" and overly probusiness (see Lawrence, 1979; and MacDougall, 1979). Lawrence (1979), for example, argues that because favorable stories are easier to do than unfavorable ones — in part as a result of news reporters' tendency to accept statements by business (e.g., press releases) without question — that far more favorable than unfavorable stories about business appear in the media. MacDougall (1979), too, argues that the news media do more favorable stories about business than unfavorable ones, not because they are easier to do but because the news media themselves are businesses in our capitalist system and thus realize that it is in their best interests in adopt conservative, status-quo, and pro-business stands in their portrayals of business. In sum, the relationship between business and the news media has been and will most likely continue to be a controversial one.

prevalence on television is grossly disproportionate to reality," (d) "television portrays workers in unionized occupations as clumsy, uneducated fools who drink, smoke, and have no leadership abilities," and (e) "the majority of workers in unionized occupations on television . . . are nameless, personality-less people who take orders, do their jobs, and disappear" (pp. 137–138). As Rollings (1983) concluded about the first phase findings, "television's denial of the importance of goods production and trades, which produce goods, is hazardous to the nation's economy" (p. 137).

During the second phase of the Media Monitoring Project, the Machinist Union was joined by two other international unions: the Operating Engineers and the Bakery, Confectionery, and Tobacco Workers Unions. If the first phase discovered a negative view of unionized labor on prime time, the second phase presented an even bleaker picture. Indeed, the second study, when compared with the first, revealed an equal level of union violence, degradation, and obstructiveness, a greater disproportion of union to nonunion occupations, and a lowered visibility of unions on prime time. As Rollings (1983) concluded, the second phase of the media monitoring project suggested that "labor as a whole was less smart, less brave, less hard-working, less friendly, less often leaders, less clean, less serious, less competent, less attractive, more selfish, less valuable, more militant, more violent, and more often victims than management and unorganized workers" (p. 141). Such a depiction, Rollings (1983) argued, was even more dangerous given the fact that "as the nation is faced with an even more critical need for increased goods production and efficiency in the workplace, television continues to emphasize service occupations to a degree that is even more hazardous to the nation's ability to sustain its economy" (p. 140).

The Machinist Union Monitoring Project suffered from methodological problems such as the overly subjective ratings of personality traits and the lack of attention to genre (e.g., comedy, drama) by coders. Moreover, union members themselves conducted the coding for the most part, and they constitute a group who are acutely interested and no doubt somewhat sensitive to the depiction of "their" union members. Nevertheless, this project suggested that members of organized labor unions are concerned about the depiction of their organizational members on prime time television. What is somewhat surprising (and rather ironic) is that studies of business on prime time have revealed similar concerns.

Stein's (1979) *View From Sunset Boulevard*

In his anecdotal account of life on television, Stein (1979) was one of the first to consider how different organizations and industries are portrayed on prime time television entertainment programs. Although Stein's methods were not systematic or comprehensive, his scanning of popular television shows of the late 1970s led him to conclude that "groups that might seem to some people to have leadership or power roles — businessmen, bankers, government leaders, military men, religious figures — are treated as bad or irrelevant, while underdog groups — the poor and criminals are treated as deeply sympathetic" (p. 127). Businessmen in particular, Stein argued, were presented as "dangerous, homicidal frauds, or buffoons" (p. 140). In sum, Stein argued that prime time television offers a very negative portrayal of American business.

Stein's support for these conclusions derived from brief anecdotal summaries of several prime time series episodes and from personal interviews with about 40 highly successful television writers and producers. Stein concluded from this that the negative portrayal of business organizations and their members was a result and reflection of the values that the Hollywood creative community responsible for creating these visions held about business. Stein characterized the values of this group as sentimental about the poor and hostile toward the powerful; he suggested that these values were held by the producers and writers because they were a "class that once was powerless, dominated by other classes — businessmen, heirs, and so forth — held in political thrall by an America dominated politically by small towns and their remnants, and [who] had then emerged into a position of power and influence" (p. 135). In short, Stein argued that television entertainment programs were antibusiness because the producers and writers of these programs were themselves antibusiness.

Although Stein's assertions were provocative at the time, his lack of methodological rigor prevents others from generalizing his findings beyond his limited sample. Moreover, as Gitlin (1983) suggested, Stein's ultimate conclusion that the television industry is antibusiness did not show a very sensitive understanding of the business of network television. Indeed, even though Gitlin himself agreed that television portrays business in a negative light, he argued that such portrayals are a reflection of the aesthetic conventions of television drama, not a reflection of antibusiness sentiment. Such conventions include the formulaic narrative structure of the victory of heroes over villains, villains who "are naturally going to be the individuals who have the power to hurt their victims" (p. 269). As Gitlin pointed out, big business executives simply make for good television villains. Indeed, Gitlin (1983) reminded business people who decry their images on television:

> What business chooses to forget, in short, is what the media never forget for a minute: that the media are businesses. As individuals, businessmen may crave recognition [and we would add positive recognition], but as advertisers they share with television an interest in the sure-fire audience. (p. 271)

In other words, Gitlin supported Stein's general conclusion that big business is portrayed negatively on television but he also argued that such is the case because these negative portrayals attract the audiences that television, as a big business, requires for economic success.

Theberge's (1981) *Crooks, Conmen, and Clowns*

While Stein's findings were interesting and provocative at the time, few researchers gave much credence to his findings because of the lack of methodological rigor employed in his analysis. In an effort to supply some of that rigor, Theberge (1981) and the Media Institute conducted a more thorough content analytic study to examine portrayals of business in 200 prime time entertainment episodes — four each of the 50 prime time programs broadcast during the 1979–1980 season. The Media Institute analyzed each character appearing on these shows whom they identified as "working in a business-related occupation" and coded as a "businessman." They analyzed these businessmen with respect to five dimensions: (a) *character status* (major regular, minor regular, one-shot part), (b) *occupational status* (owners and board members, executives and managers, small business owners, sales workers and other businessmen), (c) *economic status* (rich, middle class, unknown), and (d) *work context* (business, personal relations or a combination of the two), and (e) *business role* (positive — charitable, sympathetic helpful, or socially and economically productive; neutral; or negative — illegal, malevolent, foolish, greedy).

The demographic findings of the study were not particularly compelling and can be summarized briefly. Of the 200 programs analyzed, only 88 yielded characters that the researchers identified as "businessmen," resulting in a total of 118 such characters. In terms of *character status*, 46% were major regular characters, 12% were minor regulars, and 42% were one-shot characters. *Occupationally* speaking, 24% were heads of corporations, 14% were executives and managers, 40% were small business owners, 9% were sales workers, and the remaining 13% were "other" businessmen. In terms of *economic status*, 80% were coded as upper- or middle-class, though most of these characters were considered "rich."

The more important (and widely publicized) part of the study involved the analysis of *business role* — or overall portrayal — of these prime time businessmen. Theberge found that over two-thirds (67%) of all businessmen were portrayed *negatively* whereas only 25% were portrayed in a positive light; the remaining 8% were seen as neutral. Not surprisingly, Theberge reported that proportionately more guest (one-shot) businessmen (84%) were portrayed negatively, though over one-half of all continuing businessmen characters were still depicted in a negative manner (52% of the major regulars and 57% of the minor regulars). Heads of big business and "other" businessmen were most likely to be depicted as criminals (75% and 40% respectively) whereas owners of small businesses were more likely to be fools (43%); executives were more evenly spread across all negative categories. Similarly, upper-class businessmen were more likely to be criminals (55%) whereas middle-class businessmen were more likely to be fools (50%). In sum, Theberge (1981) found a very negative picture of business on prime time.

In summarizing the major findings of the study, Theberge (1981) noted that "two out of three businessmen are portrayed as criminal, evil, greedy, or foolish; almost one-half of all work-related activities performed by businessmen involve illegal acts, most big businessmen are portrayed as criminals; and television almost never portrays business as a social or economically useful activity" (p. vi). Indeed, Theberge argued that "if American business has redeeming social value, it is not visible on prime time entertainment" (p. x). And he concluded: "The business world in general is portrayed . . . as the embodiment of all that is wrong with American capitalism. . . . The interests of business are unalterably opposed to those of working people and consumers. What is good for business is not likely to be in the interest of American society" (p. 32).

Theberge's (1981) study, too, has been challenged severely on methodological grounds. Winston (1983) offered the most detailed critique when he pointed out that the Media Institute study suffered from unclear operational definitions for "business-related occupations" and "businessman," flawed procedures for identifying "economic status," a limited sample size, and simple-minded inferences about audience interpretations. Indeed, Winston flatly suggested that "since the work is so poor, it might be thought that it could be dismissed more succinctly" (p. 175). Nonetheless, he concluded his critique with the caution that "the findings have been given such wide and prestigious publicity that they could well enter public consciousness as received facts" (p. 175). In light of the continued coverage of the Media Institute's findings in the popular media (e.g., The Media Institute, 1981; Pollan, 1981; and the PBS special called "Hollywood's Favorite Heavy: Businessmen on Prime Time TV," March 25, 1987), we share Winston's concern.

In sum, those who have studied "business" on television entertainment programs have suggested that big business and business people have been portrayed in a limited and negative way. One purpose of this book, then, is to re-examine this finding in light of current television dramas as well as to examine other aspects of organizational life on television — other occupations, industries, and organizational activities — that are not exclusively representative of "business." In this sense, part of our examination of prime time organizational life is meant as a "replication and extension" of the Media Institute study (see Chapters 3 and 4).

Obviously, the three studies described above do not offer much extensive or comprehensive evidence about the portrayal of the broader pictures of organizational life on prime time television. Stein's inquiry was limited to prime time "business" portrayals and was conducted in an impressionistic manner which reflected his own biases about network television as much as it reflected network biases about big business. The Theberge (1981) Media Institute study, too, limited its concerns to "business" portrayals and, although it offered a more detailed analysis, it also suffered from the methodological limitations of content analysis in general and its application of content analytic techniques in particular. Finally, although the media monitoring project has displayed some promise for providing a more comprehensive analysis, it has been limited to prime time depictions of "labor" and also has several methodological weaknesses. In sum, we simply do not know very much about prime time television's presentations of organizational life in America.

This book provides more extensive and more comprehensive information about the presentations and portrayals of organizational life on prime time television dramas. In an effort to provide such a broader and deeper portrait of organizational life on television, we have employed multiple methodological approaches to the study of prime time television programs. In the next section of this chapter, we discuss two of the approaches that have been used to study television content in general and conclude with a discussion of the particular approaches we used in this examination of organizational life on television.

THE STUDY OF ORGANIZATIONAL LIFE ON PRIME TIME TELEVISION

This book answers two broad questions about prime time television's presentation of organizational life: (a) *What* features of organizational life are presented on prime time? and (b) *How* are these features of organizational life presented on prime time? Not surprisingly, the answers to both of these questions come from an analysis of the *content* of prime time television programming. In this section, we review two general approaches to the study of television content: (quantitative) content analysis and (qualitative) textual criticism. We describe these two general approaches and then discuss how these approaches informed our particular analysis of prime time television's portrayal of organizational life.

Content Analysis

Although television criticism has become more prevalent during the last decade, content analytic studies still dominate the research literature (see Adams & Schreibman, 1978; Holsti, 1969; Krippendorff, 1980; and Rosengren, 1981 for reviews). Content analysis is a research technique for making objective, replicable, and generalizable analyses of communications content (Holsti, 1969; Krippendorff, 1980). Content analysis is *objective* in the sense that it is, as Krippendorff (1980) argued, "fundamentally empirical in orientation" and "concerned with real phenomena" (p. 9). In other words, the phenomena under study in a content analysis (e.g. acts of television violence) are assumed to have an instrumental existence in the world independent of the particular researcher studying them. Second, content analysis is *replicable* because every step in the research process, including the inclusion and exclusion of categories for analysis, is based on explicitly apriori formulated rules and procedures. Any researcher, thus, can repeat any content analytic study by using the same rules and procedures and should find similar results. Finally, content analysis is *generalizable* to the extent that, as Holsti (1969) put it, the findings of any content analysis are not "purely descriptive" but also have "theoretical relevance" (p. 5). Along these lines,

Krippendorff (1980) argued that content analysis is generalizable to the extent that the researcher makes inferences from the content to a larger context, a context which could range from "a sender's intentions, to a receiver's cognitive or behavioral effects, to the institutions within which [the content] is exchanged, or to the culture within which it plays a role" (p. 24). Indeed, as Hirsch (1979) pointed out, the generalizability of most content analyses of media content is evidenced in the context of broader social problems — that is, media content analyses usually have focused on media presentations and portrayals of social issues such as violence, sexuality, ethnicity, sex roles, occupational roles, drug and alcohol abuse, and other social problems.

Perhaps the most notable and most comprehensive television content analysis project is the "Cultural Indicators Project" under the direction of George Gerbner (Gerbner, 1972; Gerbner & Gross, 1976; Gerbner, Gross, Elee, Jackson-Beeck, Jeffries-Fox, & Signorielli, 1977; Gerbner, Gross, Elee, Jeffries-Fox, Jackson-Beeck, & Signorielli, 1976; Gerbner, Gross, Jackson-Beeck, Jeffries-Fox, & Signorielli, 1978; Gerbner, Gross, Morgan, & Signorielli, 1980; Gerbner, Gross, Morgan, & Signorielli, 1982; Gerbner & Signorielli, 1979). For the past two decades, Gerbner and his colleagues have systematically analyzed the content of television drama and have provided information about the "geography, demography, character profiles, and action structures of the world of television" (Gerbner et al., 1977, p. 177). In general, the results from the Cultural Indicators Project have shown that the world of television has overrepresented males, professionals, whites, and the middle class (although there have been exceptions in certain categories and exceptions over time). However, Gerbner and his colleagues, unlike some content analysts, have used these data to argue that television drama functions symbolically (not literally) to teach collective lessons about society and to provide cultural indicators of society. (For a review of these studies, see Gerbner & Signorielli, 1979).

Content analytic approaches, as with all methodological approaches, have certain strengths and weaknesses. One strength of content analysis is that it is a particularly useful technique for describing and analyzing large samples of media content (and for making generalizations based on smaller samples of content). Second, content analysis is also an appropriate method for comparing the portrayal of a certain group, trait, or characteristic against a norm or standard (as in Gerbner's Cultural Indicators Project which reveals the way in which television drama over and underrepresents aspects of social reality). Finally, content analysis is an advantageous method because it is an unobtrusive one — that is, the use of content analysis to describe and measure communicative phenomena does not interfere with or influence the communicative phenomena under study, unlike other methodological techniques such as experiments or participant-observations.

Critics of content analysis, however, have argued that this method, as used by some researchers, has serious limitations. First, critics have charged that some content analysts place methodological elegance over theoretical relevance and thus provide efficient answers to unimportant questions. This criticism cautions researchers to recognize that content analysis is, in the end, only a *tool* for answering theoretically important questions. Second, critics have argued that some content analysts are overly concerned with quantification and thus assume that the *frequency* of content categories is necessarily related to the importance of those categories. This criticism suggests that content analysis may not be sensitive to the importance of unique communicative phenomena. Finally, and perhaps most importantly, critics have pointed out that because content analysts must treat their categories of content as exhaustive and mutually exclusive, they do not provide much insight into the multiple possible meanings of media content. Even when content analysts apply multiple coding systems to the same content, they often miss the complex levels and layers of meaning in the communicative phenomena they study. These and other limitations led us to adopt so-called "qualitative" methods in addition to content analysis in an effort to develop a richer picture of television's portrayal of organizational life.

Textual Criticism

Another approach to the study of television content is textual criticism. Actually, television "criticism" is best understood as an umbrella label which includes such varied approaches as sociocultural, genre, semiotic, aesthetic, psychoanalytic, rhetorical, literary, and ethical criticism, among others (for an overview, see Gronbeck, 1984a, and for a comprehensive bibliography of television criticism, see Deming & Gronbeck, 1985). We have employed a form of qualitative analysis in this book which may be best understood as textual criticism.

As used here, textual criticism is a research technique for making subjective, personal, and general analyses of media content (see Gronbeck, 1984a; Newcomb, 1982a; Rosenfield, 1968, 1974; Rowland

& Watkins, 1984). Textual criticism is *subjective* in the sense that it is not concerned with the instrumental status of communications content but rather with the symbolic meanings of that content. In other words, textual critics, unlike content analysts, emphasize the multiplicity of ways that socially constructed phenomena (e.g., the phenomenon labeled and understood as "television violence") are interpreted by members of the social world, including the social world of the researchers themselves. Textual criticism is *personal*, then, because every step in the research process is mediated by the researcher. Indeed, the critic *is* the instrument. That criticism is personal does not mean that the critic is necessarily less rigorous; however, it does mean that readers of any piece of criticism cannot (and should not) expect to replicate the procedures of the study but rather need to evaluate (or "appreciate" as Rosenfield [1974] and Wander & Jenkins [1972] have suggested) the *arguments* of the critic (see Brockriede, 1974; Conrad, 1985b; Gronbeck, 1984a). Finally, we would argue that textual criticism is *general* in the sense that any piece of criticism points toward a broader theoretical and/or interpretive context. Although some would say that critics are interested only in uncovering the unique aspects of particular texts, we believe that most critics ultimately are interested in locating those particular texts in a broader interpretive framework. Indeed, we believe, as do many critics, that every piece of criticism ought to be understood within the larger context of cultural myths and values (see Fiske, 1987; Fiske & Hartley, 1978; Newcomb, 1974, 1982a).

Horace Newcomb is perhaps the best known American scholarly critic of television texts (see Newcomb, 1974, 1982a, 1984; Newcomb & Hirsch, 1984). From his early studies of television formulas in his book *TV: The Most Popular Art* on, Newcomb's thoughtful theoretical analyses (e.g., "Toward a Television Aesthetic," 1979b), metacritical analyses ("On the Dialogic Aspects of Mass Communication," 1984), and close textual analyses (e.g., "Texas: A Giant State of Mind, 1982b) have provided important models of qualitative studies of prime time television. Newcomb's research, like that of Bruce Gronbeck (1980, 1983, 1984a), who also has influenced significantly the development of American scholarly television criticism, has revealed consistently his interest in and interpretations of the various ways that television, especially television drama, reflects the cultural myths and values of society.

As a method of analysis, textual criticism has many strengths and weaknesses. One strength is that it provides a richer analysis of the complexities of communicative texts. Indeed, one of the assumptions of the critic is that every text has multiple meanings and that every piece of criticism ought to reveal this polysemous (and often oppositional) nature of texts (Fiske & Hartley, 1978; Deming, 1985). Second, textual criticism allows the critic to be more creative with the analysis of texts and less confined to limited operational definitions of content categories. Although we do not endorse the idea that meaning mysteriously "emerges" from the text, we do believe that by conducting close and personal readings (and rereadings) of the text, the critic can offer more insightful and complete analyses. One final characteristic of textual criticism is that it requires a more powerful involvement of the reader/viewer than many methods of analysis. However, we believe such a requirement results in a more reflective reading of television and a more reflexive audience.

Textual criticism also has disadvantages. Those who adopt a more "scientific" bias have criticized textual criticism because there are no empirical tests to "prove" the validity of interpretations. However, as we indicated, criticism should be judged not by the application of empirical techniques but rather by the persuasiveness of the critic's arguments (including the nature and quality of the exemplary evidence the critic offers to develop those arguments). Still, there exist no conventional standards for assessing and evaluating the arguments of the critic. Certain evaluative terms such as "thick," "rich," and "insightful," are often invoked, but the meanings of these terms enjoy little intersubjectivity. Thus, readers of criticism rely on their own particular, sometimes idiosyncratic, standards for judging a piece of criticism. What one reader believes is an insightful powerful textual analysis another reader finds too impressionistic.

In summary, both quantitative and qualitative approaches to the study of television content have generated much research in recent years. And although there exist critics of each method, we believe there has been a maturing of attitudes in the academic literature such that one approach is not assumed to be necessarily superior to the other but rather that both approaches are regarded as complementary. Of course, there are those who say that quantitative and qualitative approaches derive from different assumptions and thus are in opposition to each other and cannot complement each other. However, others have explicitly called for using both approaches in an effort to "triangulate" the study of communicative phenomena (see Ford & Klumpp, 1985; and Halloran, 1983, for a discussion of using multiple methods). Indeed, as Pool (1959) argued some years ago: "It should not be assumed that qualitative methods are insightful and quantitative ones merely mechanical methods for checking hypotheses. The relationship is a circular one; each provides new insights on which the other can feed" (p. 192). In the spirit of Pool's suggestion, we have employed both methodological approaches in this book. It is to our particular use of these methodological approaches in this book that we now turn.

The Approaches Used in this Book

As noted earlier, we were interested in studying the content of prime time television's portrayal of organizational life and, thus, we were interested in *what* aspects of organizational life are portrayed on prime time television and in *how* these aspects of organizational life are portrayed. Toward this end, we used both content analysis and textual criticism.

We used quantitative content analysis techniques in this project (presented in Chapters 2, 3, and 4). Like Theberge (1981), the Machinists Union Media Monotoring Project, and other television researchers, we were interested in the demography of organizational life on television. Thus, we used selected category systems to code the types and patterns of occupations, industries, and organizational actions that were displayed on prime time television. Accordingly, content analysis techniques provided useful information about the types and patterns of organizational life on television.

However, we were also interested in considering *how* portrayals of these occupations, industries, and organizational actions in particular television texts enacted and reflected the organizational values of the larger culture. Specifically, we were interested in exploring how television enacted the cultural myths and values of organizational America. Thus, we also employed textual analysis in this project (presented in Chapters 4, 5, and 6). In sum, we believe that using both approaches provided a more complete and comprehensive study of organizational life on television.

The contents or texts for analysis in this book came from several sources: (a) descriptions of television programs from the past four decades, (b) two videotaped sample weeks of prime time programs, and (c) multiple videotaped episodes of particular programs. First, we used descriptions of television shows from the past 40 years. These descriptions are the only source of data about many television programs, especially early ones, and they provided data which allowed us to make some historical observations about television's portrayals of industries and to make some observations about how those portrayals have changed over the last four decades.

Descriptions of television content, although essential for historical analyses, are limited because they cannot provide a rich sense of the performances of organizational life on television programs. Thus, our second source of television content was a videotaped sample of 116 prime time television programs from the three major networks — one week from the spring of 1986 and one week from the spring of 1987. Sample weeks of television programs are often used in quantitative and qualitative studies alike because such samples provide a more complete source of television content for the researcher (including dialogue, behavior, characters, and plots) and allow the researcher to conduct more comprehensive analyses of that television content. As Newcomb and Hirsch (1984) argued with respect to television criticism: "By taping entire weeks of television content . . . we can construct a huge range of potential 'texts' that may have been seen by individual viewers" (p. 66).

Finally, in this book, we were also interested in studying certain prime time organizations in more detail. Thus, we used multiple videotaped episodes of programs featuring these organizations for further case analysis. Indeed, for serial programs, multiple programs were essential in order to follow particular plot lines through several episodes.

WHAT'S AHEAD

The remainder of this book offers five studies of the portrayal of organizational life on prime time television as well as a final chapter which summarizes the conclusions and implications of the book. In Chapter 2, we review studies of the portrayal of occupations on television, studies which have consistently found that managers, professionals, and service occupations are overrepresented on television while all other occupations are underrepresented. We then present the results of original content analyses which examined the types and distributions of industries portrayed on prime time television dramas during the past 40 years. We find that although regular viewers of television have certainly seen a great variety of industries on prime time over those 40 years, service and public administration industries have been overrepresented whereas manufacturing, construction, retail trade, and finance have been underrepresented compared to their distribution in the U.S. labor force.

In Chapter 3, we describe the results of another content analytic study of the demography of characters in organizations and the distribution of various types of organization actions (informational, interpersonal, decisional, political, and operational). We find that half of the organizational actors we see on prime time are background characters who fill professional and service occupations and that these background characters perform most of the operational (actual *work*) activities we see on prime time. We also find that most of the foreground characters fill professional, managerial, and service occupations and spend most of their organizational lives involved in information processing or interpersonal activities. In addition, we find the overall depictions of organizational characters and organizational actions on prime time are generally positive.

In Chapter 4, we focus on the managers of prime time organizational life, discussing the results of both content analytic and qualitative analyses of managerial characters and actions. We find that visiting (one-shot guest) managers are more likely to be villains than heroes and that managers in the finance industries are more likely than other managers to be seen as selfish or unfriendly. Thus, we find moderate support for Theberge's (1981) conclusions, though we find a lot more positive managers than suggested in the Media Institute analysis. Indeed, except for the few visiting and/or finance managers, most prime time managers are not crooks, conmen, and clowns but rather are heroes, helpers, and humanitarians.

In Chapter 5, we discuss the results of our qualitative analysis of organizational life on prime time. In particular, we examine six pairs of organizational values we find recurring repeatedly in prime time programming: work and play, individualism and community, success and failure, reason and emotion, youth and experience, conformity and deviance. We discuss how the oppositional tensions between these pairs of values are juxtaposed and mediated in the words and actions of various members of prime time organizations and in the plotlines which display these organizational values.

In Chapter 6, we offer brief case studies of seven prime time organizations including: Hill Street Police Station (*Hill Street Blues*), St. Eligius Hospital (*St. Elsewhere*), Ewing Oil (*Dallas*), NYC Municipal Court (*Night Court*), the Cheers bar (*Cheers*), the St. Gregory Hotel (*Hotel*), and the law firm of McKenzie, Brackman, Chaney, and Kuzak (*L.A. Law*). For each organization, we discuss the organizational characters and settings and then focus on one critical incident in the life of each organization which was particularly revelatory of the values, philosophy, and unique "culture" of each organization.

Finally, in Chapter 7, we offer some concluding observations about the nature of organizational life on prime time television. We discuss the recurring metaphors for organizational life we see on prime time television — the dominant organizational metaphor (the organization as "family") and three others (the organization as "machine," as "organism," and as "political arena"). We also discuss the "lessons" which prime time television presents about organizational life as well as other organizational lessons which we believe television does not (but should) present. We conclude with some observations about the ways in which individuals, organizations, and society can use these images of organizational life on television.

Chapter 2

The Portrayal of
Occupations and Industries
on Prime Time Television*

In this chapter, we examine the portrayal of two aspects of organizational life on prime time television drama — occupations and industries. As noted in Chapter 1, the portrayal of organizational life on prime time television drama is important because television drama *reflects* and *shapes* organizational reality. Television drama *reflects* organizational reality by revealing some of the cultural values and beliefs of organizational America. Thus, an examination of the types of occupations and industries portrayed on television (and the changes or lack of changes in those portrayals over time) can provide us with insights into social values and beliefs about occupations and industries in America (as well an overview of how those values and beliefs have changed over time). But television drama also *shapes* organizational reality by presenting viewers with visions of organizational America. Thus, an examination of television's portrayals of occupations and industries also sheds some light on the collective lessons that viewing audiences can learn about American occupations and industries from prime time television.

Media scholars have spent considerable time studying the portrayal of occupations on television. In the next section of this chapter, we offer a thorough review and critique of these occupational studies. However, while media scholars have examined occupations on television, surprisingly they have ignored the types of *industries* presented on television. Thus, the second part of this chapter presents an original analysis of the types of industries portrayed on

* An earlier (and much condensed) version of this chapter appeared in *Journalism Quarterly*, Fall 1987. That article reported a portion of the data reported in this extended chapter, but it did not include the 1984–87 industry data which is included in this chapter.

American television drama during the past 40 years. Specifically, we use a content analytic approach to examine the types of industries that have been presented on prime time television dramas, paying particular attention to how these industries have been distributed on television over the last four decades. We then compare these distributions of prime time television industries with U.S. Department of Labor estimates of American industries over that same period of time to examine how these industries have been over-represented and underrepresented on American television. We conclude the chapter by discussing the implications of the portrayal of occupations and industries on prime time television drama.

OCCUPATIONS ON PRIME TIME TELEVISION

As noted above, a substantial number of media researchers have studied the portrayal of occupations on television. The primary motive for studying such portrayals appears to be the assumption that people, especially children, learn about American occupations from watching television. As DeFleur and DeFleur (1967) argued: "Children, like adults, go to the television receiver primarily for entertainment rather than edification, but while being entertained they absorb much 'incidental' information about their society. One of the most significant aspects of such learning may be the information children [and adults] acquire concerning the labor force" (p. 778).

Below, we review some of the key studies of the portrayal of occupations on television, ranging from the early work of Smythe (1954) and Head (1954) to the more recent work of Greenberg (1980). We begin with a brief discussion of how the term "occupation" is used by these researchers, then turn to a summary of the key studies. We conclude this section with a discussion of the implications of these studies.

Occupations Defined

The term "occupation" is used by television researchers in a more precise manner than it is used in our everyday patois. In casual conversation, we generally use the term "occupation" as a synonym for "job"; thus, we describe as occupations the jobs people hold such as doctor, carpenter, secretary, and the like. This everyday usage of the term occupation, however, is not quite the same as the usage of the term in studies of occupations on television. In these studies, "occupation" is used to indicate *occupational role*, a rather specific term employed by the U.S. Census Bureau to indicate at least nine general categories of workers including the following: (a) professionals and technical workers; (b) managers, officials, and proprietors; (c) clerical workers; (d) sales workers; (e) craftsmen and foremen; (f) operatives; (g) service workers; (h) private household workers; and (i) laborers. As can be seen, this U.S. Bureau of the Census listing provides general worker categories but does not provide complete information regarding the types of businesses in which these workers perform their occupational roles.

Most researchers who have studied the portrayal of occupational roles on television have used some form of the above U.S. Census Bureau schema in order to compare the occupational role distribution on television with that of the U.S. labor force. However, each of these researchers has adapted this schema in a somewhat different way. Thus, even though most studies of occupational roles on television use some form of the U.S. Census Bureau occupational listing, we cannot compare directly the results of these studies because of the different ways these researchers have adapted the government listing to fit their own research purposes.

Previous Research on Television's Occupational Roles

As we noted above, studies on the portrayal of occupations on television have spanned four decades, from Smythe's (1954) early work to Greenberg's (1980) studies. Nonetheless, virtually all of these studies have found that professional and managerial roles have been substantially overrepresented on television whereas blue-collar occupations have been substantially underrepresented, with the exception of law enforcement workers. Although what follows is not an exhaustive review of the research in this area, it is a comprehensive review of the major North American studies that have been conducted on this topic.

Smythe (1954). One of the earliest examinations of occupations on prime time television was Dallas Smythe's New York Television Study. While Smythe's general interest was in analyzing the types of television content available and the "reality" that they represented, one aspect of his study was an analysis of occupational roles. Smythe analyzed 476 characters in 86 dramatic programs produced for television, a sample which constituted one-fifth of those dramatic programs produced for television which aired during one full week in 1953 on seven New York television stations.

Smythe found that television overrepresented those who work outside the home and underrepresented those at home and that while three-fourths of the television population was employed or employable, only two-fifths of the U.S. population could be so described. He also noted that managers, professionals, officials, proprietors, service workers, and private household workers were overerrepresented on television since together they constituted 51% of the television occupations but only 11% of the U.S. population. However, Smythe found that women workers were fairly represented since the most common occupation of women on television matched that of women in the U.S. population: 37% of the women on television and 42% of the women in the United States were housewives.

An interesting aspect of Smythe's study was the use of semantic differential scales to measure attitudes about occupational roles with respect to three dimensions (evaluation, potency, and activity). Smythe reported that although public officers, legitimate business executives, and illegal business executives did not differ on the potency and activity scales, they did differ on the evaluation scale with public officers rated higher than legitimate business executives who, in turn, were rated higher than illegal business executives. He found that farmers and farm managers, however, were rated higher on all three dimensions than were legitimate business executives. Furthermore, he found that among the professional occupational roles on television, teachers were rated as the cleanest, kindest, and fairest; journalists the most honest; lawyers the dirtiest; and scientists the least honest, least kind, and most unfair (p. 155).

Finally, Smythe examined how television's heroes and villains were portrayed on television. He found that "the average pattern of character or personality stereotype of all heroes was found to correspond closely with the values held by our culture, while that for villains was generally antithetical to those values" (p. 154). He also reported that villains and heroes were not appreciably different in terms of potency or activity attributes (a conclusion Fiske and Hartley (1978) echoed three decades later when they concluded that what differentiated law enforcement characters from criminals was not potency or activity but efficiency).

Head (1954). Another early content analytic study of television drama was published by Sydney Head in 1954. Although the focus of his study of 64 network programs televised in 1952 was not occupational roles, Head did provide some information about those roles. For example, Head reported that 75% of the fictional characters in his television sample had identifiable occupations. Head also found that of the protagonists in the programs, 24% were police and protection workers, 12% were housewives, 10% were white-collar workers, 10% were professionals, 7% were military personnel, and 7% were professional criminals. Head reported that of the antagonists in the programs, 70% were professional criminals, 5% were housewives, 5% were white-collar workers, 4% were professionals, 2% were military personnel, and 1% were police and protection workers.

When Head compared the fictional television society with "real society," he concluded that "the real population is relatively evenly distributed through the nine major occupational categories used by the U.S. Bureau of the Census; whereas 72 percent of the fictional population is concentrated in only three of these categories" (p. 188). However, although Head argued that television differed grossly from reality on the level of objective demographic norms, he suggested that "on the level of values, that difference may in itself be symptomatic of a close adherence to value norms" of society (p. 192). Indeed, Head concluded that television is socially reflective of society inasmuch as it is through such apparent "distortions" that the values of society (including highly regarded occupations) become visible.

Gentile and Miller (1961). Gentile and Miller's study of television's portrayal of working-class employees also offered some useful insights about the portrayal of occupations on prime time television. Gentile and Miller analyzed 26 prime time programs, which aired on the two most popular network stations in New York City plus the top 10 Nielson programs (21 hours total). Each program was analyzed in terms of program type, number of characters, character occupations, number of working-class characters, and characteristics of working-class characters (including ethnicity, speech style, consumption style, and roles performed).

Gentile and Miller reported that 18% of their program sample included working-class characters, although only 6% of the characters on nonquiz programs were working class. All of the working-class characters they identified in the nonquiz programs were males; they were portrayed in the following occupational roles: dock workers, factory worker, migratory worker, gardener, counterman-waiter, and bellhop. More importantly, Gentile and Miller discovered that "the gross tendency of these portrayals is mainly to convey negative images of working-class individuals" (p. 263) — for example, the waiter was stupid and simple-minded, the migrant worker was a drunkard, and the gardener's impracticality made him the butt of jokes. They concluded with a call for research into the occupational roles, social outlooks, and experiences of those who wrote scripts and/or made the production decisions that resulted in so few and such generally negative portrayals of working-class characters, a call that Stein (1979) and Gitlin (1983) addressed in part some 20 years later (see Chapter 1).

DeFleur (1964). DeFleur's seminal study of occupational roles was one of a series of studies he and his colleagues conducted on children's acquisition of knowledge about occupational roles. In this study, DeFleur analyzed 250 half-hours of television with respect to the types of occupations and background settings in which work was carried out, the interaction patterns of workers, and the characteristics of workers portrayed. DeFleur defined an occupational portrayal as "the appearance of a person on the television screen for at least three minutes performing some kind of recognizable occupational duty" (p. 61). Using this definition, DeFleur identified 436 usable occupational portrayals which he grouped into 12 occupational categories and which he then compared with data from the U.S. Census concerning the labor force. DeFleur found that nearly one-third of the televised labor force was involved in law-related occupations — either law enforcement or the administration of the law — which was a substantial overrepresentation of the U.S. law enforcement labor force. In addition, he found that professionals and managers were significantly overrepresented whereas sales workers, laborers, farm workers, and operatives were significantly underrepresented on television. For example, while nearly 33% of the male workers on television were managerial workers, only 9% of the males in the Indiana labor force held such occupational roles. DeFleur concluded that children do not acquire accurate factual information about the distribution of occupations in America from television drama.

In an analysis unique to his study, DeFleur classified the physical settings of work places as either glamorous, ordinary, or humble and analyzed the nature of the environments in which television characters were portrayed working. He found that personal servants, lawyers, and agents of performers worked in the most glamorous settings while service workers, unskilled workers, and ranchers worked in the most humble settings, a finding which he suggested might lead more children to grow up wishing to work as butlers, bartenders, and theatrical agents than as teachers, judges, or clergymen (p. 66). Overall, DeFleur concluded that television's portrayal of occupational roles was "selective, unreal, stereotyped and misleading" (p. 74), a depiction he interpreted as problematic given the "few available systematic sources of alternative or corrective information" with which children can correct these misconceptions about occupations (p. 72).

DeFleur and DeFleur (1967). This experimental study examined the level of occupational knowledge of children from ages 6 to 13 and the relationship among the level of knowledge, social characteristics (e.g., social class, sex, age), and three sources of occupational role knowledge — television, personal contact, and general cultural understanding. The authors found that role knowledge increased linearly with age and that upper- and middle-class children knew more about occupational roles than did lower-class children. They also found some gender differences in occupational knowledge derived from general cultural understandings; however, when boys and girls had the same opportunity to observe occupational roles either through direct personal contact or on television, there were no differences in occupational knowledge attributable to gender. In addition, the researchers noted that *children who watched television frequently had significantly more knowledge of occupational roles and status than did children who watched television infrequently.* The researchers concluded that "within the limits of the present samples of children and occupations, television is a more potent source of occupational status knowledge than either personal contact or the general community culture" (p. 787).[1]

Seggar and Wheeler (1973). Almost a decade after DeFleur published his landmark (1964) analysis, Seggar and Wheeler essentially replicated his study of television's portrayal of occupational roles by examining a sample of 250 half-hours of television spread among the same time periods as DeFleur's sample. Although their particular focus was the portrayal of minority members in network programming, Seggar and Wheeler did look at occupational role depictions as well. They found that 29% of all white males portrayed on

---

[1] Dominick's (1974) study confirmed the results of DeFleur and DeFleur (1967) regarding the role that televised portrayals of police, law enforcement procedures, and crime may play in children's knowledge about law enforcement. Dominick found that television did indeed appear to function as an important source of information for children concerning law enforcement. Specifically, he found a positive relationship between television viewing of crime dramas and children's beliefs that police are efficient, and their knowledge about arrest procedures and a concomitant lack of knowledge about those aspects of law enforcement (e.g., the judicial process) that television rarely focuses on.

television were depicted as physicians, police officers, musicians, servicemen, and government diplomats in contrast to the depictions of Chicanos and blacks, the majority of whom were depicted in service-oriented occupations. The occupational roles for females were even more limited. In general, the authors concluded that television does not accurately reflect the proportions of occupations in the national work force and that there was an underrepresentation of all low-prestige occupations except for those in protective services — police, private eyes, and so on. They summarized their findings by noting: "It is clear, as it was in DeFleur's 1964 study, that it would be exceedingly difficult for a viewer to obtain much accurate information about the distribution of occupations by watching his television screen" (p. 213).

   Greenberg, Simmons, Hogan, and Atkin (1980). Although several of the chapters in Greenberg's (1980) edited collection of prime time television content analyses include data concerning occupational roles, television's occupational role distribution is the focus of the chapter entitled, "The Demography of Fictional TV Characters." The results of Greenberg et al.'s analysis of a sample of 255 prime time episodes over three seasons from 1975 to 1978 confirmed earlier findings that managerial, professional, and service occupations (mostly law enforcement) were significantly overrepresented, while clerks and operatives continued to be the most underrepresented occupations on television. Although within the three-year period the authors noticed some drop in the professional occupational roles and a corresponding increase in managerial roles on television, they nonetheless concluded that "the job world on television is heavily that of professionals, managers, and service workers and the three are far more likely to be found on television than in the real world" (p. 40).

   Rondina, Cassata, and Skill (1983). In their edited book of studies on daytime television, Cassata and Skill (1983) made some noteworthy comparisons between daytime and prime time portrayals of occupations on television. For example, Rondina, Cassata, and Skill (1983) found that women on daytime as well as on prime time television were more likely to hold lower level positions and less likely to hold supervisory positions than men, but that women on daytime television were more likely to hold professional positions than were women on prime time. They also discovered that while managers were seen on daytime and prime time at twice the rate that this occupation occurred in the general population, other occupations which were underrepresented on prime time television — such as sales and crafts occupations — were entirely absent from their daytime sample. In short, Rondina, Cassata, and Skill concluded that although the content of daytime and prime time television were not exceptionally disparate, daytime television did paint a rather different picture of the occupational world than did prime time television.

Summary of Occupational Studies

As we noted at the beginning of this section, while these studies of television's portrayal of occupations share a common interest in exploring the portrayal of occupational roles on television, they have looked at somewhat different samples of prime time television programming using somewhat different occupational category schemas in different decades. Head (1954), for example, looked only at 64 made-for-television dramas complete in each episode during the 1950s — a time when dramatic anthologies, variety shows, quiz programs, and radio comedies adapted for television were among the most common types of programming. It is unclear whether Smythe looked only at episodic and anthology dramas or whether he looked only at serial drama in his 1950s sample of 86 television programs. However, sample differences, in addition to the apparently different versions of occupational role category systems led Head and Smythe to arrive at somewhat different conclusions about television's world of work in the 1950s. For example, while Smythe (1954) found that 37% of the women in his television drama sample were housewives, Head (1954) found only 10% of the protagonists and 5% of the antagonists in his sample were housewives. They both, however, reported that about three-fourths of television characters were employed, though they found that public officers (police and protection workers) were more likely to be protagonists than were white-collar workers and legitimate business executives.

The 1960 studies of occupational roles on television summarized above (Gentile & Miller, 1961; DeFleur, 1964) also examined somewhat different strips of television. Gentile and Miller excluded from their sample a number of programs which they described as "unlikely to portray workers," including variety shows, mysteries, and comedies. On the other hand, while DeFleur included comedies and varieties in his sample, he excluded from his analysis all programs which did not include people interacting in modern settings where "recognizeable occupational activities" were going on; that is, he excluded from his study cartoons, quiz programs, news programs, and historical westerns. Gentile and Miller found a higher percentage of working-class characters than did DeFleur, but most of the working-class depictions in Gentile and Miller's study appeared on quiz programs, which were not included in DeFleur's sample. Both sets of researchers did, however, agree that lower-prestige occupations (operatives, clerks, factory workers, etc.) were underrepresented and professional and managerial occupational role portrayals were overrepresented in comparison to the number of persons in the U.S. labor force engaged in these occupations.

Seggar and Wheeler's (1973) survey of occupational roles depicted on television in the 1970s utilized the same television units for the data sample as did DeFleur (1964) — half-hour segments chosen randomly from 3:30 to 11:00 p.m. weekdays and 10:00–11:00 a.m. on weekends — although it is not clear whether they replicated DeFleur's study to the point of excluding cartoons, quiz shows, and programs with noncontemporary settings. Their study discovered some increase in diversity between the 1960s and the 1970s; that is, they found more identifiable occupational roles than did DeFleur. This increase in the number of occupational roles in the 1970s may have been due, in part, to the shift in emphasis in the 1970s from certain types of programs which did not present many occupational roles (e.g., variety shows and westerns) to programs which did portray more occupational roles (e.g., comedies and dramas). Despite this apparent greater variety of occupational roles, however, this 1970 study reaffirmed the consistent pattern of television's depiction of organizational life: an overrepresentation of males in protective services (including law enforcement workers and private investigators), an overrepresentation of professional and managerial occupational roles, and an underrepresentation of low-prestige occupational roles. Greenberg, Simmons, Hogan, & Atkin's (1980) study of the depiction of prime time occupations in the latter half of the 1970s confirmed the general trends found in Seggar and Wheeler's study, with two qualifications; a noticeable drop in professional occupations and a corresponding increase in managerial positions as well as a slight increase in the number of characters with no identifiable occupation over the three-year period from 1975 to 1978.

In conclusion, despite all their differences, these various studies have reported consistent patterns in the portrayal of occupational roles on television. Virtually all of these studies have reported that professional and managerial workers are substantially overrepresented on television whereas lower status workers are substantially underrepresented on television. The one consistent exception has been the frequent portrayal of lower-level service workers who are primarily seen in law enforcement occupations. As Greenberg (1980) succinctly put it: "People . . . work on television, but the occupational diversity can fill two fingers of a glove. There are the professionals and the law-related service workers; a thumb can be added for the managerial-level job-holders" (p. 187).

Interpreting the occupational studies. While researchers and critics of these television occupation studies have consistently agreed that television does not represent accurately the number and types of occupations found in America, they have offered very different interpretations of these findings. Some of these researchers (most notably DeFleur, 1964) have been quite critical of television's apparent distortion of American occupations. DeFleur, for example, argued that such misrepresentation of occupations on television could have negative consequences on the attitudes that people, especially children, might form about future careers. As he interpreted his findings: "Television presents *least often* and *least desirable* (from a child's standpoint) those occupations in which younger viewers are most likely to find themselves later. . . . Television may be instructing children in ways that are not readily apparent even to close observers — ways that may lead to later disappointments as the individual enters the labor force" (1964, pp. 69–70).

However, Fiske and Hartley (1978) disagreed with DeFleur's interpretation of the occupational studies. Fiske and Hartley argued that the over- and underrepresentations of occupations on television do not and should not tell us about the social *facts* of society but rather about the social *values* of society. They have suggested that "when DeFleur (1964) tells us that one-third of the jobs represented on television were involved with the enforcement or administration of the law, we might better see this as a reflection of social values, not of objective social reality" (p. 24). As Fiske and Hartley (1978) concluded:

> The world of television is clearly different from our real social world, but just as clearly related to it in some way. We might clarify this relationship by saying that television does not represent the manifest actuality of our society, but rather reflects, symbolically, the structure of values and relationships beneath the surface. So the high proportion of middle-class occupations is not a distortion of social fact, but an accurate symbolic representation of the esteem with which a society like ours regards such positions and the people who hold them" (p. 24).

We are inclined to agree with Fiske and Hartley (1978). As noted in Chapter 1, we believe that television reflects and shapes organizational life by displaying and reaffirming the cultural myths and values of organizational America. Thus, we believe that television portrayals of occupations do not teach us about the actual distributions of occupations in the American labor force, but rather about the hierarchy of occupational values in American society.

However, we also wish to reiterate the idea that the content of television drama — including the portrayal of occupational roles— is always developed in the context of the network television industry. Thus, network television portrays some occupational roles more often than others — not solely because they are valued by society but also because they are valued by the networks themselves. And networks value certain occupations more than others because those occupations provide contexts for characters of dramatic programs which are situationally rich for audience entertainment and socially safe for advertiser sponsorship. Further, we must recognize and acknowledge that American businesses (via professional associations such as the American Medical Association and the National Education Association as well as lobby groups) have put pressure on the television industry to portray certain occupations and industries in certain ways (see, for example, Cirino, 1971; Levinson & Link, 1983; and Margulies, 1981).

The remainder of this chapter extends the findings of these occupational studies by examining the types of *industries* represented on prime time television drama over the past four decades. Specifically, we examine the types of industries that have been overrepresented and underrepresented on television and examine how these television portrayals have changed over time. We undertook this examination not so much to determine whether or not television has accurately represented American industries (although we do make such determinations), but rather because like Fiske and Hartley (1978) we believe that television's portrayal of industries offers clues as to the kinds of industries that society as a whole (and television as part of that whole) values. We now turn to our analysis of this industrial dimension of organizational life on prime time television.

INDUSTRIES ON PRIME TIME TELEVISION

As noted earlier, while researchers have spent much time analyzing television's portrayal of occupations, they have virtually ignored television's portrayal of industries. Thus, while we know that managers and professionals have been overrepresented on television and blue-collar workers have been underrepresented, we do not know the kinds of industries in which these television managers and professionals and blue-collar workers have worked. In short, we do not know which industries have been overrepresented and underrepresented on television and we do not know whether such over- and underrepresentations have changed over four decades of television.

In this section of the chapter, we summarize a content analytic study we conducted which answered the above questions. First, we briefly define the term "industry" as used in this study. Next, we discuss the methods we used to analyze television's industries, paying particular attention to the sample and procedures of our study. We then report the results of our analysis, with separate discussions regarding the total distributions of industries presented on television, the changes in these distributions across four decades of television, and the comparisons between television's industries and America's industries. We conclude with a discussion of the implications of these findings.

Industries Defined

In this study we defined the term "industry" as a general label for type of work setting or business establishment, a usage that is employed by the U.S. Department of Labor in its Standard Industrial Classification (SIC) System. The SIC system is a comprehensive one which includes 11 major categories of American industries including: (a) agriculture, forestry, and fishing; (b) mining; (c) construction; (d) manufacturing; (e) transportation, communications, and utilities; (f) wholesale trade; (g) retail trade (including eating and drinking establishments); (h) finance, insurance, and real estate; (i) services (including health, legal, and educational services); (j) public administration (including justice, public order, and national security); and (k) nonclassifiable industries (other). As can be seen, this SIC system differs from the occupational listings system described earlier since this SIC system provides information regarding the types of business contexts in which workers perform their jobs but no information regarding the types of jobs these workers actually perform.

The SIC system was a useful one with which to categorize the industries presented on prime time television for several reasons. First, it provided an exhaustive category schema — with over 90 specific subcategories — which facilitated coding of the wide range of businesses that have appeared on television. For example, it was a relatively simple decision to code St. Eligius Hospital (*St. Elsewhere*) as a health service industry, the bar Cheers (*Cheers*) as a retail (eating and drinking establishment) trade industry, and the Miami Police Department (*Miami Vice*) as a public administration (public order) industry. Second, because this system has been used by the U.S. Department of Labor to estimate the composition of U.S. industries, we were able to compare our sample of television industries with U.S. industries and, thus, to ascertain the types of American industries that have been overrepresented and underrepresented on television over the past four decades. In sum, the SIC system provided the most complete schema for analyzing the types of American industries portrayed on prime time television.

A Methodological Note

Sample of television content. As noted, we were interested in examining the types of industries that have been portrayed on prime time television drama during the last four decades. Given the historical nature of this question and the absence of comprehensive video libraries of television programming, we used descriptions of television content as the data for analysis. Our primary reference source was the third edition of Brooks and Marsh's (1985) *The Complete Directory to Prime Time Network TV Shows: 1946–Present,* a source which described virtually every prime time series program that aired during the last four decades through October, 1984. The *Directory* lists programs alphabetically by title and provides information regarding the network on which the programs aired, the genres of programs aired, the length of the programs, and the broadcast history of the programs. More importantly for our purposes, the *Directory* also provides a brief description of the regular characters as well as the types of businesses in which these characters worked and/or visited if those business were judged as important regular contexts for the program. We supplemented the *Directory's* descriptions with program listings in McNeil's (1980) *Total Television: A Comprehensive Guide to Programming from 1948 to 1980.*

To update our sample of 1980s programs, we used descriptions of television content found in *TV Guide* from November, 1984 through June, 1987. Like the *Directory*, *TV Guide* provides program information regarding the network, genre, and broadcast history of each program. So, too, *TV Guide* also provides descriptions of the regular characters and the types of businesses in which these characters work. However, *TV Guide* offers descriptions of programs on an *episode-by-episode* basis, including information about characters who appear as guest starts in individual episodes. In an effort to obtain data from *TV Guide* that was consistent with data from the *Directory*, we coded only the industries of the major regular and minor regular characters and did *not* code the industries of guest characters. Nonetheless, although the data from the *Directory* and *TV Guide* were aggregated to provide a more complete sample of 1980s programs, the 1980s sample may reflect a more comprehensive listing of industries.

Procedures. The authors read each entry in the *Directory* and made two general coding decisions regarding each of the business contexts listed in the *Directory's* program descriptions. First, each business identified in the program descriptions was coded into one of the 11 industrial categories in the SIC system discussed earlier. This coding decision was relatively easy inasmuch as the SIC manual included an alphabetical index of literally thousands of specific work titles precoded by the U.S. Department of Labor.

Second, we then coded each of these businesses as either primary or secondary, depending upon whether the business was described by the *Directory* as an important context for the program's actions and characters. We coded as *primary* industries those business contexts that were described by the *Directory* as central to the program. In these cases, most of the regular characters were described as members of a particular organization engaged in that type of business activity and most of the action was described as occurring in this organizational context. Indeed, in many of these cases, the titles of the programs themselves reflected the primary industry involved (e.g., *Medical Center, The Defenders, Magnum P.I.*, etc.).

We coded as *secondary* industries those business contexts that were described by the *Directory* as important but less central to the program than primary businesses. More specifically, we coded a business context as secondary in two cases: (a) when the business context was described as a regular context for program action but not a primary workplace of the regular characters, and (b) when the business context was described as a primary workplace of two or more of the regular characters but was not described as a context where much action took place. For example, the *Directory's* description of private detective programs usually included a brief mention of a bar or night club where the private detective would regularly "hang out" — as in the case with *Ace Crawford, Private Eye,* a situation comedy about private detective Ace Crawford who "hung out" with his assistant "at the Shanty, a sleazy club located on the wharf . . . where Ace's not-quite-girlfriend Luana was the featured singer" (Brooks & Marsh, 1985, p. 10). In the case of *Ace Crawford*, then, retail trade (eating and drinking establishments) was coded as a secondary industry because that business context was described as a regular context for the program's action but not a primary workplace of the regular (main) characters. To take another example, we coded advertising (business services) as a secondary business in *Bewitched* because two of the program's regular characters — "Darrin Stevens" and "Larry Tate, Darrin's long-suffering boss at the New York advertising agency of McMann and Tate" — were described as members of the advertising profession (Brooks & Marsh, 1985, p. 87); we did not code advertising as a primary business even though it is the primary workplace of these characters because the *Directory* describes most of the action of *Bewitched* as occurring in the home of Darrin and Samantha Stevens. To take a final example, we did *not* code architecture (miscellaneous services) or television station (communications industry) as secondary businesses in the program *Family Ties* because the *Directory* merely listed the occupations of family members "Elyse and Steve Keaton" in a parenthetical note — " (she an architect, he a public-TV-station manager)" — but offered no description of these business contexts nor listed any other characters in this program who worked with Elyse or Steve in these business contexts (Brooks & Marsh, 1985, p. 269).

In summary, our coding procedures were designed not to give an exhaustive listing of all of the industries that have ever flitted across American television screens, but rather to identify business contexts which have played important primary or secondary roles in shaping the actual content of the programs. This coding of the business contexts according to their primary or secondary function in a program involved more judgment on our part and, thus, was more difficult than the coding of the business contexts according to their SIC status. Not surprisingly, reliability estimates for coder agreement on these two types of coding decisions — using Scott's (1955) *pi* index — reflected this disparity: .87 for SIC industry coding and .76 for primary/secondary coding. Both of these estimates do, however, fall within conventionally acceptable standards for reliability.

In addition to these coding judgments, we also recorded information from the *Directory* regarding each program's broadcast history, including the *decade* in which the majority of each program's original broadcasts were aired. We identified the program's decade as the one in which the majority of the programs were aired on network television. For example, *Bonanza* (which first aired on 9/12/59 and which last aired on 1/16/73) was identified as a 1960s program — thus, the "Ponderosa" was listed as a 1960s agriculture and ranching industry. (Throughout this chapter, we have included the general broadcast dates of a program as it is mentioned in text for the convenience of the reader). We combined the 1940s programs with the 1950s programs because of the small number of primary and secondary business contexts used during the 1940s.

Finally, we coded the network and genre of each program. We eliminated programs which aired on the early DuMont network because of the small number of industrial contexts used in DuMont programs and, thus, we limited our analysis to those industries which have appeared on the three major networks of NBC, CBS, and ABC. With respect to genre, we coded each program as representing one of five genres: (a) comedy, (b) western, (c) action-adventure, (d) drama, and (e) other (including mystery, science fiction, etc.). We used the genre classifications used by the *Directory* and *TV Guide*, though we collapsed all "crime dramas," "courtroom dramas," "medical dramas," "newspaper dramas," and other dramas into a general drama category.

A 40-YEAR PORTRAIT OF INDUSTRIES ON PRIME TIME TELEVISION

Over the past four decades, a wide variety of industries have appeared on prime time television. Some of these industries have dominated prime time programming; others have appeared irregularly and infrequently. In this section, we discuss the results of our analysis of the industries portrayed on prime time television from 1946 to 1987. We look first at the total distribution of industries that cumulatively have appeared on television in the last 40 years. We then examine changes in this distribution of prime time industries over the last four decades. Finally, we compare this changing distribution of prime time industries over time with the changing distribution of U.S. industries.

The Big Picture: Total Industries on Television

One initial observation which deserves mention is the fact that a great diversity of industries have appeared, however fleetingly, on prime time television. Indeed, among the various business establishments featured on prime time television have been mainstream businesses such as banks (*Norby*, NBC, 1/55–4/55), law firms (*Owen Marshall, Counselor at Law*, ABC, 9/71–8/74), and department stores (*The Hamptons*, ABC, 7/83–8/83); relatively unusual businesses such as charter airlines (*The Bob Cummings Show*, CBS, 10/61–3/ 62), bodyguard services (*T.H.E. Cat*, NBC, 9/66–9/67), and Institutes of Oceanography (*Gavilan*, NBC, 10/82–3/83); and downright bizarre businesses such as floating casinos (*Mr. Lucky*, CBS, 10/59–9/60), pickle factories (*Thicker Than Water*, ABC, 6/73–8/73), and outer space garbage collections (*Quark*, NBC, 2/78–4/78). And although viewers may not have encountered an unusual business context, such as a brewery, on very many programs, we should remember that they may have watched a brewery or some other unusual business context on one program for quite some time (such as the brewery on *Laverne and Shirley*, ABC, 1/27/76–5/10/83).

Not surprisingly, though, certain types of industries have appeared more often while others have appeared less often on prime time. As indicated in Table 2.1, there were significant and substantial differences among the various industries with respect to their appearance on prime time television. Mining, construction, manufacturing, wholesale trade, and finance industries have appeared the least often of all prime time industries. Taken together, these industries have accounted for just over 5% of the total number of business contexts portrayed on television. Indeed, although some might remember that dock foreman Arnie Nuvo was promoted to the head of the Product Improvement Division of the "Continental Flange Company" (*Arnie*, CBS, 9/70–9/72) and others might remember the "Commerce Bank of Beverly Hills" and the assiduous attention its president Milburn Drysdale paid to the personal and financial interests of the bank's biggest depositors, the hillbilly Clampett family (*The Beverly Hillbillies*, CBS, 9/62–9/71), only the hard-core TV trivia buff would remember many other programs which featured these infrequent television industries. Indeed, we only found one example (and a secondary emphasis) of the mining industry (oil mining) that has appeared regularly on prime time television since 1946 — but that oil mining industry representation was Ewing Oil, perhaps the most widely known corporation on prime time television (*Dallas*, CBS, 4/78–present).[2]

Agriculture, retail trade, and transportation/communications in-

---

[2] We should point out, however, that the main emphasis in *Dallas* revolves around the finance industry, not the mining industry. Thus, *Dallas* was given a primary code for the finance industry and a secondary code for the mining industry.

Table 2.1. Total Prime Time Industries

Industry	Primary N	Primary (%)	Emphasis Secondary N	Emphasis Secondary (%)	Totals N	Totals (%)
Agriculture	36	(4)	7	(2)	43	(3.5)
Mining	0	(0)	1	(0)	1	(0)
Construction	5	(.5)	2	(1)	7	(.5)
Manufacturing	9	(1)	15	(5)	24	(2)
Transportation & Communications	47	(5)	13	(4)	60	(5)
Wholesale Trade	5	(.5)	5	(2)	10	(1)
Retail Trade	37	(4)	55	(19)	92	(8)
Finance	13	(2)	10	(4)	23	(2)
Service	387	(44)	125	(44)	512	(44)
Public Administration	343	(39)	54	(19)	397	(34)
Totals	882	(100)	287	(100)	1169	(100)

X^2=118.9, d.f.=9, p<.01. All percentages rounded off.

dustries have appeared more often on television than the above-mentioned industries but still infrequently in terms of the total television picture. However, although these industries have not been displayed with much frequency overall, some of these industries have enjoyed a lengthy prosperity in long-running popular shows. Examples have included the agriculture (and ranching) industries of The Real McCoys (ABC, 10/57–9/63) and Green Acres (CBS, 9/65–9/71), the retail restaurant business of "Mel's Diner" on Alice (CBS, 8/76–7/85), the transportation industry of the "Sunshine Cab Company" on Taxi (ABC, 9/78–6/82; NBC, 9/82–7/83) and the communications industry of "WJM Television" on The Mary Tyler Moore Show (CBS, 9/70–9/77).

We should point out that although the retail trade industry accounted for only 8% of the total industries on prime time, it has appeared rather frequently as a secondary business. Indeed, while retail trade accounted for only 4% of all primary industries, it accounted for 19% of all secondary industries. This finding is due largely to the regular use of retail eating and drinking establishments as background contexts and local hangouts in prime time programs. In fact, over 70% of all prime time retail industries have been eating and drinking establishments — such as "Arnold's Drive-In" on Happy Days (ABC, 1/74–7/84), the "Longbranch Saloon" on Gunsmoke (CBS, 9/55–9/75), and "Dino's" posh restaurant of 77 Sunset Strip (ABC, 10/58–9/64).

Finally, service and public administration industries have appeared more often on prime time television than any other industries and they have appeared frequently as both primary and secondary contexts. *Service* industries, for example, accounted for over 43% of the total primary and secondary industries in our sample and, thus, represented the largest group of business contexts seen on prime time television. As indicated in Table 2.2, a wide variety of services have appeared on prime time. The most common individual television service has been detective and protection services — television's private eyes —which represented about 20% of all services and which has been epitomized by such diverse agencies as those in *Barnaby Jones* (CBS, 1/73–9/80), *Charlie's Angels* (ABC, 9/76–8/81), and *Remington Steele* (NBC, 10/82–present). The "professional" services of health, law, education, and newspaper reporting and editing accounted for about 10% each and have been brought to our living rooms in such programs as *Marcus Welby, M.D.* (ABC, 9/69–5/76), *Perry Mason* (CBS, 9/57–1/74), *Room 222* (ABC, 9/69–1/74), and *Lou Grant* (CBS, 9/77–9/82) respectively.[3] Hotel services and amusement services (e.g., entertainment groups, dance halls, recreational facilities, etc.) accounted for 7% and 9% respectively and have enjoyed success on shows like *Hotel* (ABC, 9/83-present) and *The Partridge Family* (ABC, 9/70–8/74) respectively. The remaining 22% of the service industries included a variety of miscellaneous services such as automotive services (*Chico and the Man*, NBC, 9/74–7/78), dry cleaning services (*The Jeffersons*, CBS, 1/75–12/84), and photographic services (*The Bob Cummings Show*, NBC, 1/55–9/55; CBS, 7/55–9/57; NBC, 9/57–9/59).

Finally, although 43% of the *total secondary* industries (in Table 2.1) were service industries (125 of 288), only 24% of the *total service* industries in Table 2.2 were secondary industries. In other words, most (76%) of the total service industries have been presented as primary industrial contexts on prime time television. Indeed, 100% of the detective and protection services have been primary industries. In sum, service industries have represented the most frequent and arguably the most powerful industrial context on prime time television.

Public administration industries have also been frequent business contexts on prime time television. Indeed, as indicated in Table 2.1,

---

[3] Newspapers, of course, may be coded under several industrial classifications including manufacturing, wholesale trade, and professional services. The main emphasis of most newspaper television programs, however, has not been on the manufacturing or selling of the newspaper per se but on the writing and editing of the paper. Thus, in this study, newspapers were given a primary industrial classification of service and a secondary industrial classification of manufacturing.

Table 2.2. Total Prime Time Service Industries

Service Industry	Primary		Emphasis Secondary		Totals	
	N	(%)	N	(%)	N	(%)
Service-Private Investigation	100	(26)	0	(0)	100	(20)
Service-Hotel	27	(7)	11	(9)	38	(7)
Service-Health	49	(13)	8	(6)	57	(11)
Service-Legal	36	(9)	16	(13)	52	(10)
Service-Education	36	(9)	19	(15)	55	(11)
Service-Newspaper	34	(9)	21	(17)	55	(11)
Service-Amusement	34	(9)	11	(9)	45	(9)
Service-Miscellaneous	71	(18)	39	(31)	110	(21)
Totals	387	(100)	125	(100)	512	(100)

X^2=53.16, d.f.=7, p <.01

over one-third of all the industries ever displayed on prime time television have been public administration industries, and these industries have for the most part been presented as primary contexts for action. Not surprisingly, the most common public administration industry has been public order and safety — in other words, the police. As indicated in Table 2.3, cops clearly have dominated prime time public administration by accounting for over 50% of all public administration industries on prime time. These police organizations have run the gamut from *Andy Griffith* (CBS, 10/60–9/68) and *Barney Miller* (ABC, 1/75–9/82) to *Kojak* (ABC, 10/73–4/78) and *Hill Street Blues* (NBC, 1/81–5/87), with everything — most notably *Dragnet* (NBC, 1/52–9/70) — in between. National security accounted for the second largest number of public administration industries portrayed on television (27% of all public administration industries) and has been captured effectively by CBS on military shows such as *M*A*S*H* (CBS, 9/72–9/83), *Hogan's Heroes* (CBS, 9/65–7/71), and *Gomer Pyle, USMC* (CBS, 9/64–9/70) and spy shows such as *Mission Impossible* (CBS, 9/66–9/73) and *Get Smart* (CBS, 9/65–9/70). Finally, justice industries accounted for an additional 10% of all public administration industries and were been portrayed in programs such as *On Trial* (ABC, 11/48–8/52) and more recently *Night Court* (NBC, 1/84–present). As also indicated in Table 2.3, most (86%) of these public administration industries have been portrayed as primary rather than secondary contexts for prime time programs.

To summarize this section, over the medium's four decades, prime time television has presented a wide variety of American industries

Table 2.3. Total Prime Time Public Administration Industries

Public Admin.	Primary		Emphasis Secondary		Totals	
Industry	N	(%)	N	(%)	N	(%)
PA-Justice	29	(8.5)	10	(18)	39	(10)
PA-Public Order	185	(54)	28	(52)	213	(54)
PA-National Security	100	(29)	7	(13)	107	(27)
PA-Misc	29	(8.5)	9	(17)	38	(9)
Totals	343	(100)	54	(100)	397	(100)

$X^2 = 12.67$, d.f.$= 3$, $p < .05$

to viewing audiences. As we indicated, every category of the government's Standard Industrial Classification system has been portrayed on prime time television. As expected, however, not all American industries have enjoyed equal exposure on prime time television during its first four decades. Some industries — such as mining, construction, manufacturing, and finance — have had little exposure while other industries — most notably service and public administration — have enjoyed overwhelming exposure. Indeed, service and public administration industries together have accounted for 75% of the total industries portrayed on prime time television. However, have these industries consistently appeared on prime time over the last four decades or have they appeared primarily in certain decades? The next section considers this question.

The Changing Pictures: Prime Time Industries Across Time

As indicated in Table 2.4, the frequency with which some industries have been portrayed on prime time has changed very little over time, whereas the frequency with which other industries have been portrayed has changed markedly over time. For example, the proportions of mining, construction, manufacturing, wholesale trade, and finance industries on television have changed very little over time — indeed, there has been no more than 2% change for any of these industries between the 1950s and the 1980s. As we noted earlier, these five industries also represented the fewest number of television industries presented on prime time.

The proportions of prime time portrayals of agriculture and transportation/communications industries have also varied little over time with two notable exceptions. First, the proportion of prime time portrayals of agriculture increased slightly from the 1950s to

Table 2.4.   Total Prime Time Industries Over Time

Industry	1950s N (%)	1960s N (%)	Decade 1970s N (%)	1980s N (%)	Totals N (%)
Agriculture	8 (4)	23 (8)	7 (2)	5 (1)	43 (3.5)
Mining	0 (0)	0 (0)	0 (0)	1 (0)	1 (0)
Construction	0 (0)	3 (1)	0 (0)	4 (1)	7 (.5)
Manufacturing	0 (0)	5 (2)	11 (3)	8 (2)	24 (2)
Transportation & Communications	3 (1.5)	18 (6)	19 (6)	20 (6)	60 (5)
Wholesale Trade	1 (.5)	1 (.5)	3 (1)	5 (1)	10 (1)
Retail Trade	22 (12)	13 (5)	24 (7)	33 (9)	92 (8)
Finance	6 (3)	4 (1.5)	4 (1)	9 (3)	23 (2)
Service	77 (41)	107 (38)	160 (47)	168 (47)	512 (44)
Public Administration	71 (38)	106 (38)	112 (33)	108 (30)	397 (34)
Totals	188 (100%)	280 (100%)	340 (100%)	361 (100%)	1169 (100%)

$X^2=65.08$, d.f.=27, $p<.01$

the 1960s (from 4% to 8%), primarily due to the increased exposure of ranching in such long-running westerns as *Bonanza* (NBC, 9/59–1/73), *The Big Valley* (ABC, 9/65–5/69), *The High Chaparral* (NBC, 9/67–9/71), and *The Virginian* (NBC, 9/62–9/71). The increase in agriculture industries on television during the 1960s, however, was followed by a decrease in the 1970s to a low of 2% of the total industries, a percentage that has not significantly changed in the 1980s. In sum, it seems that when westerns dwindled at the end of the 1960s and we lost our prime time "Shilos" and "Ponderosas," agriculture's presence on prime time television waned.

Similarly, the proportion of prime time transportation and communications industries increased from the 1950s to the 1960s (from 2% to 6%); however, unlike television's agriculture industry, this increase was sustained during the 1970s and 1980s. Interestingly, though, we observed a inverse shift between the proportions of the transportation and communications industries from 1960 to 1980. In the 1960s, transportation industries represented slightly over 4% of the total television industries whereas communications industries represented only 2% — a ratio of two-to-one. During the 1960s, passenger transportation businesses — especially railroads (like *The Iron Horse*, ABC, 9/66–1/68) and stagecoaches (like *Stagecoach West*, ABC, 10/60–9/61) — enjoyed the greatest prosperity of these television transportation industries. In the 1970s, however, the proportion of transportation to communications industries leveled to nearly one-to-one as transportation industries dropped slightly and communications industries increased. The 1980s have continued this reversal pattern as communications industries have outnumbered transportation industries almost four-to-one during this decade — 1% for transportation, 4% for communications. Television's transportation industry apparently has fallen on hard times in recent years, a trend perhaps best prophesized at the end of the 1970s with the total demise of the railroad industry on *Supertrain* (NBC, 2/79–7/79). The outlook for the communications industry on prime time television, however, appears promising, particularly as television has continued to portray itself (in shows such as *Buffalo Bill*, NBC, 5/83–4/84 and *Max Headroom*, 3/87-present) and other media industries (as in *WKRP in Cincinnatti*, CBS, 9/78–5/81).

We also observed a moderate difference in the proportion of prime time retail trade industries over time. For example, retail industries accounted for almost 12% of all industries in the 1950s with such secondary businesses as the tobacco shop in *Martin Kane, Private Eye* (NBC, 9/49–6/54) and, most notably, the "Tropicana" and "Babaloo" Clubs of Ricky Ricardo in *I Love Lucy* (CBS, 10/ 51–9/61). But surprisingly, television's retail industries dropped sharply in the 1960s to 5% of the total businesses, a result we find difficult to explain. These retail industries recovered slightly in the 1970s (to 7%) with such businesses as the soda shop in *What's Happening* (ABC, 8/76–4/79) and the department store in *Rhoda* (CBS, 9/74–12/78) and rose again to 9% in the 1980s on the strength of primary businesses such as the bar in *Archie Bunker's Place* (CBS, 10/79–9/83) and the restaurant in *It's A Living* (ABC, 10/80–9/82). In short, television's retail industry seems to have recovered after an apparent recession in the 1960s.

Finally, service and public administration industries showed the most dramatic and the most interesting changes over time as they experienced an inverse shift from the 1960s to the 1980s. As indicated in Table 2.4, television's service industries increased by almost 10% during this period (from 38% to 47%) while television's public administration industries declined by almost 10% during this same period (from 38% to 33% to 30%). A closer look at these two industries reveals these differences.

Table 2.5 presents the breakdown for the service industry across the four decades. As is evident, the marked (albeit erratic) increase in service industries over time occurred primarily in *educational* services as they increased from 6% in the 1940s and 1950s and 5%

in the 1960s to 13% in the 1970s and 14% in the 1980s with the addition of such shows as *Welcome Back Kotter* (ABC, 9/75–8/79), *The Paper Chase* (CBS, 9/78–7/79), and more recently, *Head of the Class* (ABC, 9/86–present). Miscellaneous service has enjoyed a substantial and steady increase from 14% in the 1940s and 1950s to 26% in the 1980s with the addition of a wider range of contemporary business services. Finally, *health* services experienced an increase from 8% in the 1940s, 1950s, and 1960s to 16% in the 1970s with the addition of shows such as *Emergency* (NBC, 1/72–9/ 77) and *Medical Center* (CBS, 9/69–9/76). However, hospital industries have dropped a bit in the 1980s to 10%, though they remained healthy with medical series such as *Trapper John, M.D.* (CBS, 9/79–9/86) and *St. Elsewhere* (NBC, 9/82–5/88).

Despite the general increase in service industries over time, however, some service industries have experienced a decline over the four decades. Newspaper services and amusement services in particular have declined over the years, going from 1940s and 1950s proportions of 16% and 22% respectively to 1980s proportions of

Table 2.5. Total Prime Time Service Industries Over Time

				Decade					
	1950s		1960s		1970s		1980s		Totals
Industry	N	(%)	N	(%)	N	(%)	N	(%)	N	(%)
Service- P.I.	14	(18)	19	(18)	32	(20)	35	(21)	100	(20)
Service- Hotel	6	(8)	16	(15)	5	(3)	11	(7)	38	(7)
Service- Health	6	(8)	9	(8)	25	(16)	17	(10)	57	(11)
Service- Legal	6	(8)	15	(14)	18	(11)	13	(8)	52	(10)
Service- Education	5	(6)	5	(5)	21	(13)	24	(14)	55	(11)
Service- Newspaper	12	(16)	11	(10)	18	(11)	14	(8)	55	(11)
Service- Amusement	17	(22)	13	(12)	5	(3)	10	(6)	45	(9)
Service- Miscellaneous	11	(14)	19	(18)	36	(23)	44	(26)	110	(21)
Totals	77	(100%)	107	(100%)	160	(100%)	168	(100%)	512	(100%)

X^2=59.45, d.f.=21, $p<.01$

8% and 6% respectively. On the other hand, hotel services and legal services have experienced more erratic shifts which have resulted ultimately in relatively low 1980s proportions. Hotel industries, for example, increased dramatically from 8% in the 1940s and 1950s to 15% in the 1960s but have since declined to 7% in the 1980s, despite a strong showing by *Hotel* (ABC, 9/83–present). Similarly, legal services jumped dramatically from 8% in the 1940s and 1950s to 14% in the 1960s but have since declined to 8% in the 1980s, despite a very strong showing by *L.A. Law* (NBC, 10/86–present). In sum, while service industries have increased over the years, this increase has not been enjoyed by every category of service industries.

On the other hand, television's public administration industries have decreased over time, especially from the 1960s to the 1980s (see Table 2.6). This marked decrease in public administration industries has occurred primarily in *national security* industries which experienced a startling decrease from 42% in the 1960s to 20% in the 1970s as the networks phased out many of their spy shows and military shows such as *The Man From U.N.C.L.E.* (NBC, 9/64–1/68) and *Combat* (ABC, 10/62–8/67). Interestingly, however, while national security suffered this dramatic decline from the 1960s to the 1970s, *public order* industries enjoyed a marked increase over the same period, moving from 42% in the 1960s to 59% in the 1970s. This trend has continued as national security remains at a considerably lower proportion in the 1980s (19%) than during its glory years while public order continues to experience growth (63%) with strong additions such as *Hill St. Blues* (NBC, 1/81–5/87) and *Cagney and Lacey* (CBS, 3/82–9/83; 3/84–present).

In sum, the presentation of American industry on network tele-

Table 2.6. **Total Prime Time Public Administration Industries Over Time**

Industry	1950s N (%)	1960s N (%)	Decade 1970s N (%)	1980s N (%)	Totals N (%)
PA-Justice	11 (16)	9 (9)	9 (8)	10 (9)	39 (10)
PA-Public Order	34 (48)	45 (42)	66 (59)	68 (63)	213 (53)
PA-National Security	20 (28)	45 (42)	22 (20)	20 (19)	107 (27)
PA-Miscellaneous	6 (8)	7 (7)	15 (13)	10 (9)	38 (10)
Totals	71 (100%)	106 (100%)	112 (100%)	108 (100%)	397 (100%)

$X^2=25.51$, d.f.$=9$, $p<.05$

vision has not been static but rather has changed over the last four decades. Although the presentation of some industries has changed very little over time, the presence of other industries, most notably service and public administration, has changed rather dramatically over time. Not surprisingly, many of these changes in television's industrial portrait have reflected some of the changes that occurred in the American labor force. It is to a comparison of television industries and U.S. industries that we now turn.

Television's Reflections of American Industry: A 40-Year Comparison of Television Industries and U.S. Industries

Table 2.7 presents the distribution of industries that have been portrayed on television over the last four decades along with the distribution of industries that have characterized the U.S. labor force, as determined by the U.S. Bureau of Labor statistics. As is evident, television has offered pretty accurate representations of certain American industries but has underrepresented and over-represented other American industries.

The American industries of mining, agriculture, wholesale trade,

Table 2.7. A Comparison of Prime Time Industries and U.S. Industries

				Decade				
	1950s		1960s		1970s		1980s	
	US	(TV)	US	(TV)	US	(TV)	US	(TV)
Industry	%		%		%		%	
Agriculture	14	(4)	10	(8)	5	(2)	4	(1)
Mining	2	(0)	1	(0)	1	(0)	1	(0)
Construction	5	(0)	5	(1)	6	(0)	5	(1)
Manufacturing	29	(0)	28	(2)	26	(3)	22	(2)
Transportation								
& Communication	8	(1.5)	7	(6)	7	(6)	7	(6)
Total Trade	17	(12.5)	20	(5.5)	18	(9)	20	(10)
Wholesale	NA	(.5)	NA	(.5)	3	(1)	4	(1)
Retail	NA	(12)	NA	(5)	15	(7)	16	(9)
Finance	4	(3)	4	(1.5)	5	(1)	6	(3)
Service	10	(41)	11	(38)	26	(47)	29	(47)
Public	11	(38)	14	(38)	6	(33)	6	(30)
Administration								
Totals	100%	(100)	100%	(100)	100%	(100)	100%	(100)

Note: U.S. figures are taken from U.S. Bureau of Labor statistics. Public administration estimates do not include military industries. Breakdowns for retail trade and wholesale trade were not available for 1950 and 1960.

and transportation/communications have been only slightly under-represented on prime time television. The mining industry, for example, has employed very few people in the country and virtually no one on prime time television. So, too, although television highly underrepresented agriculture and transportation/communications industries in the 1950s (a decade when the cost and technology of television production encouraged television creators to emphasize relatively compact indoor contexts — such as houses, offices, and restaurants—rather than expansive outdoor contexts — such as farms and railways) these industries were only slightly underrepresented on television in the 1960s, 1970s, and 1980s. In short, television presented these industries on prime time with nearly the same proportions with which they appeared in the U.S. labor force.

Other industries, however, have been less accurately represented on prime time television. For example, television has moderately underrepresented the retail trade, finance, and construction industries and has highly underrepresented the manufacturing industry. Indeed, while the manufacturing industry has constituted less than 4% of the total television businesses in any decade since the 1950s, this industry has employed 22–28% of the actual U.S. labor force during that same period. Quite obviously, then, television's portrayal of the manufacturing industry has not reflected the manufacturing industry in America.

On the other hand, prime time television has substantially over-represented certain American industries, most notably service and public administration industries. According to U.S. labor figures, American service industries have accounted for 10% to 29% of the U.S. labor force during the last four decades whereas television's service industries have accounted for 38% to 47% of the total prime time labor force during that same period, although this discrepancy has lessened over time. Similarly, American public administration industries have consistently been overrepresented on prime time television over the last four decades.[4]

Television's overrepresentation of service and public administration industries shifted in an interesting way from the 1960s to the 1980s. As noted earlier, television depictions of service and public administration industries shifted inversely from the 1960s to the 1980s with television's service industry increasing by almost 10% during this time period and television's public administration industry decreasing by almost 10% during this same period. As the

---

[4] Note, however, that labor statistics estimates of public administration industries do not include military personnel.

Bureau of Labor statistics indicate, the U.S. labor force experienced a parallel increase in service industries during that period (from 11% to 26%) and a similar decrease in public administration industries during this period (from 14% to 6%). In sum, although American service and public administration industries remained highly overrepresented on prime time television from the 1960s to the 1970s, television's presentations of these two industries changed in the same direction (and about the same amount) as the U.S. service and public administration labor force during this same period.

A Note on Genre and Network Effects on Overall Industries

Table 2.8 presents the proportions of total (both primary and secondary) industries that have appeared on television over all decades by genre. As is clear, there have been significant and substantive differences among prime time industries with respect to the television genres in which these industries have been presented. On the whole, the industries which have appeared infrequently on television (mining, construction, manufacturing, wholesale trade, and finance) have been presented on comedies more often than any other genre, with the exception of the single mining industry which has been presented as a secondary context on the *drama* Dallas. On the other hand, the agriculture, transportation/communications, and retail trade industries have enjoyed limited appearances across all generic categories. Agriculture accounted for 23% of all westerns, a finding which is not surprising given the predominant use of ranching as an industrial context for westerns. The transportation/ communications industries accounted for 7% of all comedies, 10% of all westerns, and 9% of all action-adventures; however, the majority of individual transportation/communications industries (56% or 34 of 60) have been presented on comedies. Finally, retail trade accounted for 11% of all comedies and 10% of all action-adventure and other categories. Again, however, the majority (58% or 53 of 92) of individual retail trade portrayals appeared on comedies.

As is evident in Table 2.8, service and public administration industries accounted for a rather large percentage of all genres on television. Undoubtedly, these two industries accounted for most of the genre categories because they accounted for most of the programs on television period. However, when we consider each of these industries individually by measuring the percentage across each industry rather than down each genre, another implication is ap-

Table 2.8. Total Prime Time Industries By Genre

Industry	Comedy N (%)	Drama N (%)	Genre Western N (%)	Action N (%)	Other N (%)
Agriculture	10 (2)	6 (1)	17 (23)	10 (8)	0 (0)
Mining	0 (0)	1 (0)	0 (0)	0 (0)	0 (0)
Construction	5 (1)	1 (0)	0 (0)	0 (0)	1 (3)
Manufacturing	17 (4)	6 (1)	0 (0)	0 (0)	1 (3)
Transportation & Communications	34 (7)	7 (2)	7 (10)	11 (9)	1 (3)
Wholesale Trade	8 (2)	1 (0)	0 (0)	1 (1)	0 (0)
Retail Trade	53 (11)	21 (4)	2 (3)	13 (10)	3 (10)
Finance	13 (3)	8 (2)	0 (0)	2 (1)	0 (0)
Service	237 (51)	211 (44)	14 (19)	40 (32)	10 (35)
Public Administration	87 (19)	215 (45)	33 (45)	49 (39)	13 (45)
Totals	464 (100%)	477 (100%)	73 (100%)	126 (100%)	29 (100%)

$X^2 = 242.04$, d.f.$= 36$, $p < .01$

parent. Service industries, for example, have appeared in nearly equal proportions in both comedies and dramas, with comedies accounting for 46% (237 of 512) of all service presentations and dramas accounting for 41% (211 of 512) of all service presentations. However, the majority of public administration industries have appeared on dramas, with dramas accounting for 54% (215 of 397) of all public administration presentations and comedies accounting for only 22% (87 of 397) of all public administration presentations. Not surprisingly, action-adventure shows have also accounted for 12% (49 of 397) of all public administration industries, no doubt due to the relatively large number of action-adventure programs which have featured cops, spies, and soldiers. In sum, although these two industries dominated all generic categories because of their predominance on television, their individual presentations have had somewhat different generic casts.

With respect to network, we did not find any significant differences among the three networks in their presentations of industries ($X^2 = 22.8$, d.f.$= 18$, $p > .05$). In sum, it appears that no single network favors any particular industry as a context for prime time programming more than any other network.

DISCUSSION

Over the medium's four decades, prime time television has displayed a wide variety of occupations and industries to viewing audiences. As we indicated earlier in this chapter, all of the major occupational and industrial groups have been portrayed on prime time television and, in this sense, television has provided an incredible sampler of occupational and industrial life in America. As expected, however, not all American occupations and industries have enjoyed equal exposure on prime time television during the past 40 years. Some of these occupations and industries have been portrayed rarely and have been underrepresented on television, whereas others have been portrayed quite frequently and have been overrepresented on television.

We believe these studies of television's occupations and industries tell us at least two things about American society (and television as an institution in American society). First, these studies provide insights regarding the kinds of occupations and industries that American society values. As we argued earlier in this chapter and in Chapter 1, television portrayals of organizational life reflect (and shape) societal values about American business. Thus, those occupations and industries that are frequently depicted and/or overrepresented on television may very well be the occupations and industries that are held in the highest esteem by members of American culture or that symbolize the dominant values of American culture. Similarly, those occupations and industries that are infrequently depicted and/or underrepresented on television are more likely to be those that are not highly valued by American society.

However, as we also noted earlier in this chapter and in Chapter 1, television is an institution and commercial industry in American society such that the programming of television content is always guided by a number of business constraints, especially audience ratings. In other words, the types of occupations and industries featured on prime time television tell us at least as much about the preferences of the American television *industry* as they do about the preferences of American society. Those occupations and industries that are frequently depicted and/or overrepresented on television may be considered by the networks to provide better contexts for prime time television drama — that is, better contexts for keeping production costs down, for not offending various societal groups, and, most importantly, for attracting audiences and advertisers. Similarly, those occupations and industries that are infrequently depicted and/or underrepresented on television are more likely to be those that are judged to be ill-suited contexts for prime time television programs.

In sum, we hold that studies of television's occupations and industries tell us something about the preferences of American culture and the preferences of network television. In fact, we believe that both of these considerations, taken together, provide the best explanation for the frequent or infrequent appearance of certain occupations and industries on prime time television. Occupations and industries which are frequently displayed and overrepresented on prime time are more likely to be those which reflect widely shared cultural values and the commercial and aesthetic preferences of the television industry. Stated differently, each factor may be a necessary but not alone a sufficient condition for a particular occupation or industry to be frequently portrayed as a prime time work setting.

For example, in terms of the total industrial picture, television's service and public administration industries have been portrayed more than any other categories. And of these two large groups of industries, law enforcement, national security, and private detection businesses (in that order) have dominated our television screens. Not surprisingly, a wide variety of enduring cultural values are associated with such industries including justice, orderliness, nationalism, and the safety of person and property. Moreover, these industries also provide better contexts for television drama inasmuch as they feature physical action (especially violence) and adventure as well as interpersonal conflict and interaction, all of which can be effectively packaged in a dramatic formula and episodic format.

On the other hand, the industries of mining, agriculture, construction, and manufacturing have been infrequently portrayed and underrepresented on prime time television. In part, television's relative lack of attention to these industries, especially in recent years, may be due to the fact that these industries have relatively low status in contemporary society. Although the autonomy of agriculture and the efficiency of manufacturing and construction may be enduring cultural values, these industries lack the social status and glamour of many other industries. The lessened status associated with these industries has made them less desirable work contexts in American society (as indicated in the decline in their labor force and economic prosperity in recent times) and less desirable work contexts for prime time programs designed to appeal especially to status-conscious 18–34 year-olds with disposable incomes. These industries are also technically less desirable settings for television drama since they involve large industrial sites with individual workers engaged in relatively solitary work activities isolated from fellow employees by physical distance, sound/noise barriers, and machinery with few opportunities for interaction. So, too, these industries do not offer contexts which are normally associated with the chase scenes, shootouts, fistfights, and verbal battles that have constituted the best-selling actions of prime time entertainment.

As an aside, there do exist some industrial contexts that seem to be valued by society but that are not preferred by network television. To take two interesting examples, both the veterinary medicine and dentistry industries are generally valued in society. Nonetheless, these industries have not appeared very often on television, we suggest, because they are not particularly well-suited contexts for dramatic television. The portrayal of a veterinary medical practice necessitates the use of animals — animals who are rather unreliable actors and who do not talk, with the notable exception of "Mr. Ed." In the case of dentistry — a socially valued, if somewhat feared, profession — the work-located activities generally involve the interactions of professionals with individuals whose mouths are filled with instruments and who are generally unable to mumble more than "Mmhmm." Thus, both veterinary medical and dentistry industries present limited opportunities for character interaction and development, making them undesirable televisual narrative contexts.

This idea that the popular industries on television are those which reflect both widely shared cultural values as well as the commercial constraints of network television also helps us understand some of the changes in television's portrayal of industry over time. Indeed, changes in the distributions of prime time industries over the last four decades should reflect how the cultural values of American society and the business constraints of the television industry changed during this same period.

One illustration of this changing picture of American industry as reflected on prime time television is the case of television's shifting portrayal of the service and public administration industries from the 1960s to the 1970s. As Barnouw (1975) has argued, American society in the 1960s was very concerned with national security, a concern evidenced in media attention on the Bay of Pigs, on the Cuban Missle Crisis, on the Goldwater/Johnson campaign, and on revelations about CIA involvements in foreign coups (pp. 344–392). And, as our data indicated, this media and societal attention on national security was also found in the large number of military and espionage industries displayed on prime time during that decade.

Indeed, there were more national security industries on 1960s television than any other prime time industry during that period and more national security industries on 1960s television than during any other decade of television. Furthermore, Barnouw has argued that these prime time depictions of national security industries did not merely reflect societal concerns and values but shaped them as well inasmuch as they "provided the rationale and got Americans used to the idea" of national security activities (p. 367).

However, in the 1970s, things changed. As we noted earlier, the labor force itself changed as the number of individuals (the "baby boomers") employed in service industries — especially professional services — more than doubled while the number of individuals employed in public administration organizations significantly declined. The 1970s also constituted a decade when the Vietnam conflict ended, a failed national security effort that most Americans wanted to forget and did not want to be reminded about in too many military shows — $M*A*S*H$ being a notable exception (and though $M*A*S*H$ was presumably about the more successful Korean War, the program showed us the failure of that war, too). The emphasis in the 1970s was on putting the war — and national security industries — very far behind us and on finding well-paying jobs in the burgeoning service sector of the economy. In short, cultural values regarding national security industries and service industries shifted in opposite directions from the 1960s to the 1970s. It comes as no surprise, then, to observe that television's display of national security industries also dropped markedly in the 1970s, whereas television service industries increased, especially in the presumably more humanitarian areas of health and education.

Obviously, the appeal of national security as a televisual context for drama did not change from the 1960s to the 1970s. Military and espionage industries still provided action-oriented settings for prime time characters and plots (although there was concern in the 1970s about the violence of television drama, but that concern centered on the more urban violence of television's inner cities rather than on exotic spy violence). However, the televisual appeal of the national security industry was not a sufficient condition by itself for keeping television's national security industry on the air with the same overwhelming regularity it enjoyed during the 1960s. In short, although the national security industry may have continued to be esteemed by television networks as a dramatic context, the frequency of its appearance on prime time decreased as its esteem by the American public — the viewing audience — declined.

In conclusion, the studies of prime time television's occupations and industries summarized in this chapter provide information about the occupational and industrial universe of prime time characters and their activities. Unfortunately, these studies do not provide information about the types of organizational activities in which the characters who fill these different occupational and industrial contexts are engaged. In the next chapter, we focus our attention on the types of organizational actions that have been enacted in these occupational and industrial contexts and, thus, offer more information about the portrayal of organizational life on prime time television.

Chapter 3

Organizational Action on Prime Time

In the last chapter, we examined the types of occupations and industries that have been presented on prime time television. However, in addition to knowledge about the occupational and industrial demography of prime time television, we also need to know if these occupations and industries serve merely as background stage props for characters or if they shape the actions, especially the *organizational* actions, of these television characters. Unfortunately, after all the attention that has been paid to the occupations and industries portrayed on television, we still know very little about the kinds of actions that the characters who fill these occupations and industries engage in. As we noted, the occupation studies (as well as our own industry studies) focus on the demography of characters but not on the actions of those characters in organizational contexts. How often do these characters process information, make decisions, play politics, pursue office romances, and perform the work activities of their prime time occupations and industries? And, more importantly, *how* are these organizational actions depicted?

The answers to these and other questions about the portrayal of organizational action on prime time television have important implications for organizational America. To the extent that television helps develop, maintain, or change attitudes and expectations about organizational life, the lessons displayed through prime time organizational *actions* may be particularly powerful. Indeed, one of the advantages of television is that all actions, including organizational actions, are *performed* for viewing audiences. Thus, we actually watch characters interview for jobs, reprimand subordinates, spread rumors with peers, and use power to accomplish their own personal goals. In short, television viewers witness daily performances of successful and unsuccessful organizational action — performances which serve as entertaining parodies of their own organizational

67

lives as well as instructive scripts for how to (and how not to) enact their own organizational lives.

This chapter summarizes original research that we conducted to examine the types of organizational actions presented on prime time television. Specifically, we conducted content analyses of data collected from videotaped programs covering two sample weeks of prime time television programming for each of the three major networks during spring of 1986 and the spring of 1987. In the next section, we describe the types of organizational actions that we examined on prime time. We then define the other variables we analyzed as well as the procedures used to collect and analyze our sample of prime time television content. We then offer a detailed report of our findings and conclude with a discussion of some implications of our results for organizational America.

THE NATURE OF ORGANIZATIONAL ACTION

Although there exists no widely shared coding system for organizational action such as the SIC industry coding schema, Henry Mintzberg's (1973) well-known study of management has provided the most comprehensive typology for examining the *content* of organizational action. Mintzberg was interested in cataloging the job content of managerial activity as enacted by five chief executives whom he literally followed for one full week of work as they performed their day-to-day activities. From these observations, Mintzberg developed three general categories of managerial "roles" or organized sets of behaviors: "interpersonal," "informational," and "decisional." *Interpersonal* roles — including "figurehead," "leader," and "liaison" — were described as sets of behaviors which link directly to the manager's authority and which involve the development of interpersonal relationships. *Informational* roles — including "monitor," "disseminator," and "spokesman" — were described as sets of behaviors designed to receive and transmit relevant information to organizational insiders and outsiders. *Decisional* roles — including "entrepreneur," "disturbance handler," "resource allocator," and "negotiator" — were described as behaviors which influence organizational decisions. Mintzberg concluded that these roles formed an integrated and hierarchically related "gestalt" which served to classify the content of managerial action. Mintzberg's role sets have been empirically and critically examined (see Shapira & Dunbar, 1980; Trujillo, 1983) and have become the staple categories of management in organizational textbooks.

Although Mintzberg's (1973) three general roles offer a fairly comprehensive schema for classifying management action in particular, we felt that two other behavioral categories — political and operational — should be added to provide a more complete picture of organizational action. First, researchers have argued recently that "political" actions have been overlooked in most organizational research[1] (see Conrad & Ryan, 1985; Morgan, 1986; Pfeffer, 1981a; Pfeffer & Salancik, 1978). Such political actions involve the use of *power* to accomplish the particular interests of organizational members. Second, although Mintzberg's (1973) three roles represented *managerial* action, we were interested in *organizational* action, broadly cast. Thus, it seemed appropriate to examine as well the "operational" actions of organizational members; that is, those actions which contributed *directly* to the manufacturing of a product or the delivery of a service.

In summary, we concluded that Mintzberg's (1973) three general categories of interpersonal, informational, and decisional actions, combined with two additional categories of political and operational actions, constituted a meaningful typology of organizational action and an appropriate schema for examining organizational activities on prime time television. The categories of interpersonal and informational (and, to a lesser degree, decisional) actions are especially appropriate since television relies on the dialogue of characters to reveal organizational plots. So, too, the category of political actions is appropriate given the rise of prime time "soaps" such as *Dallas*, *Dynasty*, *Falcon Crest*, and *The Colbys* whose characters are notorious for using power to accomplish their own interests. Finally, the category of operational actions is appropriate given the ongoing (though decreasing) roles of physical (and sometimes violent) job performances by characters in crime dramas and so-called action-adventure shows such as *MacGyver* and *The A-Team*. These five categories of organizational action, thus, constituted our coding system for analyzing the content of prime time organizational life. We elaborate briefly on each of these five categories below.

Interpersonal Actions

Beginning with the so-called "Hawthorne studies" and subsequent "human relations" movement, the interpersonal nature of organizations has been cast as a dominant part of organizational life. The

---

[1] Mintzberg (1983) addressed the political aspect of organizations himself in a subsequent work.

Hawthorne studies, as interpreted by Mayo and his colleagues (see Roethlisberger & Dickson, 1939), marked an important break from so-called "scientific management" because they suggested that work was *socially* as well as economically motivated. And the subsequent human relations movement advocated what was at the time an entirely new set of assumptions including the ideas that informal groups in organizations exert an important influence on the work performance of employees and that managers who interact with their employees in caring ways may motivate these employees to work harder than managers who simply bark orders at employees (see Argyris, 1957; Likert, 1967; McGregor, 1960). Although the Hawthorne studies and human relations movement have been subject to extensive critique and revision in contemporary "human resource" approaches (see Carey, 1967; Conrad, 1985a; Franke, 1979), the interpersonal dimension remains a potent part of organizational life.

For this analysis, interpersonal actions were defined as activities which directly involved the development, maintenance, or deterioration of relationships among organizational members or between members and those outside the organization who had a specific connection to the organization (e.g., customers). Interpersonal activities did not include actions which were "purely" personal (e.g., actions in family settings that had no clear link to the organization of which those family members were a part).

Informational Actions

Informational actions also have received considerable attention in organizational literature. Indeed, it would be fair to say that traditional conceptions of "organizational communication" have been linked directly (if not viewed synonymously) with the sending and receiving of information in organizations. In fact, with the advent of "systems theory," communication was defined as the act of transferring and processing information in organizations (see Goldhaber, 1979; Katz & Kahn, 1966; Redding & Sanborn, 1964; Rogers & Agarwala-Rogers, 1976). While the infatuation with the systems perspective has cooled somewhat in recent years, most organizational communication textbooks still reflect an information processing bias and concern themselves with information processing issues such as message distortion, information over-(and under-)load, faulty feedback, and selective perception (see Conrad, 1985a; Koehler, Anatol, & Applbaum, 1981; Kreps, 1986; Rogers & Agarwala-Rogers, 1976).

Informational actions in this analysis were defined as activities which involved directly the sending or receiving of information to organizational insiders and outsiders. Once again, the information presented in the action needed to have organizational relevance such that information about the personal lives of organizational members was coded only if that information was pertinent to that member's organizational performance. Thus, informational actions included giving and getting of organizational facts (information about task assignments and organizational procedures), giving and getting feedback (information about job performance and employee development), and giving and getting explanations about organizational life (information about company values and philosophies).

Decisional Actions

Decisional actions also are an important aspect of organizational life, especially for managers (see Chapter 4). In classical models of decision making, organizational members were presumed to acquire all the necessary information needed to make informed choices, to weigh the various alternatives suggested by this information, and then to rationally select *the* alternative course of action which best accomplished the organizational goal. Not surprisingly, this classical model of rational decision making has come under attack in the past several decades. Such organizational theorists as Herbert Simon (1945) have argued convincingly that completely rational decision making and completely rational managers are mythical constructions and that most of the time organizational decision making involves finding "good enough" solutions rather than a single best solution. Whatever the case, decision making remains a key organizational activity.

In this study, decisional actions were defined as activities whereby organizational members assigned tasks, attempted to solve problems or resolve conflict, or made policy. We expected to see many mundane decisions on prime time such as the assignment of police officers, doctors, and lawyers to particular cases. However, given the dramatic nature of the television medium, we also expected to see a number of more involved decisions, especially problem solving and conflict resolution.

Political Actions

Although "power" and "control" have been staple concepts of management for some time, only recently have management and organizational researchers addressed the *political* aspects of power and control. Not surprisingly researchers have reached little consensus regarding definitions of organizational "power" and "politics." One of the earliest (and most parsimonious) definitions of politics was Lasswell's (1936) statement that politics is the study of who gets what, when and how. Since then, organizational researchers have defined politics in different — sometimes very different—ways (see Allen, Madison, Porter, Renwick, & Mayes, 1979; Burns, 1961; Harvey & Mills, 1970; Mayes & Allen, 1977; Pfeffer, 1981a; Porter, Allen, & Angle, 1981; Tushman, 1977). For example, Mayes and Allen (1977) defined organizational politics as "the management of influence to obtain ends not sanctioned by the organization or to obtain sanctioned ends through non-sanctioned means" (p. 675). Burns (1961), on the other hand, argued that politics is "the exploitation of resources, both physical and human, for the achievement of more control over others" (p. 278). Finally, Porter, Allen, & Angle (1981) defined politics as social influence attempts "that are intended (designed) to promote or protect the self-interests of individuals and groups (units) and that threaten the self-interests of others" (pp. 111–112). In short, although most definitions of politics have implied some sense of influence and self-interest, there remain considerable definitional incongruities.

In this study, political activities were defined as actions which displayed, developed, or used power to accomplish the self-interests of organizational individuals or groups and/or to hurt or harm the self-interests of other organizational members. Such activities included the everyday (and sometimes positive) organizational activities of negotiating and bargaining as well as clearly negative actions such as sexual harassment, physical threats, bribe offerings, and grandstanding.

Operational Actions

Operational activities in this study were defined as actions which directly resulted in the manufacture of the organization's product or the delivery of the organization's service. These operations include such mundane activities as food and drink deliveries and more dramatic activities such as medical surgeries and criminal arrests.

In summary, these five categories of organizational action constituted the coding system used to analyze the organizational actions of prime time workers and managers. We now describe the methods we used to collect and analyze the sample programs in which these actions were displayed and identify other variables that guided this analysis.

METHODS

In a sense, the study reported in this chapter is a "replication and extension" of the study reported by Theberge (1981). As summarized in Chapter 1, Theberge and the Media Institute content analyzed 118 characters in "business-related occupations" in terms of program status (regular, minor, one-shot series characters), hierarchical position (board member, top executive, salesperson), economic status (upper-, middle-, and lower-class), and business role (positive, negative, neutral). Each character was given a single coding judgment for each of these variables regardless of the number of different actions which the character performed. Theberge's major conclusions were that over two-thirds of all businessmen were portrayed negatively; and although proportionately more one-shot (guest) businessmen characters were portrayed negatively, over one-half of the major regular businessmen were also depicted in a negative manner (see Chapter 1).

Like Theberge (1981), we were also interested in how business workers with different character statuses and hierarchical positions were depicted on television. In this way, our study served somewhat as a replication of the Theberge study. However, our interests were much broader than were those of the Media Institute. We were not only interested in "businessmen," such as bankers and insurance agents, but we also were interested in managers, doctors, lawyers, waiters, police officers and other organizational members. More importantly, we also examined the types of *organizational actions* portrayed by these prime time members. Although Theberge suggested that most businessmen engaged in negative actions, his report provided no indication of the range, variety, and frequency of organizational actions which were interpreted as negative. Finally, unlike the Media Institute, we were also concerned with the *industrial* context (e.g., service, public administration, manufacturing, etc.), *occupational* context (e.g., managerial, professional, service worker, etc.), and *dramatic* context (e.g., comedic, serious, etc.) of organizational actions on prime time. We believed these contexts play an important role in shaping the meaning of the depiction of organizational life.

In sum, like Theberge (1981), we coded the overall functions of individual organizational *characters*, though we extended his study of businessmen to include all organizational members. However, we also coded all the *actions* of these characters across all scenes to provide a more comprehensive picture of the organizational lives of prime time organizational members. We turn now to a description of the sample and the definitions of variables, in addition to organizational action, which we employed in these analyses.

Sample

The sample for this study included 116 prime time television program episodes which covered two weeks of programming for each of the three major U.S. networks (CBS, NBC, ABC). One week included programs broadcast in spring, 1986; the other week included programs broadcast in spring, 1987. The sample was restricted to regularly scheduled prime time network programs, excluding all specials, movies, sports, and news programs. A complete list of these programs appears in Appendix A.

We should point out that it is virtually impossible to compile a complete sample week of regularly scheduled prime time network programs in one calendar week. As we gathered our videotaped sample, for example, we found some regularly scheduled programs were preempted for specials, others which had aired for several months were taken off the air before we could tape them, and some new programs appeared. When regularly scheduled programs were unavailable for videotaping during the scheduled week, we videotaped makeup episodes of those same programs at later dates. In several instances this was not possible, and in those cases we videotaped a comparable program (i.e., regularly scheduled, of the same length, belonging to the same genre, and appearing on the same network) and utilized it in our sample weeks. In short, these sample weeks were *composite* weeks, primarily but not exclusively composed of programs that aired during a calendar week. Nonetheless, we believe that this sampling procedure provided a reasonably representative sample of prime time programming.

In one sense, however, sample composite weeks of television content are never truly representative because some aspects of that content change from week to week. Thus, although the industries, occupations, and organizational positions of main regular characters do not change from week to week, the occupational and industrial credentials of the visiting characters change on a weekly basis. For example, although Rick and A.J. Simon (*Simon and Simon*, CBS) remained private detectives for several seasons, they worked for clients whose occupational and industrial affiliations changed each week. In short, the episodic nature of television drama makes a completely representative portrait of prime time content an impossibility.

Definitions of Other Variables

Depiction. Following Theberge (1981), we coded all characters and all actions according to their positive, negative, or neutral plot function. However, we expanded the categories previously developed by the Media Institute to include a general positive category — "friendly"—as well as the general negative counterpart — "unfriendly." The three depiction categories (and their subcategories) are defined below.

Positive actions were those in which characters behaved in ways which benefitted the organization and its members and/or relevant outsiders or which benefitted the broader society of which the organization was a part. Four positive categories were used to code characters' actions: charitable/philanthropic, sympathetic/helpful, socially/economically productive, and friendly. *Charitable/philanthropic* actions included behavior in which some financial resource or voluntary act was given to less fortunate characters. *Sympathetic/ helpful* actions were those which provided sympathy, advice, and other nonfinancial assistance to organizational others. *Socially or economically productive* actions included those which contributed to the organization or the larger society in a socially or economically desirable way. *Friendly* actions were those in which organizational characters exhibited behavior designed to support or affirm individuals; mere pleasantries were not coded as friendly but were coded as neutral.

Negative actions were those in which characters behaved in ways which hurt the organization or its members and/or relevant outsiders or which harmed the broader society of which the organization was a part. Five negative categories were used to code characters' actions: illegal, malevolent, foolish, greedy/selfish, and unfriendly. *Illegal* actions were those organizational behaviors which violated federal or state laws and included such acts as theft, blackmail, murder. *Malevolent* actions were those organizational behaviors in which organizational members or outsiders attempted to intentionally hurt the physical, emotional, or economical well-being of other characters. *Foolish* acts included organizational behaviors that were depicted as stupid or socially inappropriate. *Greedy or selfish* actions were those organizational behaviors in which the character sought to maximize his or her own interests without regard for other characters. *Unfriendly* actions were those organizational behaviors in which characters insulted or hurt others in their interactions.

Neutral organizational actions were those with no discernible positive or negative function. This category served as an "other" category within which were placed actions that could not be identified as positive or negative. Many of these neutral actions were the "operational" actions of characters simply doing their jobs (answering telephones, arresting suspects, serving food).

Industry. We coded every character and action as representative of a particular industry. As in Chapter 2, we used the Standard Industrial Classification schema to code industry. This scheme is a comprehensive one used by the U.S. Government to classify all legal industries including: (a) Agriculture, (b) Mining, (c) Construction, (d) Manufacturing, (e) Transportation and Communications, (f) Wholesale Trade, (g) Retail Trade, (h) Finance, (i) Service, (j) Public Administration, (k) Other (illegal or nonidentifiable industry).

Occupational role. The classification schema used to code characters occupations was adapted from the U.S. Bureau of the Census. Following the examples of Greenberg (1980), Cassata and Skill (1983), and others, we also added quasioccupational categories to account for characters whose primary occupational function was not recognized by the U.S. coding system (i.e., student, lawbreaker, customer/patient). In sum, the coding system we used to code occupations including the following categories: (a) Professional, (b) Managerial, (c) Clerical, (d) Sales, (e) Craftsperson, (f) Operative, (g) Service, (h) Homemaker, (i) Private Household, (j) Laborer, (k) Student, (l) Retired, (m) Unemployed, (n) Lawbreaker, (o) Customer/Patient/Client, (p) Military, and (q) Other (unidentifiable).

Hierarchical position. Hierarchical position was defined as the character's formal position in his or her organization. We combined the exclusively managerial typology of some management scholars (e.g., Hellriegel & Slocum, 1985) with broader typologies of other organizational scholars (e.g., England, 1967a) to code the presence of characters in a variety of hierarchical positions. For example, we coded two levels of "professional staff" to account for the hierarchical differences of certain professional groups (e.g., doctors vs. nurses, detectives vs. patrol officers). Thus, the 11 categories we employed to code hierarchical position included: (a) Board Member/CEO, (b) Executive/Top Manager, (c) Middle Manager, (d) First Line Manager, (e) Professional Staff — Upper, (f) Professional Staff —

Lower, (g) Staff, (h) Laborers, (i) Customer/Patients, (j) Owner of Small Business/Self-Employed, and (k) Other (not identifiable).

Character type. Theberge (1981) and the Media Institute identified and coded only those "businessmen" who had a "specified plot function"; they did not code characters who were "merely part of the setting" (p.3). They coded these "businessmen" as one of three types: main regular, minor regular, and single appearance. We coded these three character types but also coded characters with identifiable occupations and positions who were merely part of the scene in an effort to obtain a more comprehensive picture of prime time organizations. Thus, the categories used for character type included: (a) Major-Regular (star characters who appeared regularly in program episodes and held major speaking and action roles), (b) Minor-Regular (secondary characters who appeared regularly in program episodes but who held minor speaking and action roles), (c) Major-Single Appearance (guest characters appearing in a single episode of the program but who had important plot functions), (d) Minor-Single Appearance (*background* characters appearing in a single episode of the program but who appeared in very few scenes and who did not have many, if any, speaking parts).

Genre. Genre was defined as the broad televisual form which framed the program narrative. We believed that genre is an important variable because genre contextualizes the meaning of all organizational characters and actions. We employed five genre categories: (a) Comedy, (b) Drama, (c) Western, (d) Action-adventure, and (e) Other (including mystery, science fiction, and the recent "comedy-drama"). We relied on *TV Guide* classifications of genre in an effort to maintain a consistent coding, although we placed "crime dramas," "legal dramas," and "medical dramas" in a single general drama category. We found no westerns in our sample so ultimately our analysis was limited to the other four genres.

Dramatic tone. Dramatic tone was defined as the literary backdrop against which the attitude of the "author" (i.e., writer, director, producer, etc.) toward the characters and their actions was presented. Dramatic tone, like genre, also contextualizes the meaning of organizational characters and actions. Actions were coded as *comedic* when the characters and their behaviors were intended to be funny or frivolous to the viewing audience. Usually such a comedic tone was indicated by the presence of a laugh track or lighthearted music. Actions were defined as *serious* when the characters and their behaviors were intended *not* to be viewed as funny or amusing or when these characters were presented in a sober or solemn manner. Finally, organizational actions were defined as *comedic and serious* when characters and their behaviors could not be coded as purely comedic or serious but had elements of both comedy and seriousness.

Coding Procedures

Coding of characters. After viewing the entire program, the authors coded each individual character on all of the variables described above. First, the demographic attributes of each character were coded in terms of the character type, industry, occupation, and hierarchical position that he or she represented in the episode. Then, each character was assigned a code for the type of organizational action (or function) which best typified his or her overall performance in the episode as well as a code for the overall depiction and dramatic tone of that performance. This coding procedure offered information about the most important and most apparent classification for each character and was consistent with most studies of television content (Theberge, 1981; Greenberg, 1980).

This character coding procedure was not without problems (nor was it as easy a task as readers have been led to believe in the methods sections of many content analyses — including those of Theberge, 1981, and Greenberg, 1980). After all, over the course of an episode, characters engaged in multiple types of activities that were depicted in various ways (e.g., some positive, some negative) and in various dramatic tones. And on some occasions, a character's industry, occupation, and/or hierarchical position even changed during an episode. So, too, the use of overall coding treated all characters as equal (each received one code for each variable — a procedure which ignored the fact that some characters appeared often in an episode, served many roles, and had a more dominant and pervasive organizational presence while other characters were seen in few (even single) scenes. These disadvantages of the overall character coding led us also to code each character's actions on a scene-by-scene basis.

Coding of actions. In addition to the overall coding of each character noted above, then, we also coded every action on each of the variables on a scene-by-scene basis. Specifically, we assigned a code for every action which had a separate organizational function or which was performed in a separate scene (i.e., when the setting changed, when new characters entered a scene and the action changed, or when the actions within a scene changed). We did *not* code as separate actions those extended series of activities in which characters performed the same function over a period of time, even in different contexts (e.g., the long chase scenes in police and private eye shows). In this sense, our coding of separate actions in separate scenes was consistent with the procedures of media researchers who have studied such prime time behaviors as problem solving, antisocial behaviors, and illness treatments (see Cassata & Skill, 1983; Selnow, 1986; Turow & Coe, 1985).

The advantage of coding actions across all scenes was that we derived a comprehensive measure of the total number and types of organizational actions performed over the course of an episode. So, too, this coding procedure offered a more sensitive measure of the changes experienced by each character. One disadvantage of this coding procedures was that it artificially inflated the number of industries, occupations, and positions presented in the program. We are careful to note the impact of these two coding procedures as we discuss our findings.

Reliability estimates for *character* coding agreement, using Scott's *pi* index, were as follows for each variable: genre, .96; dramatic tone, .92; character type, .89; industry, .87; occupation, .84; hierarchical position, .81; organizational function, .76; and depiction, .74. Reliability estimates for *action* coding agreement, again using Scott's *pi*, were as follows for each variable: genre, .93; dramatic tone, .89; character type, .85; industry, .84; occupation, .82; hierarchical position, .79; organizational function, .79; and depiction, .71.[2] In general, coders enjoyed more agreement on character judgments than on action judgments since each coding inconsistency for character coding was magnified with the change in unitizing to action coding. Nonetheless, these estimates fall within conventionally accepted standards for reliability.

FINDINGS

Of the 116 prime time episodes viewed, 115 contained at least one character with an identifiable occupation, position, or industry who performed an organizational action in at least one scene. Even most of the domestic comedies coded, such as *Cosby* (NBC) and *Family Ties* (NBC), had at least one character who could be coded as a "homemaker" performing homemaker actions or as a "student"

[2] Reliability estimates for the general categories of depiction were .92 for character coding and .88 for actions coding. Thus, the coders were more likely to agree on the general judgment of an act or character as good, bad, or neutral but were less likely to agree on the specific type of good or bad depiction. Nonetheless, the estimates still fall within acceptable ranges.

performing student actions. Although these characters stretched the traditional conception of "organizational" members, we sought to provide as comprehensive an analysis of organizational action as possible. We hasten to note, however, that the domestic comedies which took place entirely in the context of the home produced very few characters and actions (and sometimes only a single code for the entire episode).[3]

The total number of *characters* coded was 1,944; the total number of *actions* performed by these characters was 7,601. Of these 1,944 characters, 19% were major regulars, 13% were minor regulars, 19% appeared in a single episode, and 49% were background characters.[4] In other words, about half of the characters in our sample were an important part of the foreground of organizational life whereas the other half were merely part of the background, functioning essentially as stage props. Not surprisingly, most of these background characters performed operational actions (e.g., serving food and drinks, driving taxicabs, etc.) and did so in an inconspicuous and neutral manner. Thus, although it was important to recognize the organizational contributions of these almost invisible background characters, it is more important to concentrate on the foreground characters and actions of prime time. Accordingly, in the next section we summarize briefly the distributions of background characters and actions, then focus on foreground characters and their actions in the rest of the chapter.

The Background Aspects of Organizational Life on Prime Time

Demographics of background characters. As we noted above, background characters comprised 958 (49%) of the total 1,944 individual characters coded in our sample. These background characters included such miscellaneous characters as bartenders (*Kate & Allie*), automobile assembly line workers (*Gung Ho*), nurses, doc-

---

[3] The only program that did not receive even a single code was the 1987 episode of the family comedy *Growing Pains* (ABC), an episode wherein none of the characters were seen in identifiable occupations, not even in domestic working roles of homemaker or student doing homework. The plot of this episode of *Growing Pains* revolved around the three kids' discovery of their parents' basement scrapbooks which contained references to their divorce. The episode ended as the parents revealed to their children that they almost ended their marriage because of the conflict in their careers — his as a psychiatrist, hers as a reporter. Thus, even no scene was coded, the plot had direct relevance to organizational values and is discussed in Chapter 5.

[4] All percentages have been rounded for reader convenience.

tors, and nuns (*Fortune Dane, St. Elsewhere*), patrol officers (*Hill St. Blues, Cagney and Lacey*), and migrant farm laborers (*Stingray*).

Occupationally speaking, 31% of these background characters were service workers (e.g., cops and waiters), 20% were professionals (e.g., nurses, lawyers, and entertainers), 12% were customers (e.g., patients and clients), 8% were other or unidentifiable, 6% were military personnel, 5% were lawbreakers, and 5% were operatives; the remaining occupational categories each accounted for less than 5% of the total characters. *Industrially* speaking, most background characters were employed in the service (37%) and public administration (31%) industries. An additional 13% worked in the retail trade industry, 5% worked in the transportation and communications industry, and 8% of these characters were employed in unidentifiable industries; the remaining industries each employed less than 2% of the background characters. *Hierarchically* speaking, most background characters worked at professional staff levels (30%) and were divided fairly equally among upper professional staff (17%) and lower professional staff (13%) positions. An additional 23% served at nonprofessional staff levels, 16% were workers or laborers, 12% were customers, and 12% had unidentifiable or nonorganizational positions. Only 5% of the background characters served in management levels with over one-half (3%) serving as first line managers; only 2% were self-employed or had their own small businesses.

With respect to *network*, 41% of the background characters appeared on NBC, 36% appeared on CBS, and 23% appeared on ABC. With respect to *genre*, 64% of these background characters appeared on dramas, 17% on comedies, 14% on action-adventures, and 5% on other programs. With respect to *dramatic tone*, an overwhelming 72% of these characters appeared in serious presentations while only 11% and 17% appeared in comedic and combined comedy-drama presentations respectively. It appears, then, that background characters are more likely to be seen in serious portrayals, a finding that is no doubt influenced by the fact that comedies (especially 30-minute situation comedies) generally involve fewer characters altogether than dramas.

Organizational functions and depictions of background characters and actions. In terms of the organizational function of background *characters*, 60% were *operational* actors (e.g., patrol officers who took criminals away after they were arrested by foreground detectives), 27% were *informational* actors (e.g., characters who answered questions from detectives), 10% were *interpersonal* actors (e.g., characters who chatted in hallways), only 2% were *decisional* actors (e.g., cops and soldiers who chose to use deadly force), and only 1% were *political* (e.g., those who sought personal gains in exchange for sharing information). In terms of the depiction of background characters, 67% were portrayed in a neutral manner (e.g., the competent but inconspicuous servers of food or drink), while only 19% and 14% were presented in positive and negative lights respectively.

These 958 background characters performed 1,514 separate organizational actions. Each of these 1,514 individual actions was also coded in terms of the organizational function (informational, interpersonal, decisional, political, and operational) and depiction (positive, negative, neutral). Of the 1,514 separate background actions coded, 57% were *operational*, 27% were *informational*, 12% were *interpersonal*, 3% were *decisional*, and 1% were *political*. In other words, background characters were seen primarily as serving operational — that is, actual "work"—functions. Although we sometimes saw these characters provide information and engage in interpersonal dialogue, we rarely saw them make decisions or use power to accomplish their own goals. In terms of the depiction of these background actions, 61% were neutral, 21% were positive, and 18% were negative.

Summary. The background characters of prime time organizational life accounted for about one-half (49%) of the total characters on television but they performed proportionately more of the operational activities for their respective organizations. In other words, these background characters did more of the actual *work* of prime time organizational life than anyone else. And they did this work in a competent, inconspicuous, and neutral manner. Such a finding is not surprising — indeed, the neutral operational quality of these characters is what makes them "background" and not "foreground" characters. It is precisely because they perform their jobs competently and inconspicuously that they stay in the background and are rarely noticed by viewers and are usually ignored by television researchers. For all the critiques of the exaggerated and melodramatic quality of all life (including organizational life) on television, this portion of the study indicates that we regularly witness many quite mundane performances of everyday organizational life. These competent and inconspicuous organizational performances provide the necessary — and fairly "realistic" — organizational contexts for the admittedly more dramatic — and less "realistic"—actions of foreground characters. It is to these foreground characters and their actions that we turn.

The Foreground Aspects of Organizational Life on Prime Time

Demographics of foreground characters. As noted, the total number of foreground characters (major regular, minor regular, guest
with important plot function) was 986 or 51% of the total characters
coded. Of these 986 foreground characters, 38% were major regulars,
25% were minor regulars, and 37% made one appearance on the
series, serving as guest characters with important plot functions on
the episodes. Thus, as was the case in Theberge's (1981) study,
viewers had about an equal chance of watching major regular
organizational members such as J.R. Ewing *(Dallas),* Captain Frank
Furillo *(Hill Street Blues),* and *Hotel* manager Peter McDermott as
they did of watching guest organizational members such as an owner
and manager of a minor league baseball team *(Riptide),* an insurance
sales agent *(Shellgame),* a construction company owner *(Knight Rider),* or a country western singer and her agent *(Simon and Simon).*

Occupationally speaking, most of these foreground characters filled
professional, managerial, and service occupations with proportions
of 20%, 14%, and 19% respectively. The remainder of these characters filled the following occupational roles: other/nonidentifiable
(11%), customer (10%), student (8%), lawbreaker (5%); the remaining
categories each accounted for less than 3% of the foreground characters. These occupational demographics were consistent with the
occupational studies summarized in Chapter 2 and thus were representative of prime time television's population of occupational
roles.[5]

Industrially speaking, most (70%) foreground characters in our
sample worked in the service and public administration industries,
46% and 24% respectively. Other industry demographics included
the following proportions: other or unidentifiable (14%), retail trade
(5%), and finance (5%); the remaining industries each employed less
than 3% of these characters. In general, these demographics also
were consistent with the findings from the industry study reported
in Chapter 2, especially with the 1980s figures.

Hierarchically speaking, most foreground characters filled man-

---

[5] It should be noted, however, that the percentages for these occupational categories
are somewhat lower here than in the studies reported in Chapter 2 because in this
study we have used additional categories not included in the occupational listings
of other studies — namely, students, customers, lawbreakers, as well as other. Indeed,
if we eliminated these four categories, the percentages of the other occupational
groups would be even closer to those reported in the occupational studies in Chapter
2. For example, the proportions of professionals, managers, and service workers
would increase to 30%, 21% and 30% respectively.

agement and professional staff positions in their organizations. Management positions were filled by 23% of these characters and were spread evenly among the four management levels: CEO/board members (5%), executives (5%), middle managers (6%), and first line managers (7%). Professional staff positions accounted for 19% of these characters but were found more often in the higher professional staff level (16%) which included doctors and detectives rather than the lower professional staff level (3%) which included nurses and uniformed officers. The remainder of the characters were distributed among the following positions: unidentifiable or nonorganizational (19%), customers (12%), nonprofessional staff (10%), owners of small businesses or self-employed (9%), and workers/laborers (8%).

Finally, with respect to network, 37% of the characters appeared on CBS, 36% appeared on NBC, and 27% appeared on ABC. With respect to genre, 50% of these characters appeared on dramas, 35% appeared on comedies, 10% appeared on action adventure shows (e.g., The A-Team, NBC; MacGyver, ABC), and 5% appeared on other genres (e.g., mysteries such as Murder She Wrote, CBS, and "comedy dramas" such as Moonlighting, ABC, and The Days and Nights of Molly Dodd, NBC). With respect to dramatic tone, 53% of the characters performed in an overall serious tone, 24% in an overall comedic tone, and 23% in an overall tone which was serious and comedic.

Demographically speaking, then, foreground characters constituted about half of the organizational members we saw in our sample of prime time television. These featured organizational actors were generally representative of the prime time population of industries, occupations, and positions reported in other studies and they were generally displayed in serious rather than humorous or mixed dramatic narrative contexts. We now examine the organizational functions of these foreground characters and actions.

Organizational functions of foreground characters and actions. Of the 986 foreground characters, 373 (38%) can be characterized primarily as information processors, 339 (34%) as interpersonal actors, 122 (12%) as operational actors, 103 (11%) as decision makers, and 49 (5%) as political actors; of the 6,087 foreground actions, 2,539 (42%) were informational, 2,006 (33%) were interpersonal, 821 (13%) were operational, 521 (9%) were decisional, and 200 (3%) were political. As is evident, organizational life on prime time was dominated by informational and interpersonal characters and actions. Indeed, 72% of all foreground characters could be characterized as information processors or interpersonal relators, and 75% of the total actions across all scenes were accounted for by these two categories. Operational and decisional functions characterized most of the remaining characters and actions. Thus, 12% and 11% respectively of the foreground characters were operators and decision makers while 13% and 9%, respectively, of the total actions were operational and decisional. Not surprisingly, political actors and actions constituted a small portion of organizational life on prime time, accounting for just 5% of the characters and 3% of the total actions.

The informational quality of organizational life dominated prime time as 38% of the characters were seen as information processors and 42% of the actions were informational. Not surprisingly, most of this informational activity came in the form of sending or receiving messages about organizational problems and cases. Private and public detectives such as Thomas Magnum (*Magnum, P.I.*), Mike Hammer (*Mickey Spillane's Mike Hammer*), and Chris Cagney and Mary Beth Lacey (*Cagney and Lacey*) generated much of television's information-seeking behavior as they spent most of their time gathering leads from a variety of organizational insiders and outsiders to help them solve their cases. Although these private and public detectives were themselves often coded as decision makers (they solved their cases) or operators (they apprehended their suspects), most of the characters they interacted with and most of their own total actions served informational functions.

The interpersonal nature of organizational life also dominated prime time. As noted, 34% of the characters were characterized as primarily interpersonal actors and 33% of the total action involved interpersonal relationships. The dominance of interpersonal action was an expected finding inasmuch as many prime time plots have little to do with the job performance of organizational members per se but rather involve the relational conversations and conflicts that occur among these members. If we had coded the "purely" *personal* actions of these members (e.g., when detective Lacey talked to her husband at home about their private life and not her (their) police life), the proportion of interpersonal acts would have been even higher.

As suggested earlier, operational functions dominated much of the combined foreground and background characters (35%) and actions (22%). However, as we noted above, most of this operational action was performed by *background* organizational characters. In fact, when background characters were excluded from the picture, operational actions accounted for significantly fewer characters and actions; merely 12% of foreground characters and only 13% of the foreground actions. Most of this operational action came in the form of doctors doing their medical rounds in hospitals, detectives apprehending suspects, and so on. In sum, foreground characters performed some, though not much, of the actual work of prime time organizational life.

The decisional nature of organizational life was represented by 11% of the characters and 9% of the total actions on prime time. Many of these decisions were rather mundane — such as the assignment of tasks or cases — and were embedded at various points throughout an episode. The more involved, and probably more memorable, decisions were those dramatic decisions such as the final solving of a murder case, the use of deadly force to stop an armed suspect, and the decision to perform a potentially life-saving but unproven medical procedure. These more dramatic decisions usually occurred at the end of the episode and were an integral part of the climax of the program. Thus, although decision making did not constitute a major proportion of prime time action, the decisions made often had a very important impact on the organizational lives of characters.

Finally the political nature of organizational life accounted for only 5% of the overall characters and only 3% of the total actions. Moreover, the majority of these political actors and actions were seen on a small number of programs, most notably on the prime time "soaps" such as *Dallas, Dynasty,* and *Falcon Crest.* We simply did not see many organizational characters use power to accomplish their own ends. After all, J.R. Ewing was only one character and, thus, had very little impact on the overall quantitative distributions. (But what an organizational politican he is! — see Chapters 4 and 5). Thus, although the number of political actors and actions were few, the importance of these actors and actions is probably quite substantial.

In summary, the overall nature of organizational life on prime time television was informational and interpersonal. This finding was not surprising given prime time television's emphasis on the conversational nature of organizational characters and the emphasis on the process (not outcome) of solving problems and resolving romances. Although we saw few operational and decisional actions and even fewer political actions, these types of organizational activity were important when they appeared. We now examine the depiction of these organizational actors and actions.

Depictions of foreground characters and actions. In terms of the depiction of the 986 foreground characters, 566 (58%) were depicted in a positive light, 240 (24%) in a negative light, and 180 (18%) in a neutral light. Of the 566 positive characters, 205 (36%) were friendly, 178 (31%) were helpful, 174 (31%) were productive, and only 9 (2%) were charitable. Of the 240 negative characters, 83 (35%) were selfish, 48 (20%) were lawbreakers, 44 (18%) were unfriendly, 41 (17%) were foolish, and 24 (10%) were malevolent.

In terms of the depiction of the 6,087 foreground actions, 2,826 (47%) were depicted in a positive light, 2,268 (37%) in a neutral light, and 993 (16%) in a negative light. As is evident, the proportions of positive and negative depictions of action decreased sharply from depictions of characters (by 11% and 8% respectively) while the proportion of neutral depictions of action increased by 19% from the depiction of neutral characters. Of the 2,826 positive actions, 1,444 (51%) were friendly, 682 (24%) were helpful, 665 (24%) were productive, and only 35 (1%) were charitable. Of the 993 negative actions, 376 (38%) were unfriendly, 275 (28%) were selfish, 119 (12%) were illegal, 114 (11%) were foolish, and 109 (11%) were malevolent.

In sum, over one-half of all characters on prime time organizations were presented in a positive light, one-quarter in a negative light, and less than one-fifth in a neutral light. In terms of total actions, less than one-half of the total number of actions were coded as positive, less than one-fifth were negative, but more than one-third were neutral. In short, considerably more actions than actors were depicted in a neutral manner. Furthermore, the overall picture of organizational life on prime time was a generally positive one, a finding that was not surprising given television's preoccupation with reaffirming traditional organizational and cultural values.

Organizational functions by depictions. Tables 3.1 and 3.2 present the distribution of organizational functions across the three levels of depiction for individual characters and for total actions. As you can see from the table, not all types of organizational actors and actions have enjoyed the same kind of depiction. In terms of individual *characters*, interpersonal, informational, and decisional actors were far more likely to be portrayed as positive whereas political actors were more likely to be portrayed as negative. The overall depiction of operational actors was likely to be split among positive, negative, and neutral portrayals.

On the other hand, the depictions of total *actions* shifted proportionately when compared to individual actors. Neutral depictions increased for every type of organizational action, a finding which was not surprising given the increase in total neutral actions compared with positive and negative actions. Somewhat more surprising was the finding that proportions of positive and negative actions shifted in different ways compared to positive and negative char-

acters. The high proportion of positive interpersonal actions remained virtually the same as for positive characters but the proportions of negative and neutral interpersonal actions and characters
shifted inversely. Decisional actions were also most likely to be
presented in a positive light, though the proportions of positive
decisions decreased by 12% when compared with the proportion of
positive decision makers. Informational actions displayed the most
dramatic shift as the proportion of neutral informational actions
increased by almost 30% over the neutral informational actors. Most
of the total political actions remained negative, though the proportion
of political actions decreased by 20% compared with the proportion
of negative political characters. Finally, the total number of operational actions that were portrayed in a neutral manner increased
to 47% while the proportions of positive and negative operational
actions decreased slightly.

Further examination of the different types of positive and negative
actors and actions revealed some interesting differences. As we noted
earlier, positive depictions accounted for 566 (58%) of the 986 characters and for 2,826 (47%) of the 6,087 actions on prime time. Not
surprisingly, most of the positive interpersonal actors and actions

Table 3.1. Depiction Of Characters By Organizational Functions

| | Organizational Function | | | | | | | | |
| | Interpersonal | | Informational | | Decisional | | Political | | Operational | |
Depiction	N	(%)	N	(%)	N	(%)	N	(%)	N	(%)
Positive	221	(65)	229	(61)	61	(59)	10	(20)	45	(37)
Negative	72	(21)	67	(18)	28	(27)	38	(78)	35	(29)
Neutral	46	(14)	77	(21)	14	(14)	1	(2)	42	(34)
Totals	339	(100%)	373	(100%)	103	(100%)	49	(100%)	122	(100%)

$X^2=122.17$, d.f.=8, $p <.01$

Table 3.2. Depiction Of Actions By Organizational Function

| | Organizational Function | | | | | | | | |
| | Interpersonal | | Informational | | Decisional | | Political | | Operational | |
Depiction	N	(%)	N	(%)	N	(%)	N	(%)	N	(%)
Positive	1306	(65)	951	(37)	244	(47)	62	(31)	263	(32)
Negative	268	(13)	326	(13)	116	(22)	111	(55)	172	(21)
Neutral	432	(22)	1262	(50)	161	(31)	27	(14)	386	(47)
Totals	2006	(100%)	2539	(100%)	521	(100%)	200	(100%)	821	(100%)

$X^2=777.13$, d.f.=8, $p <.01$

were friendly (61% and 69% respectively); after all, friendly inter-action is the primary vehicle for enacting relationships in a positive way. Positive informational actors were primarily depicted as helpful (37%) or productive (41%) whereas positive informational actions were friendly (42%) and helpful (31%). Positive decisional actors and actions were most often depicted as productive (62% and 60% respectively) no doubt because positive decisions usually accom-plished the social or economic goals of the organization. The few positive political actors were primarily helpful (40%) or productive (40%) whereas positive political actions were mostly productive (37%) or friendly (37%). Finally, while most of the positive opera-tional actors were both productive (33%) and friendly (33%), most of the positive operational actions coded were productive.

Negative portrayals represented 240 (24%) of the 986 individual characters but only 993 (16%) of the 6087 total actions. Negative interpersonal actors were usually selfish (47%) or foolish (33%), whereas most negative interpersonal actions were unfriendly (43%) or selfish (39%). Negative informational actors and actions were most often unfriendly (33% and 50% respectively) or selfish (34% and 26% respectively). Negative decision makers were predominantly selfish (36%) or illegal (25%) whereas most of the total negative decisions were unfriendly (31%) and selfish (22%). Negative political actors and actions were primarily selfish (40% and 43% respectively) and secondarily unfriendly (24% and 30% respectively). Finally, negative operational actors and actions were primarily illegal (54% and 38% respectively) and secondarily malevolent (29% and 27% respectively), no doubt because we coded many of the lawbreaking activities of criminals as operational — after all, those are the work actions of crime. In sum, friendliness and productiveness dominated the positive side of organizational actors and actions whereas un-friendliness and selfishness dominated the negative side of organi-zational life on prime time.

Organizational functions and depictions by character type. Not surprisingly, the organizational functions and depictions of actors and actions were closely related to the status of the prime time characters. Tables 3.3 and 3.4 display the types of organizational actors and actions by character type. Continuing roles, both major and minor, accounted for proportionately more interpersonal actors and actions than visiting roles. This finding was not surprising since continuing characters worked together on a week-to-week basis and, thus, spent more time developing their work relationships. Thus, while visiting characters did engage in a significant amount of interpersonal actions (25%), they spent proportionately less time developing interpersonal relationships than did continuing characters. On the other hand, all three character types accounted for similar proportions of informational actors and actions. Although the proportion of the major regulars who were informational actors was somewhat less than the proportions for other two character types, the proportion of informational actions of major regulars was somewhat more than the proportions for the other two character types.

Although proportionately more major regular and visiting characters were coded as decision makers, the proportion of decisional actions was slightly higher for visiting characters. Not surprisingly, visiting characters also accounted for proportionately more political actors and actions than both types of continuing characters. So, too, these visiting characters accounted for proportionately more operational actors and actions than continuing characters. Indeed, perhaps in part because their time on screen was limited, these visiting

Table 3.3. Organizational Function of Characters by Character Type

Organizational Function	Major Regular		Minor Regular		One-Shot (Guest)	
	N	(%)	N	(%)	N	(%)
Interpersonal	160	(43)	97	(40)	82	(22)
Informational	128	(34)	99	(40)	146	(40)
Decisional	47	(13)	14	(6)	42	(11)
Political	11	(3)	7	(3)	31	(9)
Operational	27	(7)	28	(11)	67	(18)
Totals	373	(100)	245	(100)	368	(100)

$X^2=67.03$, d.f.$=8$, $p<.01$

Table 3.4. Organizational Function of Actions by Character Type

Organizational Function	Major Regular		Minor Regular		One-Shot (Guest)	
	N	(%)	N	(%)	N	(%)
Interpersonal	1176	(35)	369	(40)	461	(25)
Informational	1464	(44)	352	(39)	723	(40)
Decisional	260	(8)	64	(7)	197	(11)
Political	92	(3)	21	(2)	87	(5)
Operational	360	(10)	111	(12)	350	(19)
Totals	3352	(100)	917	(100)	1818	(100)

$X^2=157.65$, d.f.$=8$, $p<.01$

characters accomplished proportionately more work than regulars and used whatever means possible to accomplish their own short-lived ends.

Table 3.5 and 3.6 present the distributions of positive, negative, and neutral depictions for these three character types. In general, continuing actors and actions were portrayed in a more positive light than were visiting actors and actions. Indeed, over 70% of the major characters were positively depicted, though only 53% of their actions were positive. Minor regulars were also cast as positive characters overall, though their actions on a scene-by-scene basis were almost as likely to be positive (46%) as neutral (42%). Visiting characters, however, were as likely to be seen as negative (40%) as they were to be seen as positive (39%); however, their actions were as likely to be depicted as positive (36%) as neutral (37%). Nonetheless, visiting characters still accounted for proportionately more of the negative action than did continuing characters. In fact, these visiting characters accounted for over 80% of the illegal and malevolent actors and actions. In other words, although visiting characters were depicted as overall "white hats" and "black hats" with the same regularity, the visiting "black hats" were particularly villainous.

Table 3.5. Depiction of Characters by Character Type

| | CharacterType | | | | | |
| | Major Regular | | Minor Regular | | One-Shot (Guest) | |
Depiction	N	(%)	N	(%)	N	(%)
Positive	268	(72)	153	(63)	145	(39)
Negative	64	(17)	30	(12)	146	(40)
Neutral	41	(11)	62	(25)	77	(21)
Totals	373	(100)	245	(100)	368	(100)

$X^2=112.48$, d.f.=4, $p<.01$

Table 3.6. Depiction of Actions by Character Type

| | Character Type | | | | | |
| | Major Regular | | Minor Regular | | One-Shot (Guest) | |
Depiction	N	(%)	N	(%)	N	(%)
Positive	1760	(53)	416	(46)	650	(36)
Negative	382	(11)	113	(12)	498	(27)
Neutral	1210	(36)	388	(42)	670	(37)
Totals	3352	(100)	917	(100)	1818	(100)

$X^2=274.52$, d.f.=4, $p<.01$

Organizational functions and depictions by occupation. Tables 3.7 and 3.8 present the distributions of organizational characters and actions by occupation. Here we note some of the highlights of the differences among these occupational groups; an extended discussion of managerial occupations is presented in Chapter 4.

Every occupational group enjoyed rather high proportions of interpersonal actors and actions, with the notable exceptions of military personnel and lawbreakers. Students, customers, household workers, and the combined group of other occupations accounted for the highest proportions of interpersonal characters whereas several occupational groups enjoyed comparably high proportions of interpersonal actions. In general, most occupational groups dedicated much of their organizational lives to maintaining and developing relationships with others; however, criminals and military personnel did not seem to share this relational concern.

On the other hand, every occupational group spent at least 20% of the time seeking or giving information, including military personnel and criminals. In fact, military personnel seemed to require the most information, followed closely by service workers (e.g., private eyes and police detectives) and characters with unidentifiable or no occupation (e.g., organizational outsiders who provided information to (rather than sought information from) private eyes and detectives). Household workers and the combined occupational group accounted for proportionately fewer information processors whereas the same two groups, along with students and lawbreakers, performed fewer informational activities. Nonetheless, it is fair to say that informational activities constituted an important part of the organizational lives of virtually every occupational group.

The same cannot be said about the decisional, political, and operational aspects of organizational life. There were not many decisional actors or actions in any occupational category. The groups which had the highest proportions of decision makers included managers, military personnel, students, and professionals whereas lawbreakers, managers, and military personnel made proportionately more decisions. Political actors and actions accounted for even less in all occupational categories. Not surprisingly, managers accounted for proportionately more political actors and actions than any other occupational group; lawbreakers accounted for the second highest proportions. Finally, operational actors and actions accounted for sizeable proportions of some groups and small proportions of other groups. Lawbreakers, military personnel, household workers, service workers, and professionals had proportionately more operational actors and actions than other groups. Not surprisingly, managers

Table 3.7. Organizational Function of Characters by Occupation

| Occupation | Interpersonal | Organizational Function | | | |
		Informational	Decisional	Political	Operational
Managers					
n=135	36	51	25	21	2
(100%)	(27%)	(38%)	(18%)	(16%)	(1%)
Professionals					
n=195	68	67	21	8	31
(100%)	(35%)	(34%)	(11%)	(4%)	(16%)
Service					
n=191	44	89	19	3	36
(100%)	(23%)	(46%)	(10%)	(2%)	(19%)
Household					
n=31	14	8	2	1	6
(100%)	(45%)	(26%)	(6%)	(3%)	(20%)
Military					
n=30	1	16	4	0	9
(100%)	(4%)	(53%)	(13%)	(0%)	(30%)
Other*					
n=47	28	12	1	1	5
(100%)	(60%)	(25%)	(2%)	(2%)	(11%)
Students					
n=77	49	19	9	0	0
(100%)	(63%)	(25%)	(12%)	(0%)	(0%)
Customers					
n=98	50	33	6	2	7
(100%)	(51%)	(34%)	(6%)	(2%)	(7%)
Lawbreakers					
n=52	1	15	5	7	24
(100%)	(2%)	(29%)	(10%)	(13%)	(46%)
No Occp					
n=130	48	63	11	6	2
(100%)	(37%)	(48%)	(8%)	(5%)	(2%)

* Includes clerical, sales, crafts, operatives, & laborers. X^2=256.96, d.f.=36, $p<.01$

and students engaged in very little operational activity; managers delegated work to their subordinates whereas students simply didn't like to work.

Table 3.9 presents the depictions of characters in these occupational groups. Characters in every occupational group except lawbreakers and military personnel were portrayed more often in a positive light than in either negative or neutral lights — and in most

Table 3.8.   Organizational Function of Actions by Occupation

Occupation	Interpersonal	Informational	Decisional	Political	Operational
Managers					
n=702	250	280	88	62	22
(100%)	(36%)	(40%)	(12%)	(9%)	(3%)
Professionals					
n=1209	453	459	96	42	159
(100%)	(37%)	(38%)	(8%)	(4%)	(13%)
Service					
n=1765	484	845	120	32	284
(100%)	(27%)	(48%)	(7%)	(2%)	(16%)
Household					
n=89	36	19	7	4	23
(100%)	(41%)	(21%)	(8%)	(4%)	(26%)
Military					
n=269	30	142	29	11	57
(100%)	(11%)	(53%)	(11%)	(4%)	(21%)
Other*					
n=245	126	66	14	6	33
(100%)	(51%)	(27%)	(6%)	(2%)	(14%)
Students					
n=291	153	103	9	10	16
(100%)	(53%)	(35%)	(3%)	(3%)	(6%)
Customers					
n=595	229	227	42	4	93
(100%)	(38%)	(38%)	(7%)	(1%)	(16%)
Lawbreakers					
n=294	25	94	53	15	107
(100%)	(9%)	(32%)	(18%)	(5%)	(36%)
No Occp					
n=628	220	304	63	14	27
(100%)	(35%)	(49%)	(10%)	(2%)	(4%)

* Includes clerical, sales, crafts, operatives, & laborers. X^2=673.55, d.f.=36, $p<.01$

cases far more often. The most positively depicted characters were service workers, household workers, professionals, and the set of combined occupations as well as the quasi-occupational categories of customers and students. On the other hand, the two occupational groups which had proportionately more negative characters were lawbreakers followed distantly by managers. Interestingly, military personnel were seen as neutral proportionately more often than any other occupational group.

In terms of the depictions of total actions, some changes in proportions from the character coding should be noted (see Table 3.10). First, most proportions of positive actions were significantly reduced, though they still remained fairly high for all categories

Table 3.9.   Depiction of Characters by Occupation

Occupation	Positive	Depiction Negative	Neutral
Managers			
n=135	69	48	18
(100%)	(51%)	(36%)	(13%)
Professionals			
n=195	117	38	40
(100%)	(60%)	(20%)	(20%)
Service			
n=191	125	28	38
(100%)	(65%)	(15%)	(20%)
Household			
n=31	20	4	7
(100%)	(64%)	(13%)	(23%)
Military			
n=30	12	6	12
(100%)	(40%)	(20%)	(40%)
Other*			
n=47	31	9	7
(100%)	(66%)	(19%)	(15%)
Students			
n=77	44	19	14
(100%)	(57%)	(25%)	(18%)
Customers			
n=98	61	23	14
(100%)	(62%)	(24%)	(14%)
Lawbreakers			
n=52	3	43	6
(100%)	(6%)	(83%)	(11%)
No Occp			
n=130	84	22	24
(100%)	(65%)	(17%)	(18%)

* Includes clerical, sales, crafts, operatives, & laborers. X^2=138.98, d.f.=18, $p<.01$

except lawbreakers. The occupational groups which performed proportionately more positive actions included students, professionals, and the combined group of other occupations. The proportions of negative actions decreased for every occupational group except household workers for whom negative depictions increased slightly. The most substantial decreases in negative actions occurred for lawbreakers and managers. Lawbreakers still engaged in more negative action but they performed proportionately more positive and neutral actions, a finding which was not terribly surprising given the frequent use of lawbreakers as sources of information for private eyes and detectives, such as the hooker in Spencer For Hire who provided key information which helped Spencer solve his murder case. Finally, every occupational group without exception had an increase in the proportions of neutral actions compared to neutral characters, though military personnel and service workers performed proportionately more neutral activities than any other occupational group.

Organizational Functions and Depictions By Hierarchical Position. Tables 3.11 and 3.12 present the breakdowns of the organizational functions of characters and actions by hierarchical position. Most hierarchical levels included a fairly large proportion of interpersonal actors and actions, though lower staff and customer levels had much higher proportions of these actors and actions. Similarly, informational actors and actions constituted a large proportion for most hierarchical positions. Self-employed characters (including private eyes) and professional staff members (including detectives and patrol officers as well as doctors and nurses) were proportionately the top two information processors, though every hierarchical position except lower staff workers spent at least 35% of their time giving and getting information. Lower staff workers spent proportionately less time engaged in informational activities and proportionately more time engaged in interpersonal activities.

Not surprisingly, management levels (including CEOs, executives, middle managers, and first line managers) had significantly more decision makers and political actors and engaged in more decision making and political actions. The second highest proportion of decision makers were found in self-employed positions (12%) but these characters engaged in decision making only 7% of the time; 10% of the organizational outsiders were seen as decision makers but they engaged in proportionately more decision making actions (12%). Finally, lower staff levels accounted for more *operational* actors and actions than any other hierarchical group. Not surprisingly, man-

Table 3.10. Depiction of Actions by Occupation

Occupation	Positive	Depiction Negative	Neutral
Managers			
n=702	298	160	244
(100%)	(42%)	(23%)	(35%)
Professionals			
n=1209	666	143	400
(100%)	(55%)	(12%)	(33%)
Service			
n=1765	724	220	821
(100%)	(41%)	(12%)	(47%)
Household			
n=89	44	14	31
(100%)	(49%)	(16%)	(35%)
Military			
n=269	104	36	129
(100%)	(39%)	(13%)	(48%)
Other*			
n=245	152	30	63
(100%)	(62%)	(12%)	(26%)
Students			
n=291	185	45	61
(100%)	(64%)	(15%)	(21%)
Customers			
n=595	286	87	222
(100%)	(48%)	(15%)	(37%)
Lawbreakers			
n=294	40	160	94
(100%)	(14%)	(54%)	(32%)
No Occp			
n=628	327	98	203
(100%)	(52%)	(16%)	(32%)

* Includes clerical, sales, crafts, operatives, & laborers. X^2=548.51, d.f.=18, $p<.01$

agement positions had less operational actors and conducted fewer operational actions.

Tables 3.13 and 3.14 present the breakdowns of depictions of characters and actions across these hierarchical categories. Once again, every hierarchical category, without exception, had more positive than negative or neutral characters. The same held true for their actions, except for professional staff members whose actions

Table 3.11.   Organizational Function of Characters by Position

Position	Organizational Function Interpersonal	Informational	Decisional	Political	Operational
Management					
n=223	53	83	44	28	15
(100%)	(24%)	(37%)	(20%)	(12%)	(7%)
Prof. Staff					
n=187	63	81	12	4	27
(100%)	(34%)	(43%)	(6%)	(2%)	(15%)
Workers					
n=175	87	42	9	1	36
(100%)	(50%)	(24%)	(5%)	(1%)	(20%)
Customers					
n=121	58	42	9	3	9
(100%)	(48%)	(35%)	(7%)	(3%)	(7%)
Own Business					
n=93	16	51	11	2	13
(100%)	(17%)	(55%)	(12%)	(2%)	(14%)
Non Org					
n=187	62	74	18	11	22
(100%)	(33%)	(39%)	(10%)	(6%)	(12%)

$X^2=136.61$, d.f.=20, $p<.01$.

were as likely to be positive as neutral. Self-employed characters were viewed as positive proportionately more often than any other group of individual characters whereas lower staff workers engaged in proportionately more positive actions than any other hierarchical group. Not surprisingly, management positions and nonorganizational others (which included most lawbreakers) were portrayed in a negative light more often than other hierarchical levels and they performed more negative actions than any other hierarchical groups.

Organizational functions and depictions by industry. We also examined organizational actors and actions by industry. As can be seen in Tables 3.15 and 3.16, the retail trade industry employed proportionately more interpersonal actors and displayed proportionately more interpersonal actions than other single industry, no doubt because this retail trade industry was represented primarily by eating and drinking establishments such as the Cheers bar (see Chapter 6) which provided a great context for friendly interaction. The service industry, too, enjoyed a greater proportion of interpersonal actors and actions, no doubt since it was represented by hospitals and classrooms which also provided contexts wherein insiders and out-

Table 3.12. Organizational Function of Actions by Position

| Position | Interpersonal | Organizational Function | | | |
		Informational	Decisional	Political	Operational
Management					
n=1251	358	531	175	96	91
(100%)	(29%)	(42%)	(14%)	(8%)	(7%)
Prof. Staff					
n=1656	523	764	99	36	234
(100%)	(32%)	(46%)	(6%)	(2%)	(14%)
Workers					
n=772	396	189	25	21	141
(100%)	(51%)	(25%)	(3%)	(3%)	(18%)
Customers					
n=773	314	277	65	4	113
(100%)	(41%)	(36%)	(8%)	(1%)	(14%)
Own Business					
n=829	222	412	59	17	119
(100%)	(27%)	(50%)	(7%)	(2%)	(14%)
Non Org					
n=806	193	366	98	26	123
(100%)	(24%)	(46%)	(12%)	(3%)	(15%)

$X^2=465.09$, d.f.$=20$, $p<.01$.

siders engaged in more interpersonal dialogue. On the other hand, the public administration industry accounted for most of the informational actions and it employed proportionately more informational actors than other industries with the exceptions of the finance and transportation and communications industries. Public order — that is, law enforcement—employed over one-half (57%) of the information processors of public administration and exhibited over one-half (53%) of all public administration informational actions. In short, law enforcement workers displayed their status as prime time's top information processors.

Finance and public administration industries displayed the decisional aspects of organizational life proportionately more often than other single industry. Although the transportation and communications industries employed proportionately more decision makers (19%), these decision makers made proportionately fewer decisions (only 7%) than their counterparts in the other two industries. Public administration workers made more decisions than workers in any other industry and most (over 40%) of these public administration decisions were made by military personnel. The

Table 3.13. Depiction of Characters by Position

Occupation	Positive	Depiction Negative	Neutral
Management			
n=223	107	67	49
(100%)	(48%)	(30%)	(22%)
Prof. Staff			
n=187	114	34	39
(100%)	(61%)	(18%)	(21%)
Workers			
n=175	104	33	38
(100%)	(59%)	(19%)	(22%)
Customer			
n=121	73	28	20
(100%)	(60%)	(23%)	(17%)
Own Business			
n=93	71	17	5
(100%)	(76%)	(18%)	(6%)
Non Org			
n=187	97	61	29
(100%)	(52%)	(33%)	(15%)

X^2=38.72, d.f.=10, p<.01.

finance industry also housed proportionately more *political* actors and actions than any other industry. This should not be surprising as most of the finance organizations were presented on prime time soaps such as *Dallas*, *Dynasty*, and *The Colbys* which featured more political players than other programs.

Finally, although retail trade employed proportionately more operational characters (including waiters, waitresses, and bartenders), operational actions were spread fairly evenly among retail trade and transportation and communications industries. Service and public administration industries were not far behind; most service operational actors and actions were represented by miscellaneous service workers (such as butlers, maids, housekeepers) whereas military and public order industries employed over 90% of public administration's operational actors and actions. Characters with no identifiable industry (including lawbreakers) also displayed proportionately high levels of operational action.

Tables 3.17 and 3.18 present the breakdowns of *depictions* across these industries for characters and actions. Once again, proportionately more characters were positive than negative for every industry.

Table 3.14. Depiction of Actions by Position

Occupation	Positive	Depiction Negative	Neutral
Management			
n=1251	539	247	465
(100%)	(43%)	(20%)	(37%)
Prof. Staff			
n=1656	720	205	731
(100%)	(44%)	(12%)	(44%)
Workers			
n=772	459	126	187
(100%)	(60%)	(16%)	(24%)
Customer			
n=773	360	108	305
(100%)	(47%)	(14%)	(39%)
Own Business			
n=829	412	88	329
(100%)	(50%)	(10%)	(40%)
Non Org			
n=806	336	219	251
(100%)	(42%)	(27%)	(31%)

$X^2=208.92$, d.f.=10, $p<.01$.

The service industry employed more *positive* characters than any other single industry (though the combined group of other industries accounted for more); however, we saw more total positive actions in the retail trade and the transportation/communications industries. Not surprisingly, the finance industry was characterized by proportionately more *negative* characters and actions than any other industry; in fact, the finance industry framed more negative actions than positive or neutral actions. The nonindustry category also presented proportionately more negative actors and negative actions — no surprise, since most prime time lawbreakers were coded in the nonindustry category. Finally, the public administration industry employed proportionately more neutral characters who performed proportionately more neutral actions than other types of actions. Military and public order personnel accounted for most of the neutral public administration actors and actions.

A note on the genres and dramatic tones of organizational life. Finally, we consider the dramatic genres and tones of prime time organizations. Briefly stated, over one-half of all prime time organizational characters and actions were presented in dramas (50% and

Table 3.15. Organizational Function of Characters by Industry

| Industry | Organizational Function | | | | |
	Interpersonal	Informational	Decisional	Political	Operational
Service					
n=457	191	150	45	16	55
(100%)	(42%)	(33%)	(10%)	(3%)	(12%)
Public Admin.					
n=234	45	110	31	12	36
(100%)	(19%)	(47%)	(13%)	(5%)	(16%)
Finance					
n=45	8	23	7	6	1
(100%)	(18%)	(51%)	(16%)	(13%)	(2%)
Retail Trade					
n=45	21	8	4	0	12
(100%)	(47%)	(18%)	(9%)	(0%)	(26%)
Trans & Comm					
n=27	3	14	5	2	3
(100%)	(11%)	(52%)	(19%)	(7%)	(11%)
Other*					
n=37	21	10	3	2	1
(100%)	(57%)	(27%)	(8%)	(5%)	(3%)
Non Industry					
n=141	50	58	8	11	14
(100%)	(35%)	(41%)	(6%)	(8%)	(10%)

* Includes agriculture, construction, manufacturing, and wholesale trade. X^2=93.99, d.f.=24, $p<.01$.

52%, respectively). Although we saw more interpersonal actors in comedies (57%), we saw more interpersonal actions in dramas (45%). We were almost three times as likely to find informational actors and actions in dramas (61% and 57%, respectively) than we were in comedies. Both decisional and operational actions appeared far more frequently in dramas than in any other genres, and political actions were overwhelmingly seriously handled — 80% of the political actors were seen in dramas and 75% of the political actions were displayed in dramas and action adventure programs combined. Similarly, most organizational actors and actions were presented in a serious tone with the exception of interpersonal actors who were more likely to be portrayed in a humorous tone. In sum, apart from the often comedic and humorous development of interpersonal relationships, prime time organizational life is a dramatic and serious business.

Table 3.16. Organizational Functions of Actions by Industry

| | Organizational Function | | | | |
Industry	Interpersonal	Informational	Decisional	Political	Operational
Service					
n=2872	1098	1104	213	89	368
(100%)	(38%)	(39%)	(7%)	(3%)	(13%)
Public Admin.					
n=1868	439	931	195	51	252
(100%)	(23%)	(50%)	(11%)	(3%)	(13%)
Finance					
n=129	42	48	12	19	8
(100%)	(33%)	(37%)	(9%)	(15%)	(6%)
Retail Trade					
n=342	194	61	15	5	67
(100%)	(57%)	(18%)	(4%)	(1%)	(20%)
Trans & Comm					
n=213	52	103	14	8	36
(100%)	(24%)	(48%)	(7%)	(4%)	(17%)
Other*					
n=161	58	67	23	7	6
(100%)	(36%)	(42%)	(14%)	(4%)	(4%)
Non Industry					
n=502	123	225	49	21	84
(100%)	(24%)	(45%)	(10%)	(4%)	(17%)

* Includes agriculture, construction, manufacturing, and wholesale trade. X^2=355.97, d.f.=24, $p<.01$.

DISCUSSION

Admittedly, there is much information presented in this chapter. Thus, in this discussion section, we will attempt to summarize the main conclusions of this study and develop their implications for the portrayal of organizational life on prime time television. We begin our discussion by considering the potential implications of background characters and actions, then turn our attention to the more important foreground aspects of organizational life.

The Background Aspects of Organizational Life on Prime Time

Almost one-half (49%) of all prime time organizational members are background characters, members who serve as background props for the foreground characters and actions. Most of these background

Table 3.17. Depiction of Characters by Industry

Industry	Positive	Depiction Negative	Neutral
Service			
n=457	286	92	79
(100%)	(63%)	(20%)	(17%)
Public Admin.			
n=234	124	53	57
(100%)	(53%)	(23%)	(24%)
Finance			
n=45	22	19	4
(100%)	(49%)	(42%)	(9%)
Retail Trade			
n=45	26	14	5
(100%)	(58%)	(31%)	(11%)
Trans & Comm			
n=27	14	8	5
(100%)	(52%)	(30%)	(18%)
Other*			
n=37	25	10	2
(100%)	(68%)	(27%)	(5%)
Non Industry			
n=141	69	44	28
(100%)	(49%)	(31%)	(20%)

* Includes agriculture, construction, manufacturing, and wholesale trade. $X^2=31.56$, d.f.=12, $p<.01$.

characters are service workers (e.g., maids, waiters, bartenders, and police officers) and professionals (e.g., musicians, lawyers, nurses, and doctors) who are employed in service or public administration industries and who hold professional and nonprofessional staff positions in their organizations. These characters mostly engage in operational (i.e., direct work) activities and are portrayed in an overall neutral manner. As noted earlier, such a portrait of the background organizational member is not surprising — after all, if these characters did not perform their operational actions in a competent and inconspicuous way, they would be "foreground" not "background" characters. But what, if anything, do we learn about organizational life from these background characters?

We believe these background members may teach us that organizational life is filled with many routine and mundane activities and that not all organizational members, not even on prime time, are

Table 3.18. Depiction of Actions by Industry

Industry	Positive	Depiction Negative	Neutral
Service			
n=2872	1473	399	1000
(100%)	(51%)	(14%)	(35%)
Public Admin.			
n=1868	721	276	871
(100%)	(38%)	(15%)	(47%)
Finance			
n=129	39	48	42
(100%)	(30%)	(37%)	(33%)
Retail Trade			
n=342	201	53	88
(100%)	(59%)	(15%)	(26%)
Trans & Comm			
n=213	126	14	73
(100%)	(59%)	(7%)	(34%)
Other*			
n=161	86	36	39
(100%)	(53%)	(23%)	(24%)
Non Industry			
n=502	180	167	155
(100%)	(36%)	(33%)	(31%)

*Includes agriculture, construction, manufacturing, and wholesale trade. X^2=306.03, d.f.=12, $p<.01$.

heroes or villains. Indeed, many workers simply blend into the organizational background and do their jobs competently and inconspicuously. And if you think about it, the public, as viewers of television or as customers/clients of organizations, often expect and prefer such competent and inconspicuous performances of work. For example, as customers in restaurants and bars, we often prefer that our food and drink be delivered *without fanfare*, positive or negative. In short, the background members of organizational life on prime time offer potential if unnoticed lessons about the inconspicuous competencies of organizational life. They are lessons that foreground characters, because they are in the foreground, cannot teach us.

There are, however, some potential negative implications of the inconspicuous presentation of background workers. First, we are presented with the possible lesson that organizational members who perform their work in a "merely" competent manner will go un-noticed and probably unrewarded. Indeed, basic competence is not celebrated in prime time organizations; only extreme positive or extreme negative performances receive attention from prime time organization members, especially managers. A second, and perhaps more important lesson, was suggested by Rollings (1983) who pointed out that many of these background characters tend to be unionized workers. And as Rollings (1983) put it:

> The overwhelming majority of workers in unionized occupations on television continued to be nameless, personality-less people who take their orders, do their jobs, and disappear. Most workers are depicted in robot-like roles and are mere "props" to the more important char-acters in the show. They continue to be of "too little value in the plot" for the audience to get to know them (p. 141).

Although we believe Rollings is overstating his case, the point that there remain very few, if any, working class heroes on prime time television is well taken.

In sum, we have assumed, as have many viewers and researchers, that the primary lessons about (organizational) life that are presented on prime time television are revealed by the *foreground* characters since these characters are the central narrative agents in their prime time programs. However, our own analysis of background characters has reminded us that one important but ex-nominated organizational "lesson" from prime time television may be the taken-for-granted expectations we develop about the competence of everyday organi-zational characters. In short, these background characters of prime time organizations may serve important — if unnoticed and ig-nored — functions in reaffirming social and organizational expec-tations about everyday work and workers.

The Foreground Aspects of Organizational Life on Prime Time

About one-half (51%) of all prime time organizational members are foreground characters, characters who are major regulars, minor regulars, and single-appearance visitors. In general, most of these characters are professionals, service workers, or managers who are employed by service or public administration industries and who hold management and higher professional staff positions in their organizations. These characters mostly engage in interpersonal and informational actions and are most likely to be portrayed in a positive manner. Familiar regular characters who fit this general profile included Dr. Donald Westphall and his staff of major and minor resident physicians at St. Eligius Hospital (St. Elsewhere) as well as Capt. Frank Furillo and his staff of major and minor lieutenants and sergeants who worked at the Hill St. precinct (Hill Street Blues).

Not surprisingly, however, different groups of foreground characters perform different organizational functions and are portrayed differentially. With respect to *character type*, continuing characters, both major and minor, engage in more interpersonal actions and are portrayed in a more positive light whereas visiting characters engage in proportionately more political and operational activity and are portrayed in a more negative light. *Occupationally* speaking, virtually all groups are concerned with organizational information, but managers engage in proportionately more decision making and politicking (see Chapter 4); all occupational groups except lawbreakers and military personnel are portrayed in a positive light more often than in a negative light, though managers and lawbreakers have proportionately more negative characters and military jobs have proportionately more neutral characters. *Hierarchically* speaking, those at higher organizational levels are more likely to be decision makers and political actors and are more likely to be presented in a negative light than those in lower positions. *Industrially* speaking, the service and retail trade industries employ more interpersonal actors who are more likely to be presented in positive ways, public administration industries employ more neutral information processors and decision makers, and finance industries employ more negative decision makers and political actors.

As noted earlier, our study was, in some ways, a replication and extension of Theberge's (1981) study of prime time business characters. Accordingly, some of the results from our study can be interpreted in the context of this earlier study. As described in Chapter 1, Theberge and his colleagues analyzed the depiction of "businessmen" and they came to the conclusion that most businessmen are portrayed in a very negative light — as "crooks, con-men, and clowns." Visiting characters and top executives in that study were especially villainous, though they found that even major regular characters were also portrayed in a predominantly negative manner.

Stated simply, we found only limited support for the findings of the Media Institute as reported by Theberge (1981). As did that study, we found that characters in higher hierarchical levels were more likely to be portrayed in a negative light than those in lower positions. So, too, we found that those in management occupations, especially visiting managers, were more likely to be seen as negative characters than nonmanagerial characters (see Chapter 4 for an extended discussion of managerial occupations). Finally, those who worked in finance industries — clearly "business" workers by any definition — were indeed the most negative characters in our sample. In sum, we agree that "business" characters are more likely to be "black hats" than are nonbusiness characters.

On the other hand, we found that prime time television offers a generally *positive* portrayal of organizational life. Indeed, we found that prime time television is more likely to present characters across all types, occupations, industries, and hierarchical levels in a more positive than negative light, with the important exceptions of law-breakers and guest managers. Even our "finance" workers were about as likely to be portrayed as positive characters performing positive actions as they were to be portrayed as negative characters performing negative actions. Quite simply, we conclude that Theberge (1981) presented an overly negative (and incomplete) portrayal of business on prime time television that should *not* be generalized to depictions of organizational life on prime time television. We believe that Theberge (1981) should take a second and more comprehensive look at prime time television organizations before he begs the rather melodramatic questions offered in his foreward: "How well is the public served by repetitious imitations of crime, greed, and other aberrations, presented as life? Is our view of life being warped by portrayals of wickedness, and colored by passion so that we are losing any sense of virtue?" (p. vii). Although these questions make for "good copy," they do not reveal a very sensitive or complete understanding of organizational America as depicted on prime time television.

This is not to say that we believe television is a golden medium which presents an idyllic view of organizational life. Indeed, as will become clearer in subsequent chapters, we believe prime time television drama could develop more interesting, compelling, and important presentations of organizational life. We also believe that television can do more to teach lessons which can help viewing audiences cope with the complexities and uncertainties of contemporary organizations. However, in terms of the depiction of organizational life, prime time television drama seems to present relatively balanced "coverage." It makes sense that the continuing characters and companies we see (and look forward to seeing) each week — like the St. Gregory Hotel and St. Eligius Hospital — would be portrayed in very positive, if not heroic, lights. These positive presentations of our continuing characters and companies reinforce mainstream American values of friendliness, helpfulness, and productiveness and they help audiences develop and maintain their own identifications with these values (and, from the network's perspective, they help audiences develop their viewing commitments to these characters and programs). It also makes sense that many of the visiting organizational outsiders will be cast as negative and often villainous challengers to these continuing characters and companies. Such is the well-established prime time formula of "white hats" against the "black hats." For prime time television to exclude the positive or the negative aspects of organizational characters and actions is to jeopardize its own organizational success.

Concluding Observations

We conclude that this analysis of prime time organizational activity tells us at least three things about organizational life in America. First, this study provides us with some insights regarding the similarities in the general types of activities that members of organizations in all occupations and industries perform. Indeed, from this study of organizational action on prime time we learn that no matter what the organizational setting in which one works — a hospital, a law firm, a hotel, a police department — the majority of work time is spent processing information and relating interpersonally with co-workers, clients, and supervisors.

The informational nature of organizational life reflects our so-called "information society." Indeed, prime time television programs suggest that the sending and receiving of information is one of the most important organizational activities in America. As one junior organizational member on *Hard Copy* told one senior organizational member, "What you know is gold to me." The pervasiveness of information processing activities in prime time portrayals may teach audiences that members in every type of organization, in every industry, and at every hierarchical level, must know how to perform various informational activities. One by-product of such a lesson may be a heightened awareness of interviewing, word processing, and analytical communication skills as important job requirements for working in American organizations.

The emphasis on the interpersonal nature of organizational life on prime time may teach audiences about the importance of human relations in American organizations and the necessity of interpersonal interactions for accomplishing organizational tasks and goals. Over one-third of all organizational activities in our prime time sample involved such interpersonal actions as small talk, comforting, counseling, and mentoring — actions which can be used to develop positive customer and employee relations. Viewers of prime time organizations, thus, may learn how such interpersonal actions can function to develop trust, loyalty, and confidence in the organization and its products and services.

On the other hand, the results of this study suggest some lessons which may be misleading to audiences. For example, we may learn that political activity is generally avoided in organizations, except for those outrageously selfish individuals such as J.R. Ewing (*Dallas*) and Angela Channing (*Falcon Crest*) who abuse power. We may also learn that decision making is an infrequent organizational activity. Indeed, decisions about job hiring, budget setting, and resource allocating are essentially ignored in prime time organizations with very few exceptions. Finally, we do not see much of the "nuts and bolts" of running organizations, except through the operational actions of nameless (and rather unimportant) background members. These and other organizational lessons which are presented and not presented on prime time are developed in more detail in Chapter 7.

The content analytic approach adopted in this chapter, however, only provided information about the general types and patterns of organizational performances that are presented on prime time. In the next chapter, we focus attention more specifically on managerial characters and their performances because these organizational leaders and figureheads play key roles in shaping the realities of prime time (and real) organizations.

Chapter 4

The Managerial Performances in Prime Time Organizations

In the last chapter, we examined the trends in prime time organizational actors and actions for all occupational categories. In this chapter, we turn our attention to managers. Managers, after all, represent the key actors of organizational life. Kotter (1982), for example, has argued that whereas managers affected very few people's lives a century ago, today "almost all working adults spend half of their nonsleeping lives being directed by managers" (p. 1). Today's manager directs a staggering array of activities. The manager "plans, organizes, motivates, directs and controls . . . adds foresight, purpose, integration of effort, and effectiveness to the contribution of others" (Strong, 1965, p. 5). The manager, in short, is the premier organizational leader who has become, according to Mintzberg (1973), "the folk hero of contemporary American society" (p. 2).

In this chapter we focus on the managers of prime time organizational life. Specifically, we first examine the "demography" of management on prime time by summarizing the quantitative content data from our sample of prime time organizations for managerial occupations only. Second, we consider the "dramaturgy" of management on prime time by focusing more qualitatively on the dramatic *performances* of these managers. Finally, we examine the types of overarching managerial styles that characterize the managerial action of prime time organizations.

THE DEMOGRAPHY OF MANAGEMENT ON PRIME TIME TELEVISION

As we noted in Chapter 3, our analyses of prime time organizational action were based on data from two sample weeks of network prime time programs (116 episodes) which aired during the spring season in 1986 and 1987. We coded the individual characters and the total actions on these programs in terms of several variables including: character type, occupation, hierarchical position, industry, depiction, organizational action, network, genre, and tone (for a more elaborate discussion of methods, see Chapter 3). In this section, we focus on the results of our quantitative content analysis for prime time characters who had managerial occupations, those who actually worked as managers in prime time organizations.

The Demographics of Management Characters

Of the 986 foreground characters in our sample, 135 (14%) were coded as working managers. Almost 50% of these managers were major series regulars while 23% and 27% were minor regulars and visiting characters, respectively. These managers were mostly employed in three industries: finance (25%), public administration (24%), and service (21%) industries. Hierarchically, managers were primarily spread among the top three organizational levels (28% were CEOs or board members, 26% were executive or top level managers, and 25% were middle managers) while far fewer were first line managers (8%) or managed their own small business (13%).

Interestingly, NBC had far fewer managers (15%) than ABC and CBS, which presented 37% and 48% of the managers, respectively. Additionally, managers were seen in more dramas (64%) than comedies (25%), with the remaining small proportion seen in action adventures or other genres. Managers were also more likely to be presented in a serious tone (70%) than in a comedic tone (18%) or combined comedy/drama tone (12%).

Organizational functions of managerial characters. In terms of the primary organizational functions of these managers, 38% were information processors, 27% were interpersonal actors, 18% were decision makers, 16% were political performers, and only 1% were operational actors. Not surprisingly, these proportions differed for different categories of managers. With respect to character type, major regular managers accounted for proportionately more interpersonal actors (37%), minor regular managers for proportionately more information processors (52%), and visiting managers for proportionately more political actors (32%); decision makers appeared in fairly equal proportions for all character types (about 10% each). Industrially speaking, there were proportionately more interpersonal managers in the service industry (42%), whereas the finance and public administration industries employed proportionately more information processors (47% and 46% respectively) and decision makers (21% and 24% respectively). Somewhat surprisingly, all three of these types of industries employed fairly similar proportions of political managers (service, 21%; finance, 18%; public administration, 15%). Hierarchically speaking, first line levels of management had proportionately more interpersonal actors (55%), middle management and self-employed levels had more information processors (44% and 47% respectively), and executive levels had more political managers (20%). Managerial decision makers accounted for 24% of the CEO, middle, and self-employed levels of management.

Depictions of managerial characters. In terms of the depiction of managerial characters, 51% were seen as positive, 36% were negative, and 13% were neutral. Positive managers were just as likely to be productive as friendly (each constituted 35% of the total positive managers), and only slightly less likely to be viewed as helpful (30%); however, not a single managerial character was coded overall as charitable. Of the total negative managers, 48% were selfish, 31% were unfriendly, and less than 10% each were illegal, malevolent, or foolish. These proportions differed, however, for different character types, industries, and hierarchical levels.

With respect to character type, major and minor regular managers were depicted far more positively (64% and 61%, respectively) than negatively (25% and 23% respectively); however, single appearance (guest) managers were far more often depicted negatively (68%) than positively (18%) or neutrally (14%). A closer look at the positive depictions revealed that major regular managers were more likely to be depicted as productive, minor regular managers as helpful, and single appearance guest managers as friendly. On the negative side, regular major and single appearance managers were more likely to be depicted as selfish while minor regular managers were more likely to be seen as unfriendly.

Industrially speaking, managers in service and public administration industries were considerably more positively depicted (57% and 49%, respectively) than negatively depicted (32% and 33%, respectively), whereas finance industry managers were depicted slightly more positively (47%) than negatively (41%); public administration industries accounted for proportionately more of the neutral managers. Hierarchically speaking, small business owners were depicted more positively than managers at any other level, whereas executive managers accounted for proportionately more negative depictions (49%) than other managerial levels.

The Demographics of Management Actions

Of the 6,087 actions performed by foreground characters, 702 (12%) were performed by managers. In terms of character type, most of these actions (61%) were performed by major regular managers while 17% and 22% of the remaining actions were performed by minor regular managers and visiting managers, respectively. Once again, finance, service, and public administration served as the industry contexts for over 70% of these managerial activities (accounting for 15%, 30%, 29% of these actions respectively). With respect to hierarchical level, the majority of these actions were performed by managers in the top three levels, with CEOs, executive/top managers, and middle managers accounting for 22%, 27%, and 28% of all actions, respectively; first line and self-employed managers accounted for 12% and 11% of the actions.

In terms of network, CBS and ABC accounted for most of the managerial actions (42% and 39% respectively) while NBC acccounted for only 19% of all managerial action. Over one-half of these actions were performed on dramas (54%) with 29% performed on comedies, 8% on action adventure programs, and 9% of all other genres. Concomitantly, most of these actions (61%) were cast in a serious dramatic tone while 21% and 18% were cast in comedic or combined comedic-dramatic tones, respectively.

Organizational functions of managerial actions. In terms of the organizational functions accomplished by these managerial actions, 40% were informational, 36% were interpersonal, 12% were decisional, 9% were political, and 3% were operational. Again, however, these proportions differed across different categories of managerial actors. Major regular managers performed proportionately more interpersonal actions (44%), minor regular managers more information processing actions (52%), and visiting managers more political actions (15%); decisional actions were performed by visiting managers 17% of the time, by minor regular managers 15% of the time, and by major regular managers 10% of the time. Industrially speaking, managers in service industries performed proportionately more interpersonal actions (53%) whereas public administration managers engaged in more informational and decisional actions (54% and 19%). Not surprisingly, finance industry managers accounted for proportionately more of the political actions (15%). Hierarchically speaking, executive level managers and self-employed managers performed proportionately more interpersonal actions (44% and 55%, respectively) while middle managers performed proportionately more information processing (53%) and decision-making (15%) actions.

Proportions of political actions were spread evenly among CEOs, executives, middle managers, and first line managers (each about 10%), though self-employed managers engaged in little political behavior (only 4%).[1]

Depictions of managerial actions. In terms of the depiction of these managerial actions, 42% were positive, 23% were negative, and 35% were neutral. A closer examination of the positive managerial actions revealed that 51% were friendly, 26% were helpful, 21% were productive, and 2% were charitable. On the other hand, of the negative managerial actions, 49% were unfriendly, 32% were selfish, 10% were foolish, 8% were malevolent, and 1% were illegal. Hierarchically speaking, all five managerial levels were more likely to perform positive rather than negative actions, though small business owners performed proportionately more positive actions (61%) than other managers. Middle managers enacted proportionately more negative actions (35%) than did other managers whereas small business managers performed the smallest proportion of negative actions (10%). The positive actions were more likely to be friendly for all but middle managers who were more likely to perform helpful actions. The negative actions of CEOs, top/executive, and middle managers were more likely to be unfriendly whereas first line managers were more likely to be selfish.

Industrially speaking, the finance industry framed more negative (39%) than positive or neutral actions (30% each); most of these negative actions were unfriendly while most of the positive actions were friendly. In public administration industries, managerial actions were proportionately more neutral (51%) than positive or negative. And in service industries, managerial actions were more likely to be positive (54%), and primarily friendly, rather than neutral (25%) or negative (21%); most of these negative actions were selfish. Finally, with respect to character type, major regular managers were proportionately more likely to perform positive (50%) than neutral (32%) or negative (18%) actions, with most of the positive actions being friendly and most negative actions being unfriendly. Minor regular managers were proportionately more likely to perform their managerial activities in a neutral manner (44%), with more of their

---

[1] The number of operational actions performed by prime time managers constituted a mere 22 out of 702 managerial actions — 3.1%. As a result we do not discuss operational action in this chapter. Goodman (1976) provides some support for our editorial decision as well as a partial explanation for the dearth of operational activities by managers on prime time television. As he observed, "It must be admitted that most managers both manage and do, but at the times they are doing, they are not managing" (p. 31).

positive actions being helpful and most of their negative actions being unfriendly. Not surprisingly, proportionately more of the actions of visiting managers were negative (40%) and these were primarily unfriendly. Of the 26% of the single appearance manager's actions which were positive, most were friendly.

Managers on Prime Time: Crooks, Conmen, and Clowns or Heroes, Helpers, and Humanitarians?

As we noted earlier, Theberge (1981) concluded from a study conducted for the Media Institute that most of prime time's "businessmen" were portrayed in a very negative light. That study found that while visiting businessmen were especially villainous, even continuing businessmen were as likely to be portrayed in a negative as positive light. In short, Theberge argued that most of prime time business people were indeed crooks, conmen, or clowns (see Chapter 1).

We did not find support for this overwhelmingly negative portrait, at least with respect to the managers of prime time organizations. Overall, the managers of prime time television are considerably more likely to be cast as positive characters than as negative characters, and they are much more likely to engage in positive actions than negative actions. Continuing characters, in particular, are overwhelmingly positive. Although J.R. Ewing was a notable managerial villain, prime time managers in this sample included such admirable characters as Peter McDermott (Hotel), Frank Furillo (Hill Street Blues), and Donald Westphall (St. Elsewhere), managers who were glorified as caring, compassionate, and ultimately heroic figures (see Chapter 6). In this sense, Theberge's findings are not representative of the managers we see on prime time television. In fact, we believe that the other AMA (the American Management Association) has almost as much right to praise network television for its portrayal of managers on prime time as the American Medical Association has to praise network television for its overwhelming positive portrayal of prime time doctors (see Gerbner, Morgan, & Signorielli, 1982, February).

However, all prime time managers are not alike. Visiting managers are more likely to be villains than heroes. So, too, those managers employed in the finance industries were more likely to be seen as selfish or unfriendly managers who were more concerned with furthering their own personal ends than accomplishing the goals of the organization, its members, or its clients. In short, while *most* of prime time managers are heroes, helpers, and humanitarians, it is worth noting that a portion of them are indeed crooks, conmen, and clowns.

We should point out that our sample of "managers" included some characters who were probably not coded by the Media Institute (e.g., managers — such as Frank Furillo or Donald Westphall—who manage public administration and health service "businesses") and did not include some characters who probably were coded by the Media Institute (e.g., visiting board members who were not seen at work in an organization). Had we dropped these nonbusiness managers and added these nonmanagerial businessmen, our findings probably would have been a bit more supportive of Theberge's findings. Nonetheless, we conclude that Theberge offered an exaggeratedly negative picture that is not representative of overall managerial action or organizational life on prime time television. Unfortunately, given the wide dissemination of the Media Institute study in popular trade magazines such as *Channels* (Pollan, 1981) and *Across the Board* (the Media Institute, 1981) as well as on PBS specials, we fear that many readers and viewers believe that organizational life on prime time is a lot worse than it is.

Our findings about the demography of prime time organizational life are instructive because they reveal trends in the presentation of managers and managerial action. However, while these demographic trends offer information about the distributions of managerial characters and their actions, they do not tell us much about *how* these managers actually performed their work actions in their prime time organizations. We now turn our attention to the dramatic performances of these prime time managers.

THE DRAMATURGY OF MANAGEMENT ON PRIME TIME TELEVISION

In recent years, the importance of the symbolic quality of organizational life has been (re)affirmed in the organizational literature. Organizational researchers, especially those who have studied organizations as "corporate cultures" (e.g., Dandridge, 1985; Deal & Kennedy, 1982; Frost, Moore, Louis, Lundberg, & Martin, 1985; Pacanowsky and O'Donnell-Trujillo, 1982, 1983; Pettigrew, 1979; Smircich, 1983) have told us that myths and stories and metaphors and other symbolic forms are important because they help all members understand the appropriate and accepted ways of the organization. Management in particular has been cast as a symbolic process. Pfeffer

(1981b), for example, argued that management *is* "symbolic action" and that the most important managerial skills "are political, dramaturgical, and language skills more than analytical or purely quantitative skills" (p. 44). Thayer (1987) suggested similarly that the effective leader is not one who merely directs or delegates organizational behaviors but rather is one "who sees himself or herself engaged in a great human drama" (p. 10). Perhaps Weick (1979) put it best when he said that the manager is better understood as an "evangelist" than an "accountant."

This emphasis on the symbolism of organizational life has led many researchers to consider the "dramaturgy" of management (see Mangham & Overington, 1983; Mitroff & Kilman, 1975; Thompson, 1963; Tompkins, 1984; Trujillo, 1985). At the heart of this dramaturgy is the metaphor of organizational action as "performance." The metaphor of human action as performance has, of course, been around for some time. Indeed, the familiarity of Shakespeare's oft-quoted passage "All the world's a stage, And the men and women merely players," indicates that the idea of human behavior as performance has been quite popular. As used here, the metaphor of performance has two distinct connotations which are vital to understanding organizational life (see Pacanowsky & O'Donnell-Trujillo, 1983).

The first sense of performance is theatricality and impression management, which suggests that managers and other organizational members do not "react" to behavioral laws but rather "act" in ways which reflect the social conventions of the organization. Thus, while there are general organizational "scripts" (and very specific prime time organizational scripts), the *performance* of these scripts (in life or on television) varies when enacted by different actors in different scenes. Such performances create (and ultimately manage) the "identities" and "impressions" of organizational characters (see Goffman, 1959).

However, performances are not merely displays of conveniently managed impressions and identities. As Burke (1969, 1972) and others (Berger & Luckmann, 1967; Putnam and Pacanowsky, 1983; Turner, 1977) have argued so eloquently, performances are the very actions through which people create their social realities. Indeed, for Burke, life *is* drama because humans are actors who experience their lives in the symbols they use. As Duncan (1968) put it in one of his familiar axioms: "Social order is created and sustained in social dramas through intensive and frequent communal presentation of tragic and comic roles whose proper enactment is believed necessary to human survival" (p. 39). Thus, performances are the very actions through which deeper visions of organizational reality are created and through which organizational members identify with these visions (see Abravanel, 1983; Cheney, 1983; Dandridge, 1983; Martin & Powers, 1983).

An examination of the dramaturgy of management on prime time television, thus, should reveal the types of organizational *identities* that are presented to viewing audiences as well as the deeper organizational *realities* that are presented. We reveal the former organizational identities in this chapter as we discuss the different managerial performances that were enacted in our sample; we summarize these identities at the end of this chapter in terms of the dominant management "styles" that are presented on prime time. We reveal the latter organizational realities in the next chapter as we discuss the "cultural values" that were enacted in our sample; we summarize these realities in our concluding chapter in terms of the dominant metaphoric "visions" of prime time organizational life.

Before we examine these management performances, however, we must reiterate two general points about the dramaturgy of televised organizational life. First, the managerial identities and realities presented on prime time are not the individual creations of television actors who star as characters but rather are composite creations which are socially constructed by television producers, directors, screenwriters, and program decision makers as well as the actors and actresses who play out the characters. As such, these dramatic composites of management characters reflect the organizational realities of television industry workers as much as they reflect the organizational realities of viewing audiences.

Second, and perhaps more importantly, viewers also participate in the dramaturgy of organizational life as (performing) audiences who witness these "staged" dramas of organizational life. As noted in Chapter 1, audiences actively and willingly suspend disbelief of the "reality" of prime time organizations, recognizing the dramatic license that television has taken by overplaying some and underplaying other aspects of organizational life. In so participating in the dramaturgy of organizational life, audiences compare and evaluate these prime time organizational performances against other prime time performances and against real life organizational performances and, thereby, develop expectations about organizational life (on and off television). We turn now to a closer look at some of these managerial performances in our sample which were enacted before viewing audiences.

Informational Performances

Information processing is invariably discussed as a fundamental managerial activity. Mintzberg (1973) was perhaps most explicit when he characterized the manager as an information "nerve center" who collects relevant information on the organization and its environment and sends this information to appropriate organizational members. As noted in the beginning of this chapter, these informational actions dominated prime time management, accounting for 40% of all managerial activity. In this section, we consider three types of informational activities that prime time managers perform: (a) giving (and getting) organizational facts, (b) giving (and getting) feedback, and (c) explaining organizational life.

Giving (and getting) organizational facts. Managers in real and in prime time organizations regularly give and get various organizational data. Such data keep managers and subordinates updated on important activities or procedures which are considered relevant to the organization. These facts include such information as task assignments, changes in organizational procedures, or new professional developments. Generally, such informational activity is positive inasmuch as it aids organizational members in their job performances. However, when such information is used to deceive (so-called "misinformation" or "disinformation"), it can be interpreted in a negative light.

We found many instances of such fact finding in our sample of managerial actions. For example, on *Scarecrow and Mrs. King*, former national security agency chief, Thornton, gave operative Mrs. Amanda King the background information she needed to accomplish her assignment — finding the missing pardon letter from President Eisenhower; on *Miami Vice*, Scotland Yard Agent Cross gave the Miami Vice unit information about an IRA fund-raiser terrorist whom the Yard suspected of visiting Miami to buy arms; on *Night Court*, city bureaucrat, Mr. Marsh, informed Judge Harry and the other court staff about Flo's mandatory retirement; and on *Hunter* the coroner provided Hunter and McCall with some unusual informational details about two homicides. And so on.

Perhaps the most notable performance of giving organizational facts occurred on *Hill Street Blues* in the well-known "roll call" ritual. Under Sgt. Phil Esterhaus, morning roll call at the Hill consisted of information punctuated by a delightful mixture of erudite commentary and, as he put it, "street patois" (see Chapter 6). In the 1986 episode from our sample, Sgt. Jablonski had taken over roll call and had enacted this ritual organizational information performance with a more folksy flavor, though its essence as an informational activity remained the same. Typically, Sgt. Jablonski began with "Item 1," and worked through a list of announcements ranging from eruptions of gang wars to introductions of new organizational members, as when he introduced everyone to "Officer Catherine McBride," who had been "transfered from the Polk." Jablonski also provided information about the officers' special personal events or honors of note (e.g., promotions) as well as about their more routine job assignments, as when Jablonski told everyone:

> "O.K. Item 7. Mick Belker is undercover at Michigan and 143. Our information is that a lone shark is operating a 6-for-5 operation out of a lunch wagon down there. He's feeding off the area factory workers and the construction workers. Now Mick's gonna be running a competition roach coach. Ahh, that's an area patrols alert."

In the roll call, giving (and receiving) information clearly served the functions of providing organizational members with needed facts to help them perform their daily jobs and of providing audiences with important contextual information about the current episode. However, roll call was also an important *ritual* which gave a very disparate group of employees some serious and some humorous grist for conversations, which provided a creative context for one lower level manager (the Sarge) to maintain his relationships with the troops, and which reminded and encouraged these officers to enact their identities as "cops" in a special way. Thus, this "roll call" ritual helped characters as well as viewers feel like "insiders," like they knew what was going on at the station and belonged there.

Giving (and getting) feedback. "In the absence of relevant feedback," Redding (1984) argued, "management may exist in a fool's paradise, believing its messages really have been received and understood" (p. 32), a state (or trait) which usually leads to trouble. As Hellriegel and Slocum (1985) summarized, feedback is important because it provides organizational members with information about their immediate work performance and about how their work accomplishes overall organizational goals; it may also motivate members to feel more involved in and responsible for accomplishing these organizational goals. These and other authors, however, have been quick to add that feedback is (or should be) two-way communication, that managers should receive feedback from subordinates as well. As Redding (1984) put it, one of the biggest challenges for managers is to "find ways of obtaining the important information, especially feedback, regarding his or her own job performance" (p. 94).

The managers in our sample of prime time organizations provided specific information to their subordinates, thereby helping those subordinates perform specific tasks or develop their skills as organizational members. These managers also received such feedback from peers and subordinates. One performance of giving (and getting) feedback occurred in the law firm of McKenzie, Brackman, Chaney, and Kuzak on *L.A. Law*, following the weekly meeting of the firm's attorneys. At that meeting, named partner Douglas Brackman questioned whether some firm attorneys, including the firm's most senior partner Leland McKenzie, were "pulling their weight" (in fees, of course). Brackman's comments ultimately led to a vote of confidence for Leland and a public, stinging rebuke of Brackman and his priorities. Subsequently, Brackman left a letter of resignation on Leland's desk, precipitating feedback from one senior manager to another (slightly less senior) manager about organizational performances and values.

When Leland opened the letter he immediately went to talk with Douglas Brackman to discourage him from resigning. However, in response to this request that he reconsider resigning, Douglas lamented that he had to resign since he would no longer "command respect from the other partners." When Leland retorted that "you don't *command* respect, Douglas, you've got to *earn* it," Douglas countered that he took it as his job to "wear the black hat" and demand economic accountability. Leland agreed that economic accountability was important but explained to Douglas that it was a question of his "style." Leland's feedback helped Douglas understand that his cold and impersonal demand for economic rationality, as well as his apparent disregard for the importance of Leland's role as figurehead, had alienated the other organizational members. Douglas had, as Leland put it, failed to "weigh the needs of the individuals against those of the firm." Leland's feedback thus assured Douglas that the firm needed both a Douglas (a voice of fiscal responsibility and accountability) and a Leland, a father-figure and mentor because the lawyers in the firm "need to feel cared for — wanted."

As a result of his feedback performance with Leland, Douglas decided both to withdraw his resignation and to revamp his own managerial style. The performance reminded Douglas (and audience members) about the importance of human values to members of this firm and to successful managerial performances. We saw the apparent benefits of this feedback when in subsequent scenes Brackman began to display greater friendliness and sensitivity toward other members of the firm in positive and supportive actions. And they, though surprised and wary, responded positively to Douglas.

Explaining organizational life. In addition to facts and feedback, managers must also provide broader information through which members can come to understand not only how to perform their immediate activities more effectively but also how those activities fit into the larger vision of the organization. Mintzberg (1973) described such information as "value information" which reveals the underlying rationale of the organization and which ultimately guides the decision-making actions of organizational members. Indeed, as Pondy (1978) concluded, such explanations are most important for the manager inasmuch as "the effectiveness of a leader lies in his ability to make activity meaningful for those in his role set — not to change behaviors but to give others a sense of understanding what they are doing" (pp. 94–95).

We saw a number of instances of such value information being offered by the prime time managers in our sample. For example, head of surgery Trapper John explained to a younger doctor why he had not forced an aging and ill doctor to resign from the hospital staff. As Trapper explained, the old doctor's wealth of experience could help younger physicians and besides: "What he does know can save lives. Come on, you don't just turn a guy out to pasture when he still has something to contribute" (*Trapper John, M.D.*). Similarly, when intern Carol Novino asked chief of staff Dr. Westphall for advice on how to tell a patient that he had cancer and would die in less than one year, Westphall explained: "Look, Carol. I don't care if the man's chances are 50/50 or 100-to-one. Patients count on us for more than just medical treatment. They need encouragement, inspiration, too. Sometimes we need another person to help us see the possibilities in life." (*St. Elsewhere*). In this way, Trapper John and Donald Westphall, as key leaders in their organizations, offered less information about formal procedures themselves and more information about the values and philosophies of the organization which framed such formal procedures.

In sum, informational performances create a sense of the knowledgeability of individual managers as well as a sense of the rationality of organizational life. Such informational actions help both managers and organizational members understand each other as well as the procedures, rationales, and values of their organizations. In this way, information giving and getting not only enacts the rationality but also the ideology of organizational life which guides and governs the actions of all members (see Tompkins & Cheney, 1985).

Interpersonal Performances

Interpersonal performances are those actions through which managers maintain, develop, or destroy their relationships with organizational others. Ever since the so-called Hawthorne studies and subsequent human relations movement, the interpersonal nature of organizations has been recognized as an important and integral part of organizational life. As Sayles (1964) concluded from his study of middle and lower level managers, "the one enduring objective of the manager is the effort to build and maintain a predictable reciprocating system of relationships" (p. 258). Indeed, the "relational" impacts of organizational messages are critical to management whether they are very apparent (e.g., when managers counsel employees about their personal problems or when managers humiliate employees in the presence of other employees) or are fairly subtle (e.g., when managers tour the organization, engaging in small talk with employees).

As we noted in the beginning of this chapter, the second largest proportion (36%) of prime time managerial actions in our sample were interpersonal in nature. However, this finding was not surprising when we considered the social nature of prime time television characters and plots. Here, we discuss three types of interpersonal performances enacted by our sample of prime time managers: (a) sociabilities, (b) counseling and mentoring, and (c) organizational romance.

Sociabilities. In "How the Boss Stays in Touch with the Troops," Meyer (1978) noted that it has become commonplace for managers to visit periodically with their employees. Visits often occur as managers "tour" or stroll through their organizations on the way to (or from) meetings. Such visits have been glorified with the label "Management by Walking Around" (Peters & Waterman, 1982) and have been characterized as informal ways of maintaining interpersonal contact with employees and of obtaining information from those employees.

Not surprisingly, we found many examples of such organizational sociabilities in our sample. Members of the St. Gregory Hotel (Hotel), the New York City courtroom (Night Court), and the Cheers bar (Cheers) were especially fond of small talk and other forms of "play" in their organizations. Through such verbal and physical playful sociabilities, organizational members developed a knowledge and trust of each other. Of course, some organizational members were less sociable than others, a situation which caused minor problems, for example, on Bob Newhart when George (the inn handyman) played a friendly prank on Stephanie (the weight-conscious part-time housekeeper and full-time college student). George turned up Stephanie's scale several pounds, a practical joke that Stephanie did not find at all amusing when she discovered it, although others at the inn thoroughly enjoyed watching the already petite young lady exercise to sweat off those "extra" pounds.

In general, most organizational members used such interpersonal sociabilities to punctuate their work, to develop a sense of community, and to relieve work tension. And for at least one minor regular prime time organizational member, these sociabilities were primary factors in job satisfaction. As "temporary" employee Herbert Viola explained to Madeline Hayes in response to her question as to why he kept working at the Blue Moon Detective Agency despite being harassed by the overtures of receptionist Agnes Dipesto: "I like this place. Hey, it's crazy. I mean it's like special class in junior high school when every day is an assembly or a field trip" (Moonlighting).

Of course, organizational sociabilities were not limited to interactions between organizational members but also characterized relations between organizational members and customers. Prime time managers in particular paid close attention to customers by remembering their names, by engaging in friendly smiles, and by asking them directly if they needed or wanted anything. Such "customer relations" sociabilities were perhaps best illustrated by the top manager (captain) and the first line managers (purser and cruise director) of the Pacific Princess (Love Boat) who greeted passengers when they first boarded the ship, who dined with passengers in the dining cabin, and who said goodbye to passengers when they left the ship. The most creative management response to customer complaints and problems in our sample, however, was enacted by TV program manager John Reed (Shellgame) who created a television program called "Solutions" whose crew of reporters, producer/investigator, and camera people investigated consumer problems and videotaped the process of solving them. In sum, such sociabilities kept our prime time managers "close to the customer" (Peters & Waterman, 1982) and made them better able to meet the needs of those customers.

Counseling and mentoring. Perhaps a more important interpersonal managerial function is that of mentoring and counseling. Mentoring and counseling involve the sharing of experience with other (usually junior) organizational members. As Hellriegel and Slocum (1985) summarized, mentoring is prevalent in well-run organizations inasmuch as about 70% of the top managers in American corporations have had mentors early in their careers (see Kanter, 1977). As Moore (1984) pointed out, however, "mentoring is important not only on the personal level but also on the institutional level" because "while the protege may look upon the mentor as a career enhancer, institutions . . . regard the mentor as a valuable talent scout and trainer" (p. 210).

We found a number of instances of mentoring and counseling in our sample of managerial action on prime time and most, though not all, of these actions were positive and helpful in nature. Such mentoring was illustrated when *Hotel* manager Peter McDermott advised receptionist Julie to continue with her outside computer classes because it would help her advance in the organization and in her career outside the hotel. Similarly, Trapper John advised a cocky young neurosurgeon to seek help with a problematic patient diagnosis from an older doctor with years of experience. As Trapper John put it: "Now maybe, just maybe, he knows something that you don't. I mean, not knowing the answer and being stupid are two different things. Don't be both" (*Trapper John, M.D.*).

One noteworthy exemplar of counseling, however, was directed from a lower level manager to a higher level manager in our sample episode of *Gung Ho*. In this episode, Mr. Cass, CEO of the Assan Motor Company, discovered that an odor problem with the hatchbacks, which nearly prevented the plant from meeting its shipment deadline, was his responsibility because his son had been leaving his traditional Japanese lunches stuffed under the various demo hatchbacks Cass had brought home. Cass arrived at this realization just as Hunt Stevenson, an employee Cass had previously demoted for irresponsible behavior with a company credit card, arrived at Cass's home to pay back the charged expenses. When Cass explained why he was upset and why he would have to demote himself, Hunt laughed and advised Cass that while striving for perfection is noble, being a stubborn perfectionist is foolish. As Hunt put it in this comedic scene: "Striving is fine. I, too, have striven. In fact, I strove every chance I got. But there are other things equally important — like compassion, fairness, a whiter-brighter wash (At which Cass's wife giggled.) And a sense of humor. Laugh at yourself. You were willing to dump your entire career over a piece of sushi." Cass took this lower level manager's advice to heart, laughed at himself, then granted forgiveness to both Hunt and himself.

In sum, counseling and mentoring are important organizational actions which were presented on prime time. Through mentoring and counseling, managers teach and inform other organizational members (and are themselves informed) about organizational procedures and organizational (and social) values. As Moore (1984) concluded, "Mentoring is one way, however imperfect, by which a single leader or a leadership group can help assure continuity and pass on to the next generation a particular brand of leadership" (p. 221).

Organizational romance. Finally, there is organizational romance, an aspect of organizational sociability which has been recognized, if reluctantly, in the organizational literature in the last few years. Given the ever-increasing number of women in the workplace, attention to issues of gender are not surprising. Most of this scholarly attention has dealt with organizational sex roles and related issues (see Bormann, Pratt, & Putnam, 1978; Broom and Dozier, 1986; Hennig & Jardim, 1976; Pilotta, 1983). Although the case of the "nonromance" of Mary Cunningham and Bill Agee, then of Bendix Corporation, was widely discussed (see Bernstein, 1982; Cunningham, 1984), organizational romance per se has not been widely studied. As Cunningham quipped: "There are certainly no Harvard Business School cases on how to deal with this" (cited by Bernstein, 1982, p. 238).

Such is not the case in prime time organizations. Organizational romances (and organizational sexuality) dominate the interpersonal relationships of many managers and members. Among the organizational romances between managers and members in our sample were those of bar manager Sam Malone and waitress Diane Chambers (*Cheers*), hotel manager-then-owner Peter McDermott and assistant manager-then-manager Christine Francis (*Hotel*), detective agency owner Madeline Hayes and detective David Addison (*Moonlighting*), hospital manager Donald Westphall and intern Carol Novino (*St. Elsewhere*), and police captain Frank Furillo and public defender Joyce Davenport (*Hill St. Blues*). Organizational romance is hardly overlooked in prime time organizations.

However, most of the romantically involved organizational couples listed above displayed the problems associated with organizational romance. In the 1986 sample episode of *St. Elsewhere*, for example, Donald Westphall was criticized by his friend and colleague, head nurse Helen Rosenthal, for "sniffing the young medical students"; ultimately, Donald and Carol terminated their romantic involvement because of the organizational complications it created. In the 1986 sample episode of *Cheers*, Sam and Diane admitted their love for each other when they thought they were about to die in a plane crash, only to deny what they had said to each other when they were safe again at the Cheers bar; and in the 1987 season finale (not in our sample) just when they had finally decided to get married, Diane received a contract to write a book and left Sam and the Cheers bar. Finally, in our 1987 episode of *Hotel*, political consultant John Granger's encouragement to manager Christine Francis to run for Congress precipitated a fight between Christine and the hotel's executive manager Peter McDermott related to the consequences of her taking such a position in Washington — Christine's resignation as manager of the St. Gregory and at least a six-month separation during the year. Although they reconciled their differences at the end of this *Hotel* episode (when Christine decided *not* to run for Congress), they actually broke up in another 1987 episode (not in our sample) when Christine's old flame came back into her life. Quite simply, on prime time most organizational romances do *not* work well.

In sum, organizational romance is a topic which has become an increasingly important issue in contemporary organizations and should become an important issue in contemporary organizational literature as well. Although prime time television admittedly glamorizes and glorifies these romances and their resultant problems and prospects, it does reflect an organizational reality in America that is at present virtually ignored by most organizational scholars. In this instance, students of organizational life may actually learn more about the interpersonal reality of organizational romance from watching prime time television than by reading organizational research.

Decisional Performances

Decisional performances are those actions in which managers and other members make organizational *choices* which normally concern the resolution of organizational conflicts or problems. Decision-making actions include such routine and mundane choices as assigning tasks, scheduling meetings, and authorizing routine requests for supplies as well as more dramatic choices such as hiring and firing employees, negotiating disputes, handling employee problems, and allocating economic resources. Such decisional actions, according to Mintzberg (1973), are "probably the most crucial part of the manager's work — the part that justifies his great authority and his powerful access to information" (p. 77).

Traditionally, managerial decision making has been cast as a highly *rational* activity. Indeed, classical conceptions of decision making rested on an "economic" model which assumed that managers could acquire *all* of the necessary and sufficient information to make *the* (single) best — most "cost effective" — decision which would accomplish the organizational goal. As Allison (1971) suggested, this traditional model of rational decision making also assumed two levels of managerial consistency: "Consistency among goals and objectives relative to a particular action" and "consistency in the application of principles in order to select the optimal alternatives" (pp. 28–29). This conception of decision making dominated early management writings and gave us familiar formulas for decision making ranging from Dewey's early "reflective thinking" format to the "PERT charts" and "critical paths" of today.

The classical model of rational decision making has been refined by several management theorists, most notably by Herbert Simon (1945). Simon argued that "economic" managers with "complete" rationality were mythical constructions since everyday organizational life was, by definition, filled with "administrative" managers with "bounded" rationality. Subsequent studies of managers and organizations have led others to concur. Indeed, as Sayles (1964) concluded, a highly rational organization is a "never-to-be attained ideal" (p. 162).

As we noted earlier, decision making did not constitute a large portion of the organizational action on prime time. Although managers were presented as decision makers more often than any other occupational group, decision making accounted for only 12% of all managerial activity on prime time. Nonetheless, these infrequent decisions constituted an important part of organizational life on prime time. In many cases, these decisions resolved the main problem or conflict at the heart of the program's plot and, thus, represented the climax of the program itself. Here we examine three types of managerial decision making presented on prime time: (a) assigning tasks, (b) solving problems, and (c) setting policy.

Assigning tasks. Many managerial decisions in our sample were routine choices involving well-defined issues. Mintzberg (1979) called these choices the "administrative" decisions of management and argued that they involve decision processes which "are typically routine, made on fixed schedules, and are sometimes even rather programmed" (p. 59). Although such routine decisions do not involve much choice on the part of the manager, they are important because they are made by the manager alone, without the aid of subordinates. More importantly, when these decisions call for task performances by subordinates, such tasks are delegated or assigned to subordinates who typically accept them. Thus, these routine choices are important because they reflect the authority of the manager.

Routine assignments were found in our sample of prime time

decision making actions. For example, police managers Captain Furillo (Hill Street Blues) and Lieutenant Samuels (Cagney and Lacey) made several routine assignments to their respective subordinates including Hill and Renko and Cagney and Lacey who, not surprisingly, carried out the orders from their superiors (even though Cagney and Lacey did not want to do so in our 1987 sample episode). Other examples were displayed by Dr. Mark Craig, director of surgery at St. Eligius Hospital, who assigned resident Victor Ehrlich to find and fetch a patient's file (St. Elsewhere, NBC), and by television station manager Thayer who approved the assignment of the "Solutions" crew to cover a particular story (Shellgame).

In sum, the routine decisions of management, because they are "routine," do not seem very important. Nonetheless, managers are seen as managers in part because they have the authority to make such decisions. And subordinates are seen as subordinates when they choose to obey these decisions (see Barnard, 1938). In this way, such routine decision making reveals organizational hierarchies and institutionalized power.

Problem solving. Managers, however, do not merely make routine choices; they also make more complex ("adaptive" or "innovative") organizational decisions. Such managerial choices require more emphasis on the processes of decision making which usually involve multiple organizational members, including subordinates. And, as we noted earlier, such problem solving is not the rational process that is described in some management textbooks. McCall, Kaplan and Gerlach (1982) have argued that "solving important problems will never be the logical, orderly process most of us strive for, no matter how orderly the plan" (p. 64). Indeed, as Deal and Kennedy (1982) frankly acknowledged, "how managers really make decisions is to put people in a room, review available information and data, and if pressed, 'decide' as best they can" (p. 69).

Although prime time managers did not engage in many (or very lengthy) performances of problem solving, we did find some instances of such decisional activity. For example, Dr. Trapper John McIntyre, chief of surgery at San Francisco Memorial Hospital, solved the problem of what to do with a problematic neurosurgeon who was experienced, knowledgeable, and crustily autocratic, but aging and physically unable to perform all his obligations, by creating a new position for that doctor: "Director of Medical Education" (Trapper John, M.D.). And Dr. Daniel Auschlander, St. Eligius hospital's most senior medical administrator and physician, utilized his years of experience to help resident Victor Ehrlich solve a very important case — diagnosing and identifying the cause of the apparently psy-

chosomatic pains that the neglected wife of Ehrlich's mentor, Dr.
Craig, had been experiencing (St. Elsewhere).

Unfortunately, these and most examples of problem solving tended
to present decision making as a fairly simple and rational process.
We failed to see more embedded decisional processes in part because
characters usually appeared on the television screen in very short
and fragmented scenes. In this sense, prime time does not provide
very nuanced pictures of organizational problem solving. Such pictures, however, may not be entirely unrealistic. In fact, Mintzberg
(1973) and others have confirmed that most of the manager's activities are completed in brief, varied, and fragmented periods of time.
In this sense, then, television's fragmented glimpses of decision
making and the focus on the final act of decision making rather
than on the lengthy process are partially reflective of organizational
reality.

Policy making. Finally, "policy making" decisions are those which
develop and reveal the deeper values and philosophies of the organization. Such activity is often referred to as "strategic planning" in
management literature and refers to "the process of making choices
about an organization's mission, objectives, strategies, policies, and
major resource allocations" (Grant & King, 1982). Such activity is
typically seen in terms of the organization's development *over the
long run* and includes such economic processes as environmental
scanning and forecasting as well as such noneconomic processes as
corporate philosophizing and philanthropizing.

This form of decision making was virtually absent in our sample
of prime time organizations. We did not observe any characters
dealing explicitly and directly with the long-term survival of their
companies in our sample weeks, though elsewhere (e.g., St. Elsewhere's nurses strike and the Ecumena take-over) we did. On the
other hand, managers did reveal the long-term values upon which
the organization itself was based in many of their decisions. For
example, hotel manager Peter McDermott's decision to "give" flower
lady Maggie a suite at no cost so that she could stay in the hotel
and not embarrass her long-separated daughter (Hotel) revealed the
bedrock values of this manager and this hotel — that people are
special and much more important than profits. Likewise, when Ian
Stone became acting head of a (CIA-front) corporation as a result
of the kidnapping of the company's board chairman by terrorists,
Stone's decisions revealed the organization's complex and paradoxical values. Indeed, Stone made two decisions — a public decision
to uphold the corporate policy not to negotiate with terrorists and

a private (but expected) decision to covertly use all the organization's resources to rescue the board chairman (Spies).

In summary, although we may not see many managerial decisions on prime time, the decisions that we do see are important in several senses. Routine decisions reveal the authority of management, problem solving decisions reveal the (ir)rationality of management, and policy making decisions reveal the ethicality of management. Most of these prime time management decisions are performed in response to particular situations that these managers and organizations experience. In this sense, television managers may be similar to those real managers who have been called "firefighters" and "disturbance handlers."

Political Performances

As we noted in Chapter 3, although "power" and "control" have been staple concepts of practicing managers for some time, only recently have management researchers addressed the political aspects of organizational power and control. From a political perspective, power is not the functional span of management but rather is constituted in social influence which promotes or threatens the self-interests of certain organizational members. For our purposes here, then, political performances were treated as attempts at managerial influence which were designed to protect the self-interests of individuals or coalitions or to threaten the interests of other individuals or coalitions.

Not surprisingly, prime time organizations did not present many explicit instances of political action. Such was expected since, as we argued in Chapter 1, television offers rather mainstream views of life in general and organizational life in particular. And the notion that organizational members use power to accomplish their own selfish ends or to hurt others is not a mainstream cultural ideal. In fact, as Pfeffer (1981b) argued, management researchers themselves have been slow to admit and study organizational politics because such a notion went against the ethic of rationality upon which mainstream management theory has been based.

Nevertheless, we did see some instances of managerial politics. Indeed, the group of programs that we have come to call "prime time soaps" (e.g., Dallas, Dynasty, Falcon Crest, Knot's Landing) have been distinct as a genre in part because they have featured an overly politicized view of organizational life. All prime time political behavior, however, was not completely exhausted by these programs, nor was all prime time political action as blatant as it was depicted on these serial dramas. Here we briefly describe three types of political action we observed on prime time: (a) bargaining, (b) showing personal strength, and (c) grandstanding.

Bargaining. Bargaining or negotiating characterizes the performance of two or more parties with competing goals who come together to reach consensus on a single goal. Such bargaining occurs in a variety of organizational contexts such as buyer-seller transactions, legal proceedings, departmental disputes, and — perhaps most obviously — labor-management conflicts. Whatever the context, most bargaining involves the general form which Sawyer and Guetzkow (1965) described as "reciprocal agreement and counter agreement, proposal and counter-proposal" (p. 479).

Although most research on bargaining has focused traditionally on the psychological aspects of bargaining, current researchers have been taking a closer (and more microscopic) look at the communicative behaviors of bargaining (Bazerman & Lewicki, 1983; Donohue, 1981; Donohue, Diez, & Stahle, 1983; Putnam, 1984). Such examinations, as Putnam and Geist (1985) pointed out, focus on "the use of arguments, reasoning, and persuasive appeals" rather than the "mere exchange of proposals and counter-proposals" (p. 226).

We saw very little bargaining in our sample of prime time organizations, and when we did, it primarily consisted of the general proposal-counter proposal form. For example, on *He's the Mayor*, Mayor Carl Burke was seen bargaining with the representative from the sanitation workers in an effort to negotiate a new contract. On *Bob Newhart*, Dick Louden, who hosted a talk show on a local television station in addition to running the inn, decided to use a "door in the face" strategy in negotiating with a station manager for new carpet in his office. Initially, though, station manager Bev foiled Bob's plan by giving him the microwave he did not want and then rejecting his request for the new carpeting he had really wanted. However, Bob eventually succeeded when he bargained for the carpeting in return for acting as substitute host on a children's program whose regular host was unexpectedly hit in the head by a sound boom. Other examples of bargaining occurred on *Hill Street Blues* (NBC) and *L.A. Law* (NBC) as district and private attorneys plea-bargained with defendants and plaintiffs. For example, in our 1986 *Hill Street* episode, assistant district attorney Irwin Bernstein and Capt. Furillo bargained with Jesus Martinez, a former gang leader who became a paralegal aide and, in this episode, an unsuspecting deliverer of illegal payments from a crooked lawyer to a crooked judge.

In sum, prime time managers occasionally engage in bargaining. Such prime time bargaining and negotiating activities have lighter moments, as was illustrated by Bob's carpet negotiations on the *Bob Newhart Show*. However, bargaining and negotiating actions are usually very serious organizational activities whose stakes — personal and professional, emotional and economic—are often very high both for the organizations and the individuals, especially the managerial negotiators (see the discussion of St. Eligius hospital in Chapter 6).

Showing personal strength. Managers have a variety of methods for getting their way. As noted in the previous section, managers often get what they want by merely assigning organizational tasks to subordinates who matter-of-factly perform these directives. Such power is understood as authority or "the power of the position." Other managers, however, use more aggressive tactics for accomplishing their organizational wishes. As O'Day (1974) summarized, managers have various "intimidation rituals" for suppressing employees including nullification, isolation, defamation, and ultimately expulsion.

Some prime time managers used some of these above intimidation rituals while others invented rituals of their own. J.R. Ewing *(Dallas)* was one major regular manager who often intimidated organizational members and clients. Others, like visiting manager Flin *(Stingray)*, used one of the oldest power tactics known to humanity — physical beatings—to intimidate Mexican agricultural workers on the prison-like farm he managed, a farm which grew illegal marijuana crops. Flin, like most of the managers who exercised negative political muscle, was one of prime time's guest managerial villains.

A number of other prime time managers were less aggressive but no less self-interested. One notable example was Harry, the manager of a hospital supply room on the short-lived comedy *Harry*. In the episode from our sample, Harry totally reorganized the hospital supply facility without a master plan, thus insuring that he was the only one who could run it. Another particularly selfish manager was principal Samuels on *Head of the Class* who "assigned" teacher Charlie to "squire" the female Board member who was to observe and inspect the school, since Charlie had a reputation as a "lady's man." As it turned out, the Board member and Charlie were former lovers who did indeed rekindle their turbulent romance. In the end, she turned in a positive review — not because of political (or romantic) influence but because Charlie really was a creative and brilliant teacher.

Grandstanding. Finally, we observed another type of political action on prime time which we have labeled "grandstanding." Such actions were not designed to protect self-interests per se but rather were designed to make broader political statements, usually at the expense of others. Again, most of these political actions were rather negative. For example, Lt. Guyla Cook (*Hard Copy*) took information she discovered in a confrontation with a reporter and called a press conference wherein she presented that information as a lead acquired through the hard work of "her" officers. Similarly, Alexis Colby, arranged for the long gone (and hated) brother of her ex-husband and business rival, Blake Carrington, to return from Australia and make a surprise appearance during Blake's public costume ball, thereby grandly upsetting Blake and ruining his gala event (*Dynasty*).

Although these grandstanding political actions were overwhelmingly portrayed as negative, we did see one positive enactment of grandstanding managerial politics in the 1987 sample episode — and season finale — of *St. Elsewhere*. This cliffhanger episode ended as a wrecking crew arrived to destroy St. Eligius Hospital (which had been purchased by a Japanese conglomerate). The final scene presented what we coded as a form of positive social protest as Westphall, Craig, and several others from the hospital staff staged a sit-in in front of the hospital. Eventually, they were all arrested by patrol officers, but not until they had made their grandstanding point that the hospital meant very much more than a paycheck to them.

While these kinds of overtly political actions by managers were infrequent, they were sufficiently dramatic that when managers did "grandstand," organizational members and outsiders usually took notice. And what they noticed was exactly what such theatrical activities were intended to convey — power. When prime time managers engaged in such activities, they were either throwing down the gauntlet and warning rivals that an intraorganizational or interorganizational battle for power and control was about to ensue or they were flaunting their political might.

In sum, the political actions of management are important activities in organizational life. Some forms of organizational politics are fairly innocuous and mundane, whereas other forms are far more serious and can involve the physical or economic life (and death) of organizational members or the organization itself. Indeed, the depiction of organizational politics on prime time generally affirmed our "real life" sense that, for better or worse, politics is often "a very dirty business."

In this section, we have presented a more extended description and analysis of the types of managerial performances that were enacted in our sample of prime time organizations. We develop a broader focus in the next section as we consider some of the general ways in which these categories of managerial performances were enacted by certain types of managers. In other words, we examine some of the general management "styles" that have been displayed in prime time organizations.

MANAGERIAL STYLES ON PRIME TIME

Organizational researchers have spent considerable time studying the nature and quality of management or leadership "style" (for a review of this literature, see Stogdill, 1974). Management style refers to the *behavioral* profiles of organizational leaders rather than to the physical or psychological traits of those leaders. Although early research on organizational leadership examined the traits of organizational managers, the failure of this research to explain management effectiveness led many researchers to consider the behaviors of effective managers. Here we consider briefly some key distinctions among types of management styles that have been discussed in the organizational literature. We then examine the types of management styles enacted by managers on prime time.

One early typology of leadership style was developed by Lewin, Lippitt, and White (1939) who identified three general styles of leadership: (a) "autocratic" (directive and task-oriented), (b) "democratic" (encouraging and social-oriented), and (c) "laissez-faire" ("laid back" and virtually powerless). A second early typology, developed by researchers at Ohio State who conducted an extensive research program on leadership style (see Schriesham & Kerr, 1977), included two basic styles: "initiating-structure" (use of well-defined standards and procedures) and "considerate" (attentiveness to subordinates' well-being, status, and satisfaction). House (1971) developed a similar model of leadership style with two categories: "task-centered" (similar to "initiating structure" which emphasized work standards) and "employee-centered" (similar to "considerate" which emphasized the overall needs of employees). Finally, Vroom and Yetton (1973) developed five styles of leadership in their model of managerial decision making, though these different styles actually represented positions on a continuum with "autocratic" and "participative" styles at the two extremes.

Although there are subtle differences among these various management styles, it is fair to say that two general dimensions of management style have emerged from the literature. One dimension is the so-called "task" dimension of leadership, presented in the "task-centered," "autocratic," and "initiating-structure" styles of management. The second dimension is the so-called "social" dimension of leadership, presented in the "person-centered," "democratic," and "considerate" styles of management. These two general styles have dominated the literature and remain the staple dimensions of management style which are summarized in most management and organizational communication textbooks (see Farace, Monge, & Russell, 1977; Hellriegel & Slocum, 1985; Rogers & Agarwala-Rogers, 1976).

We observed both task and social dimensions of leadership style enacted by the managers of prime time television and we have elected to call the corresponding styles associated with these two dimensions as the "administrative" and "relational" styles of prime time management. However, we believe that these two styles miss the political aspects of organizational life discussed earlier in this chapter and thus, we also discuss a third "political" style of management (see Husband, 1985). We turn now to an examination of three types of managerial styles that were displayed on prime time television: (a) administrative, (b) relational, and (c) political.[2]

Administrative Styles

We use the term "administrative" to characterize a style of managerial action which corresponds to the task-centered, autocratic, and initiating-structure styles noted above. Managers who adopt such an administrative style are more concerned with the successful task performances of their subordinates and less concerned with the subordinates themselves. The characteristic actions of such managers include assigning subordinates to particular tasks, informing subordinates of job requirements, and developing uniform standards for job performance. Such managers are highly concerned with the rules and procedures of the organization and do not encourage subordinates to violate these rules and procedures, even when they get in the way of successful task completion. Additionally, although

---

[2] We should note that although we draw primarily from the two weeks of prime time programs in our sample, we also have referred to examples from the prime time episodes included in the case studies in Chapter 6 to describe prime time managers who are particularly representative of these managerial styles (e.g., Peter McDermott, Frank Furillo, J.R. Ewing, etc.). We will note this use of "outside" episodes when appropriate.

these managers draw on their hierarchical authority as managers to direct the actions of subordinates, they are not typically concerned with the development of power for their own (selfish) ends. In short, although these managers are not necessarily insensitive to the needs of their employees, they do things "by the book" and experience organizational life with a bit less passion and compassion than other managers.

Several prime time managers exhibited such an administrative style including Mr. Cass, the CEO of an automotive plant (Gung Ho), chairman of the board Brady (Spies), television station manager Bev (Bob Newhart), and Lieutenant Quark on Spenser for Hire. For example, even at a masquerade ball, "C of B" Brady (as he was called by his subordinates) did not enter into the festivities; instead, he reminded Ian Stone twice that Ian should be more assiduous in his assigned task of keeping an eye on the ambassador (Spies). Similarly, after complaints resulting from Bob's performance as host of the children's show, TV station manager Bev did not hesitate to fire the show's regular host, even though he was in the hospital because the boom man had hit him on the head with a microphone (Bob Newhart). Two managers, both police captains, were particularly emblematic of this administrative style: Captain Martin Castillo and Captain Frank Furillo.

Captain Martin Castillo (Miami Vice) was a mysteriously self-contained leader, often found sitting at his desk in the dark at the headquarters for the Miami Vice Squad, a special investigative police unit that operated somewhat outside the regular Miami police organization. Castillo was the archetypal administrative style manager. His verbal interactions with his employees were as spartan as his black suits and white shirts and as economical as his movements. For example, in the 1987 episode from our sample titled "When Irish Eyes are Crying," Castillo had lunch with Scotland Yard Inspector Cross to discuss a suspected terrorist named Carroon. Castillo made few comments during their luncheon and those only after a lengthy explanation and a specific query from Cross. He was, as you can see from the interchange below, a man of few words:

Castillo: My operation is outside the department's normal chain of command.

Cross: Mine is too. England is under seige from terrorists and I know who they are. I just want the tools to strike first and strike hard.

Castillo: The Irish have rights.

Cross: The Irish, yes. Terrorists, no. Why should we give Carroon rights he never gave his victims? He's committed eight homicides I know about. God knows how many more people he's really killed. I should be able to put a bullet in his ear wherever I find him.

Castillo: Not in Miami.

Cross: You do know what's going to happen, don't you?

Castillo: No.

Cross: One day Carroon or one of his cronies is going to get so far over that line that I will be given that power. You don't like me, do you?

Castillo: That's not my job.

In the world of undercover police operations where officers dealt with huge sums of money as bait and constantly engaged in deception, Castillo was unbending in his insistence on following procedures and unflinching in his punishment of rule infractions. Thus, when Castillo discovered from a telephone trace that Cross had violated procedures and lied about talking to Carroon, Castillo arrested Inspector Cross on the spot.

Castillo's decision making behavior in the police station also epitomized an administrative style of management. In the 1987 sample episode, he reeled off assignments for each officer who immediately took up his or her assigned position, ready to act but immobile until Castillo gave the word. In the 1986 sample episode, Castillo listened silently in a strategy planning session as detectives Crockett, Tubbs, Zito, and Switek reported their information and offered their analysis of the possible courses of action. In this way, Castillo allowed and expected active participation in the planning portion of decision making. However, when it came to making the decisions about action, he retained ultimate and firm control.

One of the rare glimpses into Castillo's private life and past was provided in a 1985 episode (not in our two-week sample) titled "Bushido." In this episode, which again confirmed Castillo's administrative style, Castillo's friend and former partner in military intelligence, Jack Kretsky, returned to Miami with his wife, herself a former KGB agent, because the KGB had sent agents to kill Kretsky, his wife, and their child. Kretsky, having worked with Castillo in Cambodia, knew that Castillo was the only one who could protect his wife and child. In a dramatic scene, Kretsky (dying of cancer) pulled a gun on U.S. agents in Castillo's presence, knowing full well that Castillo would have to (and did) fire and kill him. Nevertheless, Castillo managed to protect Kretsky's wife and child, almost getting killed himself doing so. In the final scene, Tubbs and Crockett watched as Castillo put Kretsky's family on a boat with $500,000 that Kretsky had stolen from an interrupted vice squad deal. When Tubbs noted that no one would miss the money, Castillo corrected him, stating brusquely that every cent of that money would be covered and in the bank by closing time the next day. As Castillo, still bleeding from a stab wound, walked away, Tubbs sighed, "Castillo doesn't give an inch." Crockett summarized, "He can't afford to."

Frank Furillo (Hill Street Blues) was another compelling example of the administrative management style. Furillo, captain of the Hill Street precinct, demonstrated his administrative style in his overwhelming support for rules and procedures, especially when those rules represented "laws." Furillo demanded that his officers do things "by the book," even when that "book" prevented rather than enabled justice to be carried out. For example, in the 1986 episode from our sample, Jesus Martinez (a former gang leader turned paralegal assistant) had been unknowingly delivering bribes from a crooked attorney to an equally crooked judge. When Jesus discovered what was happening and confronted the lawyer, the lawyer died of an apparent heart attack, prompting Jesus to run for fear that he would be sent to prison for the lawyer's murder. Even though Furillo knew that Jesus was innocent of murder and bribery, he still refused to honor the request of Jesus' public defender Joyce Davenport (Furillo's own wife) that Furillo meet with Jesus outside the Hill Street precinct. As Frank explained to Joyce: "I can't do my job ad hominem. If I meet him outside I'll have to bust him." Additionally, Frank castigated his own detectives, especially Buntz and LaRue, who often failed to follow established procedures in their attempts to arrest suspects who were known to have committed crimes. On the rare occasions when Frank himself used questionable practices to accomplish morally justified ends, he experienced guilt and remorse (see Chapter 6). In short, Furillo, like most police captains, represented law and order, and conformity to that law and order was considered paramount.

However, although Frank Furillo served as an exhibit of the administrative style of management, he certainly did not exhibit the apparent neutrality displayed by Castillo. Furillo was a fairly compassionate manager (and passionate lover) who showed more emotion than his counterpart Castillo. Indeed, as Deming (1985) argued, "Captain Furillo articulates the values of a moral order that transcends the police bureaucracy, thus exposing the inadequacy of the political system for coping with the social disintegration that threatens to engulf The Hill, as well as the system's inability to respond adequately to individual human need" (p. 15). Indeed, Furillo was regularly frustrated and incensed by the inhumane qualities and political activities of his own boss, Chief Daniels, who often exploited Frank and his officers to accomplish Daniels' own selfish and malevolent ends. Nonetheless, Furillo symbolized law and order above all else and even remained loyal to his own unscrupulous boss, thereby protecting the order of the organizational hierarchy as well.

The characterization of Furillo as an "administrative" manager is important because it suggests that this style can be enacted in a powerful and even heroic way. For better or worse, such administrative styles are often represented by overly bureaucratic and insensitive managers who do little else than autocratically give directives to subordinates. We should point out, however, that Furillo was not a pure exhibit of the administrative style; in fact, his compassion for his officers suggested a relational style as well. In this sense, Furillo represents a hybrid management style, as do many of the major regular managers of prime time. It is to this relational style that also characterized Furillo's management activity that we now turn.

Relational Styles

Relational styles of management are similar to the person-centered, democratic, and considerate styles discussed above. Managers who adopt relational styles are more likely to express appreciation and give rewards when subordinates do a good job, to help subordinates with personal problems, to engage in ongoing friendly interaction with organizational members, and to encourage subordinates to participate in decision making. Such managers are less concerned with the rules and procedures of the organization per se and are more willing to bend such rules for the sake of important organizational insiders and outsiders. Although such managers are not necessarily less concerned with the successful completion of organizational tasks, these managers are more likely to tolerate the unsuccessful performances of workers who give their best efforts.

Prime time television is filled with such relational managers. Examples from our sample included Captain Merrill Stubing (*Love Boat*), Judge Harry Stone (*Night Court*), Dick Louden (*Bob Newhart*), and Sam Malone (if his actions can be described as "managing" his bar on *Cheers*). Captain Stubing was most often seen "touring" his cruise ship, monitoring through informal observation and conver-

sation his crew's personal happiness and organizational performances. Judge Harry was seen wearing crazy hats, performing magic
tricks, and generally creating a warm, fun, caring environment for
the courtroom family. And Sam Malone's relational style of managing
entailed organizational romances with employees and customers as
well as jocular interactions with employees and customers. However,
the two prime time managers who displayed particularly exemplary
enactments of the relational style were Dr. Donald Westphall (St.
Elsewhere) and Peter McDermott (Hotel).

Dr. Donald Westphall served as director of medicine at St. Eligius
Hospital, a position which kept him busy as a physician as well as
an administrator (until his unceremonious resignation in the fall of
1987). He was the most compassionate and caring of all the hospital's
managers, one who "favored conciliation over confrontation, negotiation over pontification, and communication over authoritative
administration" (Schatz, 1987, p. 93). Indeed, head nurse Helen
Rosenthal told Westphall in the 1986 episode from our sample that
he represented a "higher order" at St. Eligius. As Schatz (1987)
concluded, Westphall's primary management function "was to hu-
manize a traditionally insensitive bureaucracy, to transform a group
of disparate and potentially alienated wage slaves into a working
family" (p. 93).

During his tenure at St. Eligius, Donald counselled various staff
members, including orderly Luther, whom he encouraged to pursue
first paramedic and later physician's assistant training, and fellow
doctor and administrator Daniel Auschlander, whom he helped deal
with ongoing flare-ups related to Auschlander's liver cancer. We
saw Westphall remain one of the few (perhaps only) close friends
of Dr. Craig, the ascerbic chief of surgery, despite Craig's frequent
insulting accusations that Westphall's managerial style was weak
and "overly sensitive." To Donald, patient care and compassion
were especially important values which he regularly instilled in his
staff. And although he acted a little foolishly when he fell in love
with Carol Novino, a former nurse who became an intern at the
hospital after his encouragement, Westphall generally did represent
the "higher order" of St. Eligius on professional and moral grounds.

Most impressive about Donald Westphall was his passion and
compassion toward the hospital itself. As we learned in the award-
winning prequel special titled "Time Heals," Donald grew up at St.
Eligius, having essentially been adopted by the hospital's founding
father, Father Joseph McCabe, after Donald's mother and siblings
were killed in a fire. Donald's lifelong relationship with St. Eligius
helped us understand why he alone tried frantically to save St.

Eligius from the wrecking ball in the 1987 finale while Dr. Craig planned his farewell party and other residents worried about their own future jobs. As Schatz (1987) put it, "His fate is with St. Eligius, inexorably bound to a kinship system that penetrated his personal and professional well-being, that extends indefinitely into his past and future" (p. 100). In short, St. Eligius was Westphall's personal and professional life. As he himself explained to organizational members at the 50th anniversary celebration of the hospital in the last scene of the prequel episode: "They call us a teaching hospital, but I find it's a learning place. And whether it be nurses or doctors or orderlies or surgeons or patients, we all have something to offer each other. I want to salute those people who have brought us to this celebration and to those who will lead us into the future."

Another manager who epitomized the relational style of management was Peter McDermott, general manager of the luxury St. Gregory hotel (Hotel). Indeed, so powerful was his devotion to and love for the organization that hotel owner Mrs. Trent left him half ownership in the hotel in her will. Thus, when she died at the end of the 1985–1986 season, Peter became the executive manager and part owner of the St. Gregory.

Peter McDermott exemplified a participative style of management. He interacted with his employees in supportive ways and helped them develop a sense of self worth and esteem by giving them great latitude in performing their jobs and by allowing them to try out unusual ideas. Furthermore he regularly explained his actions to other organizational members, thereby teaching and sharing key organizational values. For instance, in one episode not in our sample, McDermott explained to director of hotel relations Mark Danning that he wanted flowers and "the works" in one of the suites because the guests, a grocery store owner and his family, had saved up for the vacation of a lifetime and he wanted to make sure they had the "royal" treatment.

McDermott also listened empathically to his employees. For instance, McDermott patiently listened while Danning explained that he had just given the presidential suite, at no charge, to a young singer fresh from the country who believed her "agent" had booked an engagement at the hotel for her with Mel Torme. When Danning asserted that he would pay for the suite, McDermott laughed and asked, "Out of what, your next decade's salary?" McDermott then told Danning that he was being overly sentimental and that he had made a mistake in giving the young woman the suite. Nonetheless, McDermott supported Danning's decision, partly because he realized that the young man had fallen in love and that "taking care of" the naive young singer was personally important to Danning. McDermott also backed Danning's "giving" of a suite because in acting as he had, Danning was indeed performing his managerial duties in accord with the organization's corporate credo: "The St. Gregory is a place where everyone is special." Indeed, in our 1986 sample episode, McDermott himself gave a suite, at no cost, to a lady who worked at a flower cart outside the hotel in a way that preserved her dignity and allowed her to "impress" a long lost daughter (see Chapter 5).

In sum, Peter was a humane, ethical, caring manager of the sort that Frederick (1960) characterized as willing "to see that human and economic resources are utilized for broad social ends and not simply the narrowly circumscribed interests of private persons and firms" (p. 60). In this way, he epitomized the type of manager that Geller (1985) argued was essential for the success of real-life hotels — a manager who cultivates positive employee and customer attitudes and morale.

Political Styles

As noted earlier, the social-task dichotomies that have characterized much of the management literature on styles miss the political nature of organizational life. We use the term political style, then, to characterize those managers who appear predominantly concerned with the development and use of power and control to protect their own interests (and, in the very negative sense, to hurt the interests of others). These managers are very concerned about their relationships with organizational others but only insofar as the manipulation of these relationships can help them accomplish their own ends. Not surprisingly, these managers are also likely to be more autocratic than democratic in their decision making. In short, these managers tend to be depicted as devious, demanding, and manipulative.

Not surprisingly, many of the managers who exhibited political styles came from the prime time soaps and included, among others, J.R. Ewing, Cliff Barnes, and Jeremy Wendell of Dallas, Angela Channing and Richard Channing of Falcon Crest, Blake Carrington, Stephen Carrington, and Alexis Carrington Colby of Dynasty, and Zach Taylor of The Colbys. Other less notable yet eminently political managers from our sample included Chief Daniels (Hill Street Blues), Inspector Nolan (Cagney and Lacey) and hospital supply room manager Harry (Harry). These managers regularly engaged in actions which promoted their own self-centered purposes and, in many cases, which hurt other organizational insiders or outsiders. Two managers in particular who epitomized this political style were J.R. Ewing (Dallas) and Angela Channing (Falcon Crest).

J.R. Ewing was the prime time manager audiences loved to hate. The popularity of his character with the American public has been well documented. The so-called "Who Shot J.R.?" episode was watched by about 80 percent of the U.S. television viewing audience. "J.R. For President" bumper stickers can still be seen on our (especially Texas) highways. And Larry Hagman was named "Texan of the Year" in 1986 for his contribution to Texas lore. Of course, more important than J.R.'s popularity per se was his importance to the program itself. As the central character in Dallas, he and his political actions served as the focal point for all other characters. As Goethals (1981) summarized, "His avarice and hard-living, hard-loving ways keep the show resplendent in sin" (p. 53), which also, no doubt, kept the series in the top 10 for almost a decade.

Over the years, J.R.'s political actions have run the gamut from underhanded negotiations with his nemesis Cliff Barnes and manipulative displays of personal strength to exploitive performances of negative grandstanding. In the 1987 episode in our sample, for example, J.R. was under investigation for his role in a CIA plan to disrupt the flow of oil from the Middle East and thereby corner the market for Ewing Oil (see Chapter 6). Quite simply, he has engaged in virtually every type of political action. As Newcomb (1982b) characterized him: "He pushes civility to the limits, strains every family tie, every sign of love, overlooking basic morality, the law, and business ethics. If there is something to grab, J.R. grabs it" (p. 172). J.R. was the antithesis of mainstream American values.

Or was he? Newcomb (1982b), for example, argued that J.R. "believes in tradition and family" (p. 172). Indeed, although he alienated all of the members of his own family with his selfish, unfriendly, malevolent, and often illegal actions, J.R. also appeared to cherish their love and affection. For example, after he gained control of Ewing Oil when Pam sold her stock to him after Bobby's mythical death in the episode from our 1986 sample, J.R. asserted to himself as he looked at Bobby's portrait: "I would give it all up if you were here to fight with me, Bobby." We could not believe him entirely when he said this, but we could not disbelieve him either. Clearly, however, the most dominant aspect of his love for his family was his affection for his son. Again, as Newcomb (1982b) explained: "There is no contradiction in character when J.R. tenderly holds his infant son. He is holding his world together until his son can take over. That is J.R.'s one and only business, hobby, dream, and burden" (p. 172). As J.R. himself affirmed to his son as the two of them gazed at a picture of founding father Jock Ewing in J.R.'s office: "I'm going to build you an empire and nothing can stop me now."

In sum, J.R. was the epitome of prime time's political managers. He engaged in virtually every form of positive and negative organizational politics. Although some have pointed out that he was an overly-dramatized political manager, he has provided a telling caricature of the aberrant high finance manager. As Newcomb (1982b) quipped, only half-jokingly, "When we see the brothers W. Herbert and Nelson Bunker Hunt bluff Congress on the evening news we understand them better because we now know J.R." (p. 171).

Another prime time political manager in our sample was Angela Channing (Falcon Crest), one example of a long tradition of serial villainesses who actively manipulated power and people. According to Modleski (1982), such characters have sought to "make the most of events that render other characters totally helpless" in order to transcend the essentially powerless state in which most women have found themselves (p. 97). Angela, like other coldly political managers, allowed neither kinship nor sentiment to deter or deflect her from the acquisition of power, wealth, and status.

When television viewers first met Angela, she was trying to ruin her nephew Chase Gioberti, who had just inherited 50 acres of vineyards near her sprawling Falcon Crest vineyards, by blocking a bank loan he needed and by alienating his son. When Angela failed by these means, she then dangled promises of future ownership before her grandson Lance Cumson and manipulated him into marrying Melissa Agretti in order to consolidate Falcon Crest and the equally large neighboring Agretti vineyard; Lance and Melissa later separated, divorced, remarried, reseparated, and so on, and so forth.

During the 1987 season, Angela secretly embarked on a landgrab deal and tried to disrupt her nephew Chase's political campaign. In the episode in our sample, for example, Angela hired a private investigator to gather information about Melissa, who had left Lance to try her wings on stage. When the private investigator turned up some dirt on Melissa, Angela's pleasure surprised him, and he commented that she seemed "to relish all this cloak and dagger business." Her response was vintage 1987 Angela Channing: "I especially like the dagger part."

Angela's ambition led her to lose control of her vineyard to her nephew Chase, but she ultimately used every means at her disposal — fair and foul — to regain it, including buying up the land in the Tuscany Valley to monopolize the water supply and force Chase (who then had the controlling interest in the vineyard) to sell Falcon Crest back to her. In short, Angela epitomized the corrupt, duplicitous, manipulative manager who uses bribery, blackmail, and psychological bullying to enhance her organizational power. Angela expected her employees and her family, many of whom were her employees as well, to be "good little corporate soldiers" and to do whatever Angela required of them in order to further her own selfish ambitions. If they did not, she deprived them of their benefits (she took away handsome Lance's handsome salary and allowance), their freedom (she kept her daughter Emma confined for years in the house), and their happiness (she used information to destroy Lance and Melissa's marriage and thereby destroy their business relationship). Angela was, as Ang (1985) noted, the female counterpart to J.R. Ewing, both of whom symbolized the potentially villainous quality of the political style of management.

DISCUSSION

Management has consistently been described as a richly communicative endeavor, and our analysis has confirmed the pervasively communicative nature of managerial action on prime time television. Prime time managers spent over three-quarters of their time engaged in interpersonal and informational communicative activities. And if we include two other richly communicative endeavors — decision making and political performances—the proportion would rise to over 95%. In this regard, prime time presentations of managerial action reflect closely the findings of researchers who have studied managers in "real" organizations who have argued that communicative activities take up as much as 90% of the managers work time (see Burns, 1954; Lawler, Porter, & Tannenbaum, 1968; Mintzberg, 1973). As Tompkins (1977) put it, management is synonymous with communication in successful organizations. In short, prime time portrayals of managerial work reflect the communicative nature of American management.

Perhaps more importantly, all types of managers, with the exception of visiting managers and finance managers, were more likely to be depicted in a positive rather than a negative or neutral light. Overall, the prime time managers in this study performed nearly twice as many positive as negative actions, with slightly over one-third of their activities depicted as neutral. In terms of the managerial ethos, over half of the managers in this study were depicted as positive personae. In short, this study provides more empirical support for Mintzberg's (1973) characterization of the manager as "the folk hero of contemporary American society" (p. 2) than it does for Theberge's (1981) characterization of businessmen (including managers) as "crooks, conmen and clowns."[3]

In sum, prime time television portrayals of managers are, like television itself, a mixture of the real and the ideal. Our analysis has convinced us that prime time depictions of the broad dimensions of managerial activity — managerial character, action, and style — reflect both the real and the ideal. Prime time television, thus, may be a useful pedagogical tool for illustrating management principles in academic class periods and management training sessions alike. And for the home viewers, these involving (sometimes verisimilar, usually dramatic) displays of prime time management may serve as entertaining narratives reminiscent of our own bosses (who themselves are often dramatic or comedic characters) as well as potential rehearsals for dealing with these bosses. In the next chapter, we continue our exploration of television's lessons about organizational life by examining some of the dominant values displayed through the actions of managers and other organizational members.

---

[3] We do wish to note, however, that Theberge's (1981) study looked only at businessmen and not all managers. Keeping this in mind, we did find some limited and qualified support for some of Theberge's general observations. For example, when we looked only at those managerial characters who fit into more traditionally "business" industries (like finance), we find that they are depicted as more negative than other types of managers, though overall they were still depicted as more positive than negative. However, single appearance managers were depicted more negatively than positively.

Chapter 5

The Dramatic Enactment of Organizational Values on Prime Time Television

Television is a ubiquitous institution of American culture which, like other mainstream secular or sacred institutions, reflects and shapes social and organizational reality for American audiences. As we argued in Chapter 1, television's most powerful role in our society may be as a socializing agent which teaches and reinforces lessons about social *values* of American culture and organizational values which are part of that culture. To the extent that television does indeed help to shape our social and organizational values, it is important to understand the types of values that are displayed on television as well as the ways in which these values are enacted.

In this chapter we examine some of the social and organizational values that are enacted in television's prime time portrayal of organizational life. We begin with a discussion of the importance of values to organizational life, noting the impact of broad cultural values on organizations as well as the impact of particular values which are developed by individual organizations. We then describe some of the metacritical assumptions and critical tools which guided this "qualitative" analysis of organizational values on prime time television. Next, we offer an extended analysis of several of these organizational values, focusing especially on the oppositional tensions among these values. We conclude with a discussion of the implications of this analysis for television and organizational research.

VALUES AND ORGANIZATIONAL LIFE

The concept "value" has been a focus of researchers in a variety of academic disciplines including anthropology, sociology, psychology, political science, organizational behavior, and communication studies. Not surprisingly, given that the concept has been adopted by so many diverse scholars, there exists no single accepted definition of value. Indeed, as Williams (1970) has pointed out, the term has been used to refer to likes, wants, needs, pleasures, desires, interests, and other selective orientations. For our purposes here, we agree generally with Rokeach (1979) that values are core ideas about "desirable end-states of existence" (e.g., security, equality, salvation) or "desirable modes of behavior" (e.g., honesty, loyalty, forgiveness) which "are capable of being organized to form different priorities" (p. 49). In other words, values constitute moral and/or competence standards that we use to guide personal, social, and organizational actions, to inform our attitudes and opinions on social, political, and religious issues, to shape our self-presentations to others, to judge and evaluate ourselves and others, and to rationalize our actions, thoughts, and judgments. In short, values, as Gerbner (1977) succinctly summarized, help us understand what is related to what, what is important, and what is right and wrong.

Values affect organizational life in at least two general ways. First, the broad cultural values of society influence organizational life inasmuch as all organizations reflect, to a greater or lesser degree, the values of the cultures of which they are a part. Second, each organization can be said to create its own unique set of values which shapes the actions of individual organizational members and frames that organization's corporate philosophy and goals. We turn now to a discussion of these two general relationships between values and organizational life.

American Cultural Values and Organizational Life

The American value system has been described by many scholars as a complex cultural matrix consisting of various value clusters and dimensions. Based on a substantial body of historical, political, and sociological data, sociologist Robin Williams (1970) has identified 15 major value clusters that American society as a whole generally endorses, including the values of achievement and success, activity and work, morality, progress, humanitarianism, efficiency and practicality, material comfort, equality, freedom, external conformity, science and secular rationality, nationalism, democracy, individual and group superiority. Psychologist Milton Rokeach (1973), too, has investigated societal values and has offered a similar map of American cultural values including terminal or "ends" values (such as freedom, equality, accomplishment, security, comfort, and salvation) and *instrumental* or "means" values (such as honesty, responsibility, independence, ambition, logic, and courage). In addition, Rokeach identified two types of terminal values — personal and social — and two types of instrumental values—moral and competence. Likewise, communication scholars Steele and Redding (1962) painted a similar portrait of American culture in their examination of American presidential addresses. They identified several similar "clusters" of enduring American values including puritan and pioneer morality, patriotism, achievement and success, change and progress, equality of opportunity, science and secular rationality.

These and other students and critics of American culture and society (e.g., Edelman, 1964; Gans, 1979; Gerbner, 1977; Kluckhohn, 1958; Parsons, 1951) have argued that although Americans may share these values, the emphasis on particular values changes over time. So, too, they have asserted that many of these enduring values in America are oppositional in nature (e.g., freedom and conformity, tradition and change) and thus create value conflicts for different groups. Given that American society is built around a dynamic and shifting set of individuals and groups, such changes and conflicts in value priorities are inevitable. Not surprisingly, these cultural values and their changes and conflicts have important implications for organizations in American society.

Perhaps most obviously, American cultural values distinguish American organizations and organizational members from those found in other cultures. England and his colleagues have conducted the most extensive research program on the impact of national culture on organizations and have found that organizations generally reflect the broader cultural values of their respective societies (see England, 1967a; 1967b, 1975; England & Lee, 1971; England, Dhingra, & Agarwal, 1974). England (1967b), for example, found a "general value pattern characteristic of American managers," a value pattern he described as "pragmatic" since American managers, more than managers in other cultures, tend to emphasize the values of organizational stability, profit maximization, and organizational efficiency. Cultural differences between Japanese and American societies have received considerable attention in recent management literature (see Ouchi, 1981; Pascale & Athos, 1981) as authors have tried to explain the increased successes of Japanese organizations and the increased failures of American organizations by looking at the respective values of these two societies. In sum, it has been well documented that organizations in general reflect the broader cultural values of the societies in which they exist. For those who study or practice multinational management, an understanding of these cultural values is crucial.

The finding that organizations reflect the cultural values of their societies is important inasmuch as these values affect the day-to-day actions of organizational members. As Udy (1959) argued some time ago: "Each individual member of any organization has been socialized relative to a larger society, and thus brings with himself into the organization from the outside various expectations and values which inevitably enter into the way he plays his role and interacts with others" (p. 10). Contemporary organizational researchers have found that cultural values do indeed influence a wide variety of organizational actions including decision making (Beyer & Lodahl, 1976; Haberstroh & Gerwin, 1972), innovation (Blau & McKinley, 1979), formal structure (Lincoln, Olson & Hanada, 1978), legitimation (Meyer & Rowan, 1977) the establishment of new programs (Hage & Dewar, 1973), and the use of oral and written communications (McMillan, Hickson, Hinings & Schneck, 1973; Pascale, 1978). Indeed, the effects of cultural values on organizations are pervasive and powerful.

The effects of cultural values on organizational life, however, are by no means static or universal. As American cultural values have changed over time, so, too, have organizations changed. As Hay and Gray (1974) have charted, the value systems of American management have gone through at least three historical phases as American culture has changed: (a) "profit maximization" management (emphasizing the values of economic success and organizational efficiency), (b) "trustee" management (emphasizing paternalistic authority and stockholder equity), and (c) "quality of life" management (emphasizing the enlightened interests of employees and corporate social responsibility). Hay and Gray (1974) concluded that each subsequent phase has not replaced but rather has been "superimposed" on the earlier phase, though there are contemporary managers who subscribe to each of these value positions. In a similar manner, Maccoby and Terzi (1979) recently argued that the so-called "work ethic" has gone through at least four phases over time, each one stressing different values: (a) the "Protestant" ethic (emphasizing self-discipline and rugged individualism), (b) the "craft" ethic (emphasizing moderation and humility), (c) the "entrepreneurial" ethic (emphasizing risk-taking and opportunism), and (d) the "career" ethic (emphasizing specialization and professionalism). However, Maccoby and Terzi (1979) concluded that although the values of the work ethic have shifted, organizational members have remained committed to the overall value of hard work. In sum, these and other organizational researchers have agreed that organizational changes reflect broader cultural changes.

Finally, the effects of cultural values on organizational life are not universal but vary for different members in different positions in different organizations. Researchers, for example, have discovered that even though the value patterns of organizational members are more homogeneous in some cultures than in other cultures, there are value differences *within* organizations in virtually every culture. As England and his colleagues (1974) summarized about managers:

> Some managers have a very small set of important values, while others have a large set and seem to be influenced by many strongly held values. The important values of some managers include concepts which are almost solely related to their organizational life. Other managers include a wide range of personal and philosophical concepts among their important values. Some managers have what might be termed individualistic values as opposed to group-oriented values. Some managers are highly achievement-oriented as opposed to others who value status and position more highly. (pp. 84–85)

In sum, the idea that one grand set of cultural values typifies *the* American worker (or manager) or *the* American organization is a cultural myth. Indeed, as researchers interested in "corporate cultures" have argued, every organization has its own unique set of values. We now consider the individual values of corporate cultures in more detail.

Individual Values and Organizational "Cultures"

In recent years, the idea that organizations themselves are cultures which develop their own unique values has received considerable attention in the scholarly and popular literature (see Deal & Kennedy, 1982; *Fortune*, 1977, November; Frost, Moore, Louis, Lundberg & Martin, 1985; Krefting & Frost, 1985; Peters & Waterman, 1982; Pettigrew, 1979; Smircich, 1983). Although organizational culture researchers have been interested in a wide variety of cultural symbols in organizations (including myths, stories, rites, rituals, and metaphors), the organization's set of *values* has been presented as the "heart" of any organizational culture. Deal and Kennedy (1982), for example, described values as "the bedrock of any corporate culture" inasmuch as they "provide a sense of common direction for all employees and guidelines for their day-to-day behavior" (p. 21). Indeed, as Peters and Waterman (1982) put it: "Every excellent company we studied is clear on what it stands for and takes the process of value shaping seriously. In fact, we wonder whether it is possible to be an excellent company without clarity on values and without having the right sort of values" (p. 280).

Organizational culture researchers have agreed generally that organizations create their own distinct values for at least two reasons. First, these values create "a sense of identity for those in the organization, making employees feel special" and give them "a sense of pulling together" (Deal & Kennedy, 1982, p. 23). Second, these values instruct organizational members about the aspects of work which are the most important: "They suggest what kinds of information is taken most seriously for decision-making purposes" and "they define what kind of people are most respected" in the organization (Deal & Kennedy, 1982, p. 31). As Peters and Waterman (1982) concluded, successful organizations focus on a few key values because this "lets everyone know what's important so there's simply less need for daily instructions" (p. 65). In sum, an organization's distinct set of values may have pervasive and powerful effects on the organizational activities of members.

Not surprisingly, organizational culture researchers have offered rich and compelling descriptions of the distinctive value systems of particular companies. Thus, we have learned that IBM's most important values are "respect for the individual" and "productivity through people"; that Walmart operates on the "empty headquarters rule" — going into stores and listening (Peters & Waterman, 1982); that General Motors demands respect for authority, invisibility, and loyalty (Martin & Siehl, 1983), that Bendix played "dirty politics" (Velasquez, Moberg, and Cavanaugh, 1983), that Silicon Valley companies concentrated on innovation of new products and "getting [them] out the door" (Gregory, 1983), and that "Dextor" (a pseudonym for a facility for emotionally disturbed children) employees thought of their organizational lives in terms of the "Rumpelstiltskin" fairy tale (Smith & Simmons, 1983). And so on.

Organizational culture researchers have argued convincingly that individual organizations develop and maintain their own unique visions and values which guide and govern the actions of organizational members. Although researchers' descriptions of organizational cultures tend to be impressionistic and anecdotal, they do offer rich portraits of the unique value structures of individual American organizations. Such research has helped us understand how similar types of organizations and organizational members can have very different levels and types of success.

In summary, values are important to organizational life in two different ways. First, the broader cultural values of the society in which the organization exists exert an influence on the organization's ability to survive in that society as well as on the actions of organizational members who have been socialized in that society. On the other hand, particular organizations also develop and maintain their own unique cultural values which likewise influence the actions of organizational members who are socialized into these organizations. Not surprisingly, these two senses of values create certain tensions for organizations, especially when they are in opposition to each other. Indeed, as Blau (1977) has suggested, organizations must often choose between adapting to the broader (and often readily accepted) values of American culture or developing and maintaining a distinctive set of values unique to the organization. As Beyer (1982) summarized, "The second alternative is riskier, but can be successful if organizations can choose or create suitable environmental niches that support their ideologies and are able to defend and maintain those niches over time" (p. 173). However, she also pointed out that many organizations, "especially large ones dependent on diverse environments, do not pursue distinctiveness in culture" (p. 173).

Our study of organizational life on prime time television involves similar tensions between broader cultural values of society and the individual values of particular prime time organizations. We noted in Chapter 1 that television, as an institution in American society, reflects the values of society in its portrayals of organizational life. By the same token, however, television portrays particular prime time organizations as unique places with distinct values. Thus, "San Francisco General" (*Trapper John, M.D.*) and "St. Eligius" (*St. Elsewhere*) are both fictional American hospitals which reflect some of the health care values in America; on the other hand, these hospitals are also very distinct prime time organizational cultures. In short, any analysis of organizational values on prime time television should include considerations of values at both the societal and individual levels.

In the remainder of this chapter, we focus on the former level; thus, we examine some of the broader cultural values that are reflected in prime time television's overall portrayal of organizational life. In the next chapter, then, we examine more closely some of the particular values of unique prime time organizational cultures. We now turn to a discussion of the methods we used to examine the broader cultural values reflected in prime time organizational life.

STUDYING ORGANIZATIONAL VALUES ON PRIME
TIME

Although academic and popular critics have not always agreed about the values and preferred meanings invited by particular television programs, they unanimously have agreed that television does reflect and shape cultural values. Indeed, as Haffner (1973, September) has argued, television "is profoundly instrumental in our lives — not in terms of the stories it tells, but more importantly the values it portrays" (pp. 25-26). Not surprisingly, then, many television critics have been concerned with the broad range of values presented on prime time in general or with particular values displayed in certain programs and program genres. In his analysis of popular television, for example, Chesebro (1979) concluded that while prime time television overrepresents some values and underrepresents other values, television as a whole portrays a wide variety of American values. Indeed, Chesebro argued that 10 of the American cultural values identified by Steele and Redding (1962) are regularly reflected in prime time mimetic dramas, including "puritan morality . . . achievement and success, effort and optimism, sociality and considerateness, external conformity, generosity, and patriotism" (p. 30). On the other hand, Newcomb (1974) has suggested that although prime time may reflect a broad range of values, those values "grounded in the belief of the family as a supportive group" have been the central values of most television genres, a finding that has been supported by other critics including Roiphe (1979), who examined The Walton's, Williams (1979), who examined The Mary Tyler Moore Show, and Schatz (1987), who examined St. Elsewhere.

These above examples, of course, represent a small sample of the scholarly critics who have focused on the cultural values of prime time television. Arlen's (1974) The View From Highway 1, Marc's (1984) Demographic Vistas, Sklar's (1980) Prime-Time America, and Gronbeck's (1984b) "Audience Engagement in Family" represent more examples in a growing body of critical studies which have explored values on American prime time television. Unfortunately, for our purposes, most of these critics have either focused on the broader sociocultural and ideological values (e.g., Katz & Liebes, 1987; Newcomb, 1984; Schudson, 1987; Schwichtenberg, 1987) or on the aesthetic values (e.g., Barker, 1985; Deming, 1985; Feuer, Kerr & Vahimagi, 1984; Schatz, 1987; Thorburn, 1976; Timberg, 1982) which are displayed on prime time programs, while very few critics have concerned themselves with *organizational* values per see (see Alley, 1976; Real, 1977; Schrag, Hudson, & Bernabo, 1981). The remainder of this chapter, then, examines some of these organizational values displayed on prime time television. Before we turn to these values, however, we describe the metacritical assumptions and critical tools which guided our analysis.

Metacritical Assumptions of Our Study

We made three assumptions about the nature of organizational values and television drama that have particular relevance for this analysis. First, as we argued in the last chapter, we assumed that organizational values are revealed in television drama *only as they are enacted in symbolic performances*. That is, like many rhetorical and organizational scholars (see Bormann, 1983; Brummett, 1976; Burke, 1969; Denzin, 1983; Gronbeck, 1980, 1983, 1984a; Mangham & Overington, 1983; Pacanowsky & O'Donnell-Trujillo, 1983), we assume that communicative performances are the very actions by which organizational members (on television and in "real" life) create and reveal organizational reality to themselves and to others. In other words, organizational members, clients, and outsiders (including television viewers) understand values only as they are articulated in particular performances. As Gronbeck (1983) advised, "We can understand good and evil, friendliness and strangeness, and the seamlessness of time only as those concepts are given expression in actuality" (p. 236). Thus, our analysis of organizational values displayed on prime time television programs began with a close reading of characters' verbal actions, one means by which organizational and cultural values are communicated.

Second, we assumed that organizational values, like general cultural values, are displayed on television drama through overt or implied opposition with other values. In other words, the meaning of any value displayed on television is understood in the context of a related but opposed value. A value does not represent a preference or cluster of preferences because of the innate properties of the value itself but rather because of the differences between the value and related but opposed values. As Saussure (1960) argued, "Concepts are purely differential and defined not by their positive content but negatively by their relations with other terms" (p. 117). Thus, for example, the value "prosperity" (i.e., economic success) is best understood in its relationships with the oppositional concepts of "human success" and "economic failure"; similarly, heroic characters are recognized as such by virtue of the differences between them and villainous characters. In sum, we believe that an analysis of organizational values displayed on prime time television programs necessitated an examination of the relationships among oppositional pairs of values.

Finally, we assumed that television dramas which feature organizational contexts reveal multiple values and value oppositions characteristic of organizational cultures. As Geertz (1973) has suggested, culture is a "multiplicity of complex conceptual structures, many of them superimposed upon or knotted into one another, which are at once strange, irregular, and inexplicit" (p. 10). Television, as a reflection of American culture, must be open to a multiplicity of readings or interpretations. Thus, we assumed that each individual television program simultaneously reveals a wide rather than a narrow range of organizational and cultural values.

In summary, the three metacritical assumptions discussed above had important implications for our analysis of the enactment of values in television's portrayal of organizations. First, as we viewed our two sample weeks (116 individual program episodes) of prime time programming, we paid particular attention to the symbolic performances of each program's characters since it is through the interpersonal, informational, decisional, political, and operational performances of organizational insiders and outsiders that organizational values are enacted and affirmed. Second, we identified pairs of values and examined the oppositions and mediations among these values through the performances by the organizational members featured in our sample. Finally, we explored a range of interpretive possibilities for these organizational values, even for those programs that appeared to present obvious or simplistic portrayals of organizational life.

Critical Indicators of Organizational Values

In this study, we analyzed the displays of organizational values in prime time television programs by using a set of four critical observational tools: (a) dialogue, (b) character, (c) situation, and (d) plot. These critical tools are well-established dramatistic constructs and serve as particularly revealing indicators of organizational values. Although we introduce each of these critical constructs separately in this section, they were used together as a cumulative analytical system with which we discerned some of the values of prime time organizations.

Dialogue, as Chatman (1978) has noted, "is the preeminent enactment" (p. 32). Indeed, since we are presumed to consciously control the language we employ — including the vocabulary we use, the metaphors we invoke, and the stories we tell — language is the most direct and accessible indicator of values and beliefs. In the same way, characters on dramatic television, including members of organizations, reveal themselves — and their apparent values and beliefs — to the viewing audience most directly through the explicit (and highly scripted) language they use on a prime time program.

Character refers to that composite of values, beliefs, and emotions that represent an individual's personae. As Chatman (1978) argued, character is inferred or "read" through the symbolic actions of various performers. In dramas, characters are not simply individuals but rather they are types of individuals who represent broader social roles (e.g., father, mother; manager, subordinate; rich, poor; male, female; young, old, etc.). Moreover, as Gronbeck (1984a) has advised, these social actors are "larger-than-life personae (heroes, villains, divine or semidivine helpers) who embody virtue and vice" (p. 23). Thus, as Gronbeck illustrated, Matt Dillon of *Gunsmoke* (1955–1975) "is more than an historical figure, even more than a 'Lawman' who solved the problems of Dodge City . . . he is the frontier mythic hero personifying American virtues (honesty, quietness, legality, concern for others, public service) not only for nineteenth-century America but for our own times as well" (p. 23).

Setting refers to the organizational context in which the action of a television drama occurs. In a surface sense, setting refers to the situational aspects which help the viewing audience understand the meaning of the characters' actions in the television program. However, as used here, the term setting also refers to the deeper symbolic context of the program or, as Gronbeck (1984a) has put it, the "generalized *environmental forces*" used "for understanding mythic oppositions or struggles" (p. 23). Thus, "the city" is not merely a context for particular chase scenes and shootouts but is "the setting for the struggle between order and anarchy" (Gronbeck, 1984a, p. 23).

Finally, the *plot* (narrative structure) may be the most important analytical tool used by critics to examine television texts. In a surface sense, the plot refers to the particular syntagmatic structure or sequences-of-action which constitute the chronological storyline in a television drama — usually concerning a personal or organizational problem which is revealed then solved. Yet, as Chatman (1978) and others have asserted, every plot "exists at a more general level than any particular objectification, any given movie, novel, or whatever" (p. 43). These general plots (which are repeated in various particular stories) are timeless structures through which the broader values of organizations and societies are dramatically enacted for viewing audiences (see, for example, Cawelti, 1976; Fiske, 1984, 1987; Fiske & Hartley, 1978). It was through a close analysis of the organizational plots that we came to understand many of the social values which were enacted in our prime time organizations.

The sample. As noted in the last chapter, our sample consisted of two composite weeks of regularly scheduled prime time television dramas which aired during the spring of 1986 and 1987, a total of 116 episodes. Not included in this sample were nondramatic or nonfictional programs, such as *60 Minutes* and *20/20*, nor prime time specials and movies. (See Chapter 3 for a complete discussion of the sample and sampling procedures).

The remainder of this chapter discusses six sets of values that were displayed in our sample weeks of network prime time television: (a) work and play, (b) success and failure, (c) individualism and community, (d) reason and emotion, (e) youth and experience, and (f) conformity and deviance. These values are discussed in pairs because they appeared often in opposition to each other, one value being functioning as an interpretive frame for the other.

WORK AND PLAY

The values of work and play form an interesting oppositional cluster in American society. Perhaps the dominant sense of work in American organizations is the so-called "work ethic" — the notion that with hard work, discipline, and perseverance, *anyone* and any organization can be successful. Indeed, so powerful is the work ethic in American culture that hard work is often understood as an *end* value in and of itself as well as a *means* value for achieving some preferred end state of success. Concomitantly, however, both organizations and American society also esteem "play," a value usually subsumed under the so-called "leisure ethic." As new technologies made work time more efficient, workers began to have more "free time" and, in the process, organizations and society glorified the value of leisure (see, Kaplan, 1960; Smigel, 1963). Still, organizations have also recognized the value of "play" on the job. As David Ogilvy reportedly told his employees: "Try to make working at Ogilvy & Mather fun. When people aren't having any fun, they seldom produce good advertising. Kill grimness with laughter. Maintain an atmosphere of informality." (Peters & Waterman, 1982, p. 291). In a limited (and negative) sense, play means "idleness" or "frivolity" and ultimately refers to activities that are "unproductive."

However, in a richer (and more positive) sense, play means enjoyment and self-fulfillment and ultimately the development of positive working climates and cultures. In sum, work and play are pervasive values in organizations and in American society and both of these values are displayed in prime time organizations.

Working Hard: Satisfaction and Pain in Going That Extra Mile

As noted in Chapters 3 and 4, we did not find a large proportion of actual work ("operational") activities on prime time, especially from foreground organizational members. Nonetheless, the value of hard work was glorified in prime time organizations. As Sklar (1980) has suggested, television's work force itself has risen the last few years, thereby reflecting the values and concerns of American workers:

> Television programs certainly don't "reflect" American society in any precise sense, but to be popular they do need to express, in their various conventional stylized ways, some of the real feelings and concerns of their audience. And some of those real feelings these days have to do with getting and keeping a job, putting bread on the table, having money in the pocket." (p. 20)

Although Sklar (1980) made these remarks to explain the rise in television's working-class characters in the 1970s, we also observed the value of hard work displayed by a variety of prime time organizational members. For example, we watched a harried mayor in He's The Mayor negotiate a contract and interview job candidates; we watched an idealistic young doctor in St. Elsewhere do rounds in St. Eligius Hospital in the morning only to go to a local prison in the afternoon to treat prisoners; and we watched one dual-career couple on Growing Pains — she a journalist, he a psychiatrist — miss the opportunity to celebrate their wedding anniversary because both of them worked overtime. Not surprisingly, hard work was also evident in law enforcement and public administration shows where cops such as Cagney and Lacey and Hunter and government agents such as MacGyver and Scarecrow and Mrs. King did not simply work hard but also risked their lives as part of the everyday job of public protection and national security.

Television's affirmation of the work ethic, however, was perhaps best displayed in prime time characters who had the choice not to work but who worked anyway — characters such as the bailiff in Night Court who, on her 65th birthday, could have retired but chose not to do so; characters such as the 60-plus-year-old physician on *Trapper John, M.D.* who suffered a heart attack, recovered and chose to work even harder in a new hospital position; and characters such as the wealthy J.R. Ewing (*Dallas*) and Jason Colby (*The Colbys*), executives who undoubtedly had enough money to quit working yet who continued to run their family businesses. In these and other examples, television drama affirmed and reaffirmed the value of hard work.

Playing: Fun, Frolic, and Family at and Away From Work

However, prime time organizations were not just forums for televised Horatio Algers; there was much playtime on prime time as well. In some cases, the enactment of this value of play was relatively obvious. For example, we saw workers such as Diane Chambers (*Cheers*) and David Addison (*Moonlighting*) specifically ask their respective employers for time off to "play" when former lovers re-entered their lives. Although these characters were predictably back at work before the close of their respective programs, their actions gave the viewing audience at least an indication that time away from work is sometimes more important than time at work. Even more obvious endorsements of the value of play were provided in series which featured organizational contexts specifically designed for the leisure pursuits of clients and customers such as *Cheers* bar and *The Love Boat* cruises.

The value of leisure was also affirmed in a more subtle way in domestic comedies where the main characters had jobs but rarely (if ever) were seen at work. For example, although both of the "Huxtable" parents in *Cosby* worked outside the household — she as a lawyer, he as a medical doctor—as did both of the "Keaton" parents in *Family Ties* — she as an architect, he as a manager of a public television station — we did not see these characters at work or even talk about their work. Instead, the Huxtable and Keaton parents spent all of their prime time with their families, thereby indirectly affirming the importance of leisure.

Working and Playing on Prime Time

Prime time organizations displayed themes of work and play through individual characters seen hard at work or hard at play. However, work and play were not merely revealed as discrete themes but were also integrated in some interesting ways in prime time organizations.

Fun things happen to people who work hard. The oppositional tension between work and play was enacted beautifully in an episode of *Foley Square*, a short-lived comedy about organizational life in a New York City district attorney's office. In the episode from our sample, all of the regular characters who worked at Foley Square, except the program's principal protagonist Alex, took off for a playful three-day weekend celebration of President's Day. Alex, however, stayed home on-call because a drug arrest on her caseload had been planned for that weekend. After the second day of waiting in her apartment, however, Alex treated herself — beeper in hand—to dinner in an elegant French restaurant in the city where she met and shared an enjoyable dinner with a similarly dedicated, attractive, single male obstetrician — also with beeper in hand — who was treating himself to dinner after working all weekend delivering babies. Rather conveniently, Alex's beeper went off just as they finished their meal (and made plans to see each other again) and she left for the drug bust, a bust which we later discovered was a complete success.

The tension between work and play was meaningfully and humorously mediated in the epilogue when all the D.A. office employees returned after their weekend. Almost everyone who had played over the holiday weekend had a miserable time — one was caught in a snowstorm at the airport and never made it to Bermuda, one had a miserable visit to her family's farm after being awakened daily at 4:30 a.m. by roosters, and one shot himself in the foot with a shark gun while deep-sea fishing. In contrast, dedicated worker Alex experienced a professionally productive and personally enjoyable weekend. In short, *Foley Square* affirmed the value of work and reinforced the work ethic through a narrative with the moral that fun things happen to those who work hard.

Work can be fun. Another way in which the values of work and play were juxtaposed in prime time organizations was through the enactment of a playful working environment. Two prime time organizations with especially fun work contexts were the *Cheers* bar and *The Love Boat* cruise ship. The title songs of *Cheers* and *The Love Boat* provided immediate clues that these organizations were playful environments. The title song from *Cheers* told us that the "Cheers" bar was a place where you could take "a break from all your worries" and a place "where everybody knows your name, and they're always glad you came." Indeed, Cheers' workers did call people by name and did engage in witty interpersonal repartee among themselves and with customers. So, too, the title song of *The Love Boat* promised "something for everyone," including "adventure" "new romance," and assured us that on this boat, "Love won't hurt anymore; It's an open smile, on a friendly shore." The employees in this organization (listed as "your" crew in the opening credits) were instrumental in arranging these "adventures" and "new romances" for passengers and, in some cases, for themselves. Indeed, in the *Love Boat* episode in our sample, members of "our" crew ate a leisurely dinner with passengers and enjoyed a floor show — a dancing performance by the ship's "Mermaids" — with passengers in the ship's lounge. In sum, the *Cheers* and *Love Boat* employees enacted work *as play* (and demonstrated that the title songs of programs can offer clues about the values of prime time organizations).

   All work and no play: Getting aced, iced, and isolated. Prime time television, however, also presented powerful, and certainly less positive, pictures of life in organizations which were not very fun work contexts. During our sample weeks, several characters discussed and/or displayed the negative side of organizational life as they enacted hard work with absolutely no play. For example, the overpowering commitment to hard work (i.e., workaholism) was presented as stressful and destructive for some members of St. Eligius hospital (*St. Elsewhere*). For Dr. Mark Craig, work was so all-consuming that his personal life — including a 20-plus-year marriage began to fall (and ultimately did fall) apart. So, too, resident Dr. Jack Morrison paid an even greater price for his hard work and dedication — his wife had been killed in an accident, his son had been kidnapped in the hospital because Jack was busy doing rounds, and in our episode, he was beaten and raped at a prison where he had volunteered to treat patients. For these and other organizational members, hard work did not have good or fun consequences at all.

   In sum, work and play are key organizational and cultural values. Not surprisingly, then, these values and their resulting oppositional tensions were reflected in television's portrayals of organizational life. In general, television drama reaffirmed the so-called work ethic by demonstrating the importance of work and by revealing the enjoyment of work, though it did not present an entirely positive view of working hard.

SUCCESS AND FAILURE

It seems self-evident from the plethora of books and other materials on how to succeed at everything from stock investing to making friends and losing weight that achieving success and avoiding failure are key organizational and cultural values in America. And despite Cooley's early observation that success "is whatever men think it is" (1889, p. 167), two distinct and (often opposing) formulations of success as an organizational value have been evident: "economic" success and "human" success.

On the one hand, organizational success is often defined as economic achievement and measured in the form of company profits. Steele and Redding (1962) argued that such economic success has been "the ultimate criterion" of organizational achievement in America as well as a "crucial measure of personal merit" (1962, p. 86). Indeed, in their search for "excellent" American companies, Peters and Waterman (1982) stated flatly that "no matter what prestige these companies had in the eyes of the rest of the business world, the companies were not truly excellent unless their financial performance supported their halo of esteem" (p. 22).

Economic success has long been associated with such traits as initiative, aggressiveness, and competitiveness. In its most admirable form, economic success is exemplified by individuals and organizations whose energy, inventiveness, and initiative have produced benefits for themselves and for others — benefits which have included wealth, power, status, and improved quality of life. In its less attractive form, however, economic success is exemplified by self-centered and ruthless organizations and individuals who pursue power, profit, and position irrespective of the social or personal cost to others (see Cawelti, 1965).

However, there is a second conception of success also present in American organizations which we term "human success." Although this human vision of success was not a dominant one in very early America, Cawelti (1965) has observed that by the mid-20th century "few areas of American culture failed to show some sign of this new mood which, if not explicitly critical of the idea of business success, placed primary emphasis on a different range of values: health, leisure, fun, family life" (p. 202). This alternative version of success is associated with such traits as altruism, cooperation, and social responsibility, and focuses on moral obligations rather than on wealth or status. Indeed, as Cawelti (1965) summarized, a distinction came to be made in American culture between *true success* (the socially responsible use of one's material and intellectual means) and *false success* (mere acquisition of land, money, popularity, or influence).

These two visions of economic and human success are not necessarily opposed to each other. Indeed, as Peters and Waterman (1982) argued, excellent American companies must, by definition, integrate these two visions of success: "Of course a business has to be fiscally sound. And the excellent companies are the most fiscally sound of all. But their value set *integrates* the notions of economic health, serving customers, and making meanings down the line" (p. 103). We now turn to presentations of these visions of organizational success on prime time television.

Success: Economic Empires and Caring Companies

Both economic and human success values were enacted in prime time organizations. The preeminent and overt display of the economic success ethic occurred on prime time serials such as *Dallas* and *Dynasty*. *Dallas* character J.R. Ewing, for example, has been prime time's embodiment of the economic success ethic for the 1980s. J.R. not only strove to become "captain" of his family's oil company, he wanted to build an oil *empire*. J.R. made no secret of his single-minded efforts to make Ewing Oil the "biggest independent oil company in Texas"; and, as noted in the last chapter, he employed every legal, illegal, and unethical means available to him. J.R. reiterated this position in the 1986 episode from our sample when he purchased additional shares of Ewing Oil from Pam (who was then alive and still "dreaming" that Bobby was dead) and, thus, obtained a controlling interest in the family corporation. That evening, J.R. took his son (John Ross III) up to the Ewing corporate offices and promised him: "I guarantee you, I'm going to build you an empire and nothing can stop me now." In short, as Himmelstein (1984) concluded, "The new frontier of *Dallas* is a reflection of our social conservatism and of the 'me' generation of Americans — it is the current celebration of doing one's own thing, except that rather than the 1960 anthem, which meant seeking personal experience, the 1980 anthem signals a search for personal wealth and success" (pp. 185–186).

The value of *human success* was also displayed in many prime time organizations. Perhaps the most humanistic prime time organization in our sample was the luxurious St. Gregory Hotel (*Hotel*), a place where organizational members from owners and top executives to bellhops and desk clerks showed concern and respect to kings, socialites, and flower-ladies alike — indeed, to all who entered the hotel (see Chapter 6). St. Eligius hospital (*St. Elsewhere*), too, was a place which displayed concern for human success via characters such as Dr. Daniel Auschlander (chief of hospital services) and Dr. Donald Westphall (chief of staff) who chose to work in the run-down St. Eligius rather than in their own private and more lucrative practices because of their belief that human and personal fulfillment were more important than mere economic success. Finally, several prime time private detectives in our sample — including Maddie Hayes and David Addison (*Moonlighting*), Thomas Magnum (*Magnum, P.I.*), and A.J. Simon and Rick Simon (*Simon and Simon*) accepted cases from people who could not afford their services because these private detectives were as concerned with other people as with their own pocketbooks. In these and other instances and programs, the human success ethic was dramatically enacted and affirmed.

Failure: Permanent Losses and Temporary Setbacks

Two visions of failure were presented in our sample of organizations. *Permanent failures* were those losses which resulted from phenomena beyond the organization's control or from an individual's single-minded, unbalanced, ruthless pursuit of economic success. Failures resulting from phenomena beyond one's control appeared in medical dramas when patients died or contracted deadly diseases despite the competent and caring attention they received from heroic medical professionals, as in the case of the cartoonist who came to St. Eligius with respiratory problems but was found to have cancer. Permanent failures, however, also resulted from phenomena within human control, as on *Miami Vice* when one bad cop's pursuit of monetary success through drug trafficking caused his own and others' deaths.

Second, *temporary failures* were those temporary setbacks which arose from phenomena within human control — misunderstandings, crises of confidence, or misplaced priorities. Moreover, organizational members "learned" lessons from these temporary setbacks about how *not* to fail in the same way in the future. Thus, on *Love Boat*, one passenger, a radio psychologist, found herself unable to give advice to patients after she temporarily lost her professional confidence; not surprisingly, this confidence was restored when the ship's own physician (and armchair psychologist) gave her some good advice.

Success and Failure on Prime Time

These apparently oppositional values of success and failure were mediated in at least three ways in our sample prime time organizations: by learning through losing, by presenting apparent success as real failure, and by presenting apparent failure as real success.

Learning through losing. In prime time television's depictions of organizational life, temporary failures were often cast as useful steps on the way to future successes. Indeed, many prime time organizational members learned from their mistakes and ultimately became better workers and human beings. In the *Love Boat* episode mentioned above, the radio psychologist learned from her temporary failure not to be so self-centered and involved in her business so that in the future she could maintain her relationships with family and friends. And on *He's The Mayor*, Mayor Carl Burke and Wardell, his chauffeur, learned from their temporarily failed work relationship and friendship not to allow selfishness and false pride to prevent them from appreciating their friendship and each other's work contributions. In these and other ways, prime time organizational members learned how better to succeed in the future by understanding their temporary failures.

Seeing is believing I: Apparent failure as real success. One vivid juxtaposition of the values of success and failure occurred when apparent economic failure was presented as human success. In the 1986 episode of *Hotel* from our sample, for example, Maggie Lewis, a flower lady who had operated a fresh flower stand at the hotel's rear entrance for years, was helped by the St. Gregory staff to demonstrate to her long-separated daughter that Maggie's lack of wealth did not mean that she was a failure. As the episode began, we learned that Maggie gave her daughter Lisa up for adoption 25 years earlier when the child's father deserted them. However, when Maggie read that Lisa's adopted parents had died, she wrote to her daughter and arranged to meet with her to let her know that she had a real mother who did care. Since Maggie wrote to Lisa on St. Gregory stationary, Lisa (who was about the marry a local San Francisco scion) assumed that her mother was living in a hotel suite and invited her mother to attend the prenuptial reception which was to be held at the St. Gregory. Maggie, not wanting to embarrass her daughter, decided to check into the hotel for the two days before her daughter's wedding.

When hotel manager Peter McDermott saw Maggie at the reception desk and discovered why she was checking in, he immediately directed the front desk clerk to put "Miss Lewis" into a just-cancelled reserved suite. He explained to Maggie, with a conspiratorial wink to the desk clerk, that the prepayment for the room was forfeited with the cancellation, so there would be no cost to Maggie for the room. In addition, later McDermott asked Maggie if she would help him out and let a just-hired beautician get some practice by doing Maggie's hair. In this way, McDermott aided Maggie in a gentle manner that allowed her not only to retain her dignity but also to feel like she was doing rather than receiving a favor. Indeed, both through his words and actions, McDermott revealed that although Maggie was not wealthy, she was a successful human being whom he valued as a friend and who should not be ashamed to meet her daughter.

Maggie finally met Lisa, Lisa's fiance Roger Easton, and Roger's very rich, snobbish, and domineering mother, Ruth Easton. Ruth Easton investigated Maggie's background and discovered that Maggie was actually a flower lady, and then used the information to publicly humiliate Maggie at the engagement reception in an attempt to end her son's engagement to this girl who was not a wealthy socialite. The plot concluded when Roger reprimanded his mother for trying to have her own selfish way without regard for other people. He then told her that Lisa and he would be marrying in Rome, their home, and at *their* convenience, not hers. As Lisa and Roger left the St. Gregory hotel the next morning, they gave Maggie a plane ticket so that she could attend their wedding in Rome. Thus, the self-centered actions of the economically successful Ruth Easton contrasted markedly with the other-centered concerns of humble Maggie Lewis and caring manager Peter McDermott.

Seeing is deceiving II: Apparent success as real failure. The theme that economic success may serve, at least initially, as a smokescreen for real failure as a human being was also enacted in the prime time organizations in our sample. This lesson was enacted elegantly in the 1986 episode of *Dallas*. As described earlier, in this episode Pam Ewing sold her stocks to J.R., thus giving him controlling interest in Ewing Oil, a goal that J.R. had sought to attain for several melodramatic years of *Dallas*. But surprisingly, even J.R. Ewing recognized that his apparent economic success was really a human failure. Indeed, after signing the stocks and gaining controlling interest in Ewing Oil, he went to Bobby's former office by himself and addressed the portrait of his (apparently) dead brother: "Well, Bobby. I finally control it all. But it's not the way I wanted to get it. And I'd give it back in a minute if I could have you here to fight with." In this eloquent soliloquy, J.R. himself revealed that economic success alone is not really success.

In summary, prime time organizations offered visions of organizational success and failure. Interestingly, prime time organizations revealed that economic success is both a cultural value and a cultural problem. Indeed, viewers of *Dallas* (see Ang, 1985; Katz & Liebes,

1987) have varied in their reasons for watching the program, and researchers have suggested that these viewers have been both attracted to and repelled by the vision of organizational life enacted by J.R. Ewing, the so-called "man we love to hate." As we suggested earlier, the negative enactments of economic success were usually presented on prime time as opposed to the positive enactments of human success. Thus, although the grandeur and elegance of the St. Gregory hotel implies that human and economic success can be complementary values, prime time television usually casts the two visions of success as opposed, even contradictory, values. While this may make for good drama, it does not reinforce Peters and Waterman's (1982) lesson that excellent companies are successful in economic *and* human ways. In short, success and failure are an interesting but problematic pair of cultural values in the organizational lives of Americans and prime time characters.

INDIVIDUALISM AND COMMUNITY

Individualism and community constitute another interesting pair of organizational values which are frequently displayed in prime time organizations. In its most positive enactment, the value of individualism is exemplified by self-reliant, capable organizational members who distinguish themselves by their initiative, courageousness, and abiding sense of personal responsibility. This form of individualism is epitomized by the cultural "hero" who is celebrated in organizations and in society. However, individualism has a negative dimension as well, one that is enacted by self-centered individuals who are often so selfish and ruthless that they are seen as "villains." Not surprisingly, prime time organizations are populated by both positive and negative individualists.

The value of community is exemplified on prime time by the *cooperation* of individuals working together and is celebrated by organizations who see themselves as "teams" or "families." Indeed, this value of community is so vital to organizational life that it is usually incorporated into so-called corporate credos (Ouchi, 1981; Peters & Waterman, 1982). Both values of individualism and community, and their oppositional tensions, were reflected in the prime time organizations from our sample.

Individualism: Heroic Professionals and Visiting Villains

Prime time organizations were filled with members who enacted the positive and often heroic sense of individualism. Although ordinary employees occasionally acted in heroic ways (see Chapter 6), we agree with Himmelstein (1984) who argued that most of our prime time heroes are professionals and managers. Indeed, most leaders in prime time organizations, especially the major regular character leaders, represented literally and symbolically the ideal values of their organizations. Frank Furillo, the precinct captain in *Hill Street Blues*, was one such heroic individualist (see Chapter 4). A recovered alcoholic, he was an intelligent, politically astute professional cop and a strong yet fair manager who made hard administrative decisions and took personal responsibility for those decisions. Although Furillo was firm, he was both compassionate and passionate. He was a religious person who, despite living "between the rock of dangerous criminals and the hard place of public abuse" (Marc, 1984, p. 95), did not lose his faith either in God or in human potential. Not surprisingly, he was also capable of separating the personal and professional aspects of his life even though he and Joyce Davenport, the public defender who was his lover and later his second wife, had professional confrontations on a daily basis. As Marc concluded, Furillo's "three piece suits, trips to the gym and capacity to make effective judgments under pressure with equal parts of pragmatism and morality, coupled with tireless energy that allows him to put it to the public defender both in court and in the bedroom make him a candidate for college-educated, middle-management-executive Man of the Decade" (1984, pp. 95–96).

Other members of prime time organizations who embodied the positive sense of individualism included Dr. Donald Westphall (*St. Elsewhere*) and Captain Merrill Stubing (*Love Boat*). As noted in the last chapter, Westphall (chief of staff at St. Eligius Hospital) was a dedicated, self-disciplined, and other-centered professional who cared about the physical, emotional, and professional well-being of his employees and patients and, thus, represented the quintessential relational leader. Captain Merrill Stubing, too, although treated a bit less seriously than Westphall — in part because he appeared in a comedy rather than a drama — also exhibited the same kind of integrity, competence, and concern for his *Love Boat* crew and passengers.

In sum, although these organizational members worked in very different organizational settings — police stations, hospitals, and cruise ships — all were honest, competent, and honorable individuals who took a personal interest in and felt a personal responsibility for others. They displayed this positive form of individualism in their organizational words and their actions.

Not all members of organizations on prime time television, however, were presented as heroic individualists. As noted in Chapters 3 and 4, there were a variety of unfriendly, selfish, and malevolent individuals as well. Not surprisingly, most of these rather villainous individuals were lawbreakers who were organizational outsiders. As noted in Chapter 4, the negative individualists who did belong to organizations were usually found in management levels of these organizations. Although a small portion of these selfish or malevolent managers were organizational regulars (such as J.R. Ewing), most of them were visiting villains who exhibited virtually no concern for the welfare of the people they used, abused, and exploited. One visiting managerial villain from our sample was Mr. Hayward, an old college buddy of Peter McDermott who was hired as "director of hotel operations" for one episode of *Hotel*. However, when McDermott found out that Hayward had been sexually harrassing Julie, one of the regular hotel desk clerks, McDermott gave him "fifteen minutes to pack your things and get out of my hotel." So much for selfish individualism and a managerial career at the St. Gregory.

Of course, not all visiting villains were managers. Bad cops and bad spies also made for appropriate one-shot bad guys. The 1986 sample episode of *Miami Vice*, for example, featured a federal agent named Cates who was so burned out from watching too many drug dealers get rich and go free that he stole $3 million from a drug dealer and tried to frame Sonny Crockett for the theft. Similarly, in our 1986 episode of *Scarecrow and Mrs. King*, the selfish individualism of one greedy double agent threatened to destroy the entire U.S. government intelligence agency. In sum, prime time individualists were usually depicted as either very good or very bad.

Community: Coordination, Cooperation, and Caring

The organizational value of community was displayed in prime time organizations when members worked together to accomplish tasks and goals. On medical dramas such as *St. Elsewhere* and *Trapper John, M.D.*, for example, the hospital personnel — staff physicians, resident physicians, interns, nurses, aides, and hospital administrators — cooperated and coordinated their efforts to deal with medical crises and patient problems. Similarly, on crime dramas, detective partners such as Crockett and Tubbs (*Miami Vice*), LaRue and Washington (*Hill Street Blues*), and Cagney and Lacey (*Cagney and*

Lacey) cooperated and coordinated their efforts to investigate criminal misconduct and restore public safety and security.

The essential element of organizational community is "cooperation." As Newcomb (1974) has noted, the value of cooperation pervades both television's traditional kinship families and television's nontraditional "work families." Although such work families are not united by ties of kinship, they are "united by ties of love, warmth, and of mutual concern" (Newcomb, 1974, pp. 50–51). And members of these work families cooperate with each other in order to give and get physical assistance, emotional support, and social identification.

Of course, members of these work families cooperate not only to help each other but also to help organizational outsiders, as our 1987 episode of *Fortune Dane* illustrated. In this episode, the "Bay City" city council debated the issue of declaring their city a sanctuary for political refugees, an issue which the mayor and three council representatives regarded as a moral issue and which two other council representatives regarded as an economic issue (encouraging illegal aliens to take away Bay City jobs). Yet when Mayor Harding requested it, all five members of the council appeared publicly the following week presenting a united front in support of protection for all residents of the city — even South American opposition leader Ortello who had taken refuge in Bay City.

In short, the value of community was displayed as a key value in prime time organizations. As Newcomb and Alley (1983) noted about the prime time WJM-TV organization (*The Mary Tyler Moore Show*) in particular but also about prime time organizations in general: "These people supported one another in ways usually reserved to families. . . . Even in their arguments, in the times when they are estranged from one another, the working group remains familial in its anger. While they portray the peculiarities of individuals, the overarching theme of this show, and many others . . . is compassion for one another" (p. 206). In sum, the value of community enacts and affirms a "humane collectivity" in prime time organizations (Schrag, Hudson & Bernabo, 1981).

Individualism and Community on Prime Time

Individuals as team players. One way in which prime time dramas integrated the oppositional values of individualism and community was by depicting individuals as "team" players. Prime time dramas displayed this integration through the words and actions of skilled professionals who placed their organizations and its members and clients above their own feelings and self-interests. In so doing, individualism and community were integrated through teamwork — individuals working together in a way that did not call attention to their individual actions. Thus, physicians at St. Eligius (*St. Elsewhere*) wheeled patient beds and hotel managers (*Hotel*) answered the reservation telephone at the front desk when those actions helped accomplish organizational tasks and goals.

The *Miami Vice* episode described earlier provided an especially noteworthy example of the integration of individualism and community. In this episode, detectives Sonny Crockett and Ricardo Tubbs were called into Lt. Martin Castillo's office to talk with two outside drug enforcement agents about a big drug dealer whom they had been tracking for several months. Even though Crockett and Tubbs decided that they did not want to work with these agents because it would not "work out compatability-wise," they nonetheless displayed reluctant cooperation after Castillo told them to work together. Furthermore, we later discovered that arch-individualist Lt. Castillo was himself being a team player. Shortly after Crockett and Tubbs left Castillo's office, Cates extended his hand to Castillo and said, "I appreciate the cooperation." Castillo ignored the proferred handshake, signifying his distaste for Cates who was actually working with an Internal Affairs officer under the guise of a drug agent in order to investigate Sonny's integrity. Yet Castillo cooperated with the Internal Affairs investigation because he was a team player who put aside his personal preferences for the good of the organization. In this case, his actions were indeed in the best interests of the Miami Vice P.D., for the resulting investigation confirmed that one of its premiere undercover drug detectives, Crockett, was "clean." When Crockett learned some time later about the IA investigation, he affirmed Castillo's actions, telling him, "You had a responsibility to the unit."

A team of individual heroes. In a similar manner, the values of individualism and community were integrated in depictions of prime time organizations as "teams of individual heroes." There is a subtle but important distinction between an individual who is a team player and an organization that is a team of individual heroes. In organizations in which members are "team players," each member subsumes his or her individual identity for the good of the organization. In contrast, organizations that are teams of individual heroes are loosely coordinated groups of very distinct individuals — often "outlaw heroes"—who work together to accomplish short-term organizational goals.

One such team of individual heroes from our sample was *The A-Team*. This group of freelance soldiers of fortune was comprised of outlaw former special-mission soldiers whose unique coalition of individual skills enabled them to successfully right the wrongs of their clients. The A-Team included such distinct members as Colonel Hannibal Smith — leader, organizer, strategist; B.A. Baracus — a macho mechanic of forbidding size; "Howling Mad-Dog" Murdock — an expert pilot whom the team periodically "borrowed" from a mental hospital because he could fly anything from a cropduster to a 747; and Lieutenant Templeton "Face" Peck — a handsome, suave provisions expert who could hustle almost anything from almost anyone. Together this team of "outlaw" heroes undertook seemingly impossible tasks and often risked their lives to help individuals in need. In the 1986 episode from our sample, for instance, *A-Team* members combined these unique skills to help a group of senior citizens protect an old Texas mission they were running as a tourist attraction in order to avoid being banished to nursing homes. The senior citizens were being intimidated by a greedy former military official who wanted to buy their land for almost nothing in order to resell it at a huge profit to the military for a new base site. Thanks to the creative, if eccentric, combined efforts of the heroic *A-Team* individualists, the elderly citizens and their mission were rescued.

Becker (1975) has asserted that humans constantly experience dual needs and desires — on the one hand, humans need and want to stand out — to be individual stars; and on the other hand, humans want the security of being members of winning teams — part of something and not isolated out front. Members of prime time organizations meet these dual needs through teamwork and organizational activities which integrate individualism and community, thereby benefitting themselves as individuals as well as their collective organizations.

REASON AND EMOTION

It comes as no surprise that American organizations have a reverence for reason. As March and Olson (1976) have argued, an "ethic of rationality" pervades organizational life inasmuch as the performances of all organizational behaviors are interpreted within a preferred context of reason and logic (p. 21). This value of reason is reflected in so-called "economic rationality," the organizational preference for "efficiency" and "cost-effectiveness," as well as in the organizational preference for "systematic" and "analytic" decision making. On the other hand, organizational researchers have also argued that organizations are not as rational as our models tend to suggest. Indeed, organizations are also contexts for intuition, irrationality, sentimentality, and even "passion" (see March, 1980; Mintzberg, Raisinghani, & Theoret, 1976; Peters & Austin, 1986; Weick, 1980), all of which affirm the value of emotion in organizational America. Not surprisingly, both of these organizational values were reflected in prime time television.

Reason: Cold Pragmatism and Systematic Analysis

"Economic rationality" was presented in our sample of prime time organizations most often in the actions of so-called "administrative" managers (see Chapter 4). One obvious instance of this "bottom-line" sense of reason appeared on the 1986 episode of *Trapper John, M.D.* when one higher level hospital administrator confronted resident physician J.T. McIntyre regarding the payment for the treatment of one of his patients — an indigent can collector (a "canner") known only as "Fellah." The hospital administrator argued that treating indigents like Fellah was not rational because they do not have insurance and because they usually skip out of the hospital without paying. Thus, she did not feel that the hospital should provide Fellah with the expensive care that J.T. had ordered. J.T., on the other hand, argued that the hospital was a public service organization that should serve all of the public by providing the best health care available. He also argued that Fellah was an honorable person who would pay for his treatment, somehow. Thanks to Dr. J.T., Fellah did receive the needed health care, and he did try to pay his bill, though his mode of payment (in thousands of aluminum cans) was somewhat unorthodox (and no doubt incomplete). Nonetheless, the episode revealed the conflict between the economic rationalities of hospital administration and the operational realities of quality health care (see Turow, forthcoming).

A second sense of reason — reason as systematic analysis—was also displayed in our prime time organizations. For example, the detective series *Remington Steele* overtly and humorously illustrated the problems encountered when systematic reasoning was not followed. Agency detective Remington Steele almost always leaped to a premature conclusion by grandly announcing that he had solved the case, based on a "life imitates art" analogy between the case being investigated and one of his favorite movies. Viewers were invited to laugh at Steele's hasty generalizations, mistaken conclusions, and general lack of rationality. Equally predictably, Laura Holt — the owner of the detective agency—usually provided a contrapuntal positive illustration of the results of analytic reasoning as she explained how she systematically had collected and analyzed information which led her to an alternative, and almost always correct, solution. In our 1986 episode titled "Steele at Your Service," for example, Laura indeed stepped in with the correct solution to a murder after Steele had accused nearly half of the members of a wealthy household and its staff of blackmailing and murdering the former butler. Steele had leaped to these mistaken conclusions because he again had failed to use either common sense or logic, while Laura arrived at the correct solution because she had used both.

Emotion: Sound Sentiments, Instincts, and Irrationalities

The emotionality of prime time organizational life was displayed in several ways in our sample. First, organizational members revealed their own genuine, heartfelt sentiments as they performed their jobs. In one St. Elsewhere episode, for example, internist Carol Novino displayed sadness and anger when she discovered that her patient had terminal cancer. Subsequently, relational manager Dr. Donald Westphall affirmed the importance of such emotion when he encouraged her to continue to feel genuinely concerned for her patients and to channel this concern into action — in particular, by giving her patients another important emotion — hope.

Another sense of organizational emotion was displayed when prime time characters used their instincts to solve organizational problems. In one episode of Scarecrow and Mrs. King, for example, Thornton (the then-retired head of the U.S. government intelligence agency) summoned espionage operative Amanda King to his office to enlist her aid in finding a letter of pardon from former President Eisenhower which had been stolen from his files. Without this letter, Thornton explained, both he and all the agents would be discredited because Thornton had actually been a triple agent for the United States, a status known only to President Eisenhower. Thornton selected Amanda to help him because, as he explained, only a person with good instincts would be able to understand right from wrong on this case and he believed that Amanda had such instincts. Not surprisingly, Amanda's instincts did indeed enable her both to save her partner's life and to find the missing letter.

Thus, emotion as trustworthy instinct was affirmed as an important organizational value which helped members accomplish their goals and helped the organization survive.

A final sense of emotion which appeared on prime time television was that of irrationality. Emotion in this sense was often displayed by organizational members who blurted out knee-jerk reactions to surprising, scary, or disappointing situations. Irrationality was usually cast in a negative light and thus was not depicted as a positive organizational value. One humorous enactment of irrational emotion appeared on the episode of *Bob Newhart* mentioned earlier, an episode in which George, the inn handyman, played a practical joke on Stephanie, the college student and part-time housekeeper at the inn, by adjusting her scale to make it appear that Stephanie had gained three pounds. So, when Stephanie — who was very petite and who was obsessively concerned with her weight — stepped on her scale, her shriek was heard all over the inn. And viewers were invited to laugh as she spent the entire day jogging, doing situps, and fasting; displaying irrational (re)actions which temporarily disrupted her job performance and personal relationships.

A more serious depiction of organizational irrationality occurred on our 1987 episode of *L.A. Law*. Douglas Brackman, one of the law firm's named partners, submitted a letter of resignation to senior partner, Leland McKenzie. Brackman had decided to resign after his own irrational outburst at a firm meeting prompted an immediate and unequivocal castigation by Leland and the other partners, both for Brackman's outburst and its selfish content. As Brackman told Leland, "How can I command respect from the other partners after a humiliation like that?" Ultimately, however, Brackman retracted his resignation and learned to avoid similar irrational outbursts and to be more sensitive to others in the future.

Reason and Emotion on Prime Time

Cold-blooded passion. One way in which the often antithetical values of reason and emotion were integrated involved the systematic use of passion for some nonpassionate end. This opposition was evident in the negative, usually criminal, actions of individuals with whom members of law enforcement agencies, public administration agencies, law firms, and private investigation organizations regularly interacted. In our 1986 episode of *Moonlighting* entitled "Knowing Her" — which intertextually referenced the movie *Body Heat* — detective David Addison's former lover (for whom he still carried a torch) systematically looked him up, hired him to investigate a fabricated crime, and set him up as the trustworthy alibi and witness to an apparently passionate killing of her husband in "self-defense." When David realized that she had really murdered her husband and had cold-bloodedly sought him out to exploit his true love for her, members of the Blue Moon Detective Agency (David and Maddie) and the viewers were given a powerful lesson in "cold-blooded passion."

Reasoning with instincts. Reason and emotion also were integrated in prime time organizations when members reasoned with their instincts. In the episode of *Scarecrow and Mrs. King* described above, Amanda King enacted this synthesis of seemingly opposing values in several scenes. In one scene she secretly trailed her partner Scarecrow to Thornton's house. But just as Scarecrow entered the house, Amanda noticed that Thornton's warning signal of imminent danger was in use — a flower pot on the balcony rail. Amanda reasoned with her instincts by tempering spontaneous emotion (her initial impetus to yell at or run after Scarecrow to warn him) with reason (her realization a split-second later that either of these actions would not alert Scarecrow to the potential of danger from someone inside Thornton's house but merely to the fact that she was following him). Instead, Amanda spotted a baseball in her car and threw it through the upstairs window in time to alert Scarecrow, who ducked and managed to elude the hidden intruder's attempt to kill him.

In summary, both reason and emotion were values that prime time organizations held in high esteem. However, as this discussion has indicated, excessive rationality or excessive emotionality were depicted in negative ways as preventing individuals and organizations from functioning effectively. Thus, prime time organizations presented the lesson that reason and emotion should be combined in moderation for effective organizational action.

YOUTH AND EXPERIENCE

It should come as no surprise that the value of youth, with its associated qualities of strength, eagerness, and idealism was celebrated in prime time organizations. Recently, however, prime time television has experienced a shift toward the presentation, and positive depiction, of older individuals. As McFadden (1985, October 19–25) quipped about senior citizens in a *TV Guide* article focusing on the success of NBC's *The Golden Girls*, "[senior citizens] are trendy right now, having supplanted yuppies as the demographic darlings of the media" (p. 6). While older workers certainly have not yet upstaged younger workers on prime time, both youth and experience were portrayed as multiaccented values in the prime time organizations in our sample.

The Idealism (and Naivete) of Organizational Youth

The value of youth was revealed on prime time through youthful organizational members who embodied qualities such as optimism and idealism. Young Dr. Jack Morrison of St. Eligius Hospital (*St. Elsewhere*) was one prime time organizational member who displayed these attributes. Throughout the history of this hospital (melo)drama, Jack was one of the most optimistic and idealistic characters at the hospital. In the 1986 episode from our sample, Jack enthusiastically agreed to treat patients at a local prison as his community service activity because "prison reform is something I care about." And, as he told his colleagues at the hospital: "I've got a lot to be grateful for. I passed my remedial. My knee is okay. My son is safe and sound. It's time to give something back." At the prison, however, Jack's youthful naivete and idealism were cast against the experience and cynicism of a middle-aged veteran prison doctor who told Jack: "I was just like you when I came here. Work within the system. Change things. [pause] Nothing ever changes." When Jack criticized this grizzled veteran about being "burned out," the veteran added: "No, son, I'm way past burned out. Worst part of it is that I don't even feel like a doctor anymore. I'm a veterinarian." Thus, the youthful idealism, and perhaps naivete, of Jack was contrasted in a powerful way with the cynicism of this perhaps too-grizzled veteran. Regrettably (at least for Jack), his idealism didn't save him from being beaten and raped during a prison riot.

The idealism of youth was often associated with an accompanying naivete which, in Jack's case, resulted in very painful consequences. In other situations, however, such naivete was cast in a humorous light, as was the case in *Mr. Sunshine*, a short-lived comedy about a blind college English teacher named Paul Stark. In the episode from our sample, one of Mr. Stark's female students came to a class party at his house. She stayed at Mr. Stark's house after all the guests departed, asked if she could read a poem that she had written especially for him, then slipped into another room to "get the poem." She returned in a silk negligee only to discover that Mr. Stark's current love, Janice (a woman closer to his middle age), had stopped by for a visit. Although this event was temporarily quite embarrassing for Mr. Stark and for the student, it did not disrupt his relationship with Janice; after all, as he explained to Janice, the student's actions merely represented "a school girl's crush." In summary, the organizationally esteemed value of youthful, enthusiastic idealism was often accompanied by the naivete of youth and its painful or humorous consequences. Thus, youth was not portrayed unilaterally as an unproblematic value in organizational life.

The Maturity (and Cynicism) of Organizational Experience

In contrast to the idealism and naivete of youth, experience and a cluster of related values — such as maturity, seasoned judgment, and sometimes cynicism — were also displayed by organizational members in prime time programs. Peter Fischer, executive producer of the successful *Murder She Wrote* (CBS) series, which starred 60-year-old Angela Lansbury, explained that television's concern for the value of experience was a relatively recent phenomenon: "It's a matter of youth versus experience and generally, maturity seems to be losing out. But there's been a big change in TV viewing habits lately. The kid stuff is losing favor because the teens and subteens are watching MTV or youth-oriented movies on tape, and many of them have dropped out of the Nielson network-viewing audience." (Davidson, 1986, February 15–21, p. 26).

The value prime time organizations placed on experience often was revealed when seasoned organizational veterans offered advice to less experienced members. In our sample, for example, we watched Ms. Colby (*The Colbys*, ABC), the Colby family matriarch, offer advice to her brother and fellow stockholder Jason Colby — himself a pretty powerful patriarchal figure; we watched the older and experienced female assistant of the newly hired (but short-lived) director of hotel operations (*Hotel*, ABC) advise reservations clerk Julie to beware of sexual harrassment by this new director, suggesting "if you're going to give at the office, make sure you know what you're getting back in advance"; and we watched older doctors on *St. Elsewhere* (NBC) and on *Trapper John, M.D.* (CBS) give medical and personal advice to younger doctors. In sum, in giving sound advice — both personal and occupational — to their younger colleagues, these veterans revealed and affirmed experience as a positive organizational value.

As suggested earlier, however, the value of experience was also enacted in a negative way as cynicism. In our 1987 episode of *Hard Copy*, for example, rookie reporter David DeValle took his first assignment on the police beat — covering the latest in a string of recent freeway murders. There he joined Andy Omar, a 40-year-old veteran who was considering quitting the newspaper business to take a cushy public relations job. At the beginning of the episode, DeValle sought assistance from Omar, because, as he told Omar: "You're supposed to be the veteran. You're supposed to have instincts on this kind of stuff. You're supposed to pass that down like, uh, heirlooms. What you know is gold to me." But Andy Omar, who was burned out on investigative reporting, explained to his young colleague: "You picked the wrong role model. I mean, I'm the guy who never made editor. See, my life's a disaster. . . . I'm all out of answers. Sorry. End of story."

Of course, that was not the end of the story. DeValle's youthful persistence and hard work turned up the only significant lead in the case and seemed to rejuvenate the cynical veteran Omar. Predictably, they decided to work "together" on the case and pursued different leads which did indeed solve the case. But unpredictably, this experience-plus-youth plotline had an unexpected twist as Omar filed an *exclusive* byline while DeValle was in the field covering the arrest. In short, the youthful DeValle learned a bitter lesson — that experience can turn some organizational members into cynical and selfish veterans.

Youth and Experience on Prime Time

Teaching old docs new tricks (and young docs old tricks). The values of youth and experience were integrated positively on our sample episode of *Trapper John, M.D.* Appropriately titled "The Curmudgeon," this episode focused on Dr. McDuffy, an older and very grouchy neurosurgeon who offended almost everyone in the hospital with his arrogant and nasty demeanor except for the older and very sturdy Nurse Andrews (who, as we later learned, had been stood up at the altar 38 years before by McDuffy, an act which McDuffy never had explained to Andrews). As the plots unfolded, tensions developed between McDuffy and a younger neurosurgeon, especially after the younger neurosurgeon had to finish an operation that McDuffy was unable to complete when he became ill. After the operation, the young neurosurgeon complained to Trapper John, the hospital's chief of staff, that McDuffy was "too old" to be working and that he was "dangerous to the patients in the hospital." Trapper agreed that McDuffy's work load had been too strenuous but lectured the young doctor that "you don't turn a guy out to pasture when he still has something to contribute."

As it turned out, Trapper did not need to cut McDuffy's case load because McDuffy suffered a heart attack. He survived the heart attack and spent several weeks recuperating in the hospital under the supervision of Nurse Andrews. And after McDuffy fully recovered, he returned to work in a new position — director of medical education — created for him by Trapper so that other organizational members could benefit from McDuffy's experience. Even in this new position, though, McDuffy still overworked himself and alienated nearly everyone around him, including the young neurosurgeon, until a hospital executive asked Trapper to fire McDuffy. When Trapper told him of his dismissal, McDuffy became quite depressed — he had lost an important job in the hospital, he still had not explained to Andrews why he had left her, nor had he told her that he was still in love with her.

Not surprisingly, McDuffy's conflicts with Andrews and the young neurosurgeon were resolved at the end of the program. McDuffy resolved his conflict with Andrews when he finally explained to her that he had stood her up at the altar 38 years ago because he was too embarrassed to tell her that he had dropped out of medical school (temporarily) to work in a meat packing plant to support his mother and family after his father died; he then asked Andrews to forgive him and marry him now, and she accepted. McDuffy also resolved his conflict with the young neurosurgeon when, on Trapper's recommendation, the young neurosurgeon consulted and received advice from McDuffy which allowed the youthful physician to correctly diagnose and treat a patient whom he had been unable to help. McDuffy also asked for and received the promise of a second chance from Trapper at being the director of medical education. In the end, both the youthful physician and the experienced old curmudgeon learned new things and grew — as professionals and as people.

In sum, youth and experience were presented on prime time as values that many organizations esteem — the former for the energy, enthusiasm, and idealism that youthful members bring with them, the latter for the irreplaceable wisdom and maturity that comes from the experience of organizational veterans. However, both youth and experience also presented problems for organizations — the former with the dangers and misunderstandings resulting from the naivete of youthful members, the latter with the intractibility and loss of morale resulting from cynical veterans. In short, youth and experience offer mixed problems and potentials for organizations in American culture and on prime time television.

CONFORMITY AND DEVIANCE

That the value of conformity, defined here as compliance with public laws and organizational rules, is featured regularly and affirmed in positive ways in prime time organizations is not surprising. After all, most scholars of American television have agreed that prime time drama generally presents a "mainstream" view of American society (Cantor, 1980; Comstock, 1980; Fiske & Hartley, 1978; Gerbner, Gross, Morgan, & Signorielli, 1980; Gitlin, 1983; Turow, 1984a). As Cantor (1980) put it, television drama "is consistent with public norms, evasive where there is overt controversy, and supportive of the economic interests of the industry where they are clear" (p. 118).

However, images of deviance are also displayed in prime time organizations. Much of this deviance is, of course, presented negatively in the antisocial, violent, and illegal actions of villainous antagonists, actions which stand in marked contrast to the sociable, productive, and law-abiding actions of heroic organizational protagonists. Indeed, as Carlson (1985) has argued, prime time law enforcement programs valorize a "norm of compliance" inasmuch as criminals usually embody very undesirable and violent qualities in potent opposition to the generally heroic and morally courageous law enforcers who normally arrest (or kill) these criminals by the end of the program. Although the lines between these negative criminals and positive police officers have blurred in some recent cop shows (as will be discussed momentarily), deviance continues to be featured predominantly as a negative value in prime time organizations.

However, not all organizational deviance on prime time is portrayed as negative. In fact, prime time organizations, including law enforcement agencies, often present and endorse a positive sense of deviance that resembles Steele and Redding's (1962) "rejection of authority." As they put it, this more positive sense of deviance refers to "a deep aversion to the acceptance of any coercive restraint by established social organizations or by personal authorities" (p. 88). Perhaps Marc (1984) put it best in his recent analysis of television's public safety industries when he argued, "The continuing glorification of laissez-faire competition and social Darwinist ideology since the realization of the manifest destiny has fostered a heroic vision of the man of action that often engenders a benevolent indulgence of rule breaking" (p. 66).

Conformity: Playing It Straight

Prime time television frequently affirms the value of organizational conformity through the presentation of relatively mainstream actions and characters. We found the value of conformity affirmed in manifestly obvious ways when organizational characters engaged in actions which complied with specific organizational rules and societal norms. For example, detectives Sonny Crockett and Ricardo Tubbs (Miami Vice) decided not to arrest a suspect, even though they knew he was a major dope smuggler, because they had no hard court-admissible evidence against him. In Trapper John, M.D., the curmudgeon director of medical education described earlier refused to bend the rules and give education credits to a doctor who slipped out of a medical training class early. And, in Murder She Wrote, an English professor (suspected of murder but ultimately proved innocent) conformed with scholarly norms of respectability when she wrote romance novels under her daughter's name rather than her own name so as not to undermine the academic integrity of herself or her university.

More powerful enactments of conformity were revealed through moral and courageous organizational heroes such as Captain Merrill Stubing (The Love Boat), hotel manager Peter McDermitt (Hotel), police chief Frank Furillo (Hill Street Blues), and hospital chief of staff Dr. Donald Westphall (St. Elsewhere). Yet even the somewhat off-color protagonists such as Moonlighting's private eye David Addison — who found it difficult to work without double entendre joking — and Hill Street Blues' undercover cop Mick Belcher — who found it difficult to work without insulting criminals or colleagues with labels such as "dirtbag" and "dogbreath" — endorsed conformity as a necessary, if inconvenient, organizational value.

Deviance: Breaking Laws and Bending Rules

Television's law-breakers, most of whom were not regular members of a prime time organization, were generally portrayed as very negative characters. Indeed, this was the case with many of the visiting antagonists in our sample: on Airwolf, a deranged mountain man stalked a group of paraplegics who set out on a mountain climb with protagonist Hawke; on Highway to Heaven, a neo-Nazi group terrorized an elderly survivor of Auschwitz and killed his son; and on *Riptide*, a cold-blooded male-female pair of antagonists attempted to murder the female's brother-in-law and frame an innocent person for the murder. There are indeed some very nasty deviants on prime time. However, most of these visiting criminals are arrested (or killed) by rule-abiding members of prime time law enforcement or private investigative organizations.

On the other hand, television's rule-breakers, most of whom were regular members of prime time organizations, were portrayed in a far more positive light. These rule-breakers generally rejected the rules and conventions of authorities and institutions for altruistic purposes. In this sense, these rule-breakers integrated conformity and deviance by conforming to a higher set of mores. We now turn to a further explanation of this positive integration of deviance and conformity.

Conformity and Deviance on Prime Time

Conforming to a higher set of rules. As just noted, most of the rulebreakers of prime time organizations violated organizational or institutional conventions for the sake of some higher value and ideal. One such juxtaposition of conformity and deviance was enacted beautifully on our 1987 episode of *Night Court* (also see Chapter 6). This episode displayed the zany New York City night court presided over by Judge Harry Stone on New Year's Eve. On this festive occasion, marked by the presence of streamers, noisemakers, and party hats, the judge prepared to exercise some holiday generosity in the case of an older gentleman named Walter Wyse. Mr. Wyse, an escapee from a New Jersey prison hospital, had been arrested for indecent exposure after the Times Square wind had whipped up the hospital nightgown he was wearing. Wyse had escaped the prison hospital with only two months left until his parole because he feared that since he had cancer, he might never get another chance to celebrate New Year's Eve at Times Square, where he had met his late wife 40 years earlier.

Judge Harry's willingness to let Mr. Wyse return to Times Square for the New Year's countdown was stymied by New Jersey prison officer Lt. Gerard, who insisted that he take Mr. Wyse directly back to prison with no detours, as the rules required. Despite Harry's appeals, Gerard refused to honor Mr. Wyse's request. That is, until another arrestee — "Mr. 1987"—dressed only in a diaper, mugged Lt. Gerard in the courthouse bathroom and escaped with the lieutenant's clothes, including his identification. Judge Harry and the rest of the *Night Court* staff then hoist Gerard by his own petard. Without identification, they had no legal proof that Gerard was indeed a prison officer. Thus, they argued that strictly following the law meant they would need to send a polaroid picture of Gerard, dressed as he was in diapers, back to the prison for corroboration before they released him or released Mr. Wyse into his custody. The thought of the verbal indignities that he would suffer if his fellow prison officers saw this picture prompted Lt. Gerard to agree to deviate from the precise rule-governed procedure and to return Mr. Wyse to prison via Times Square (escorted by *Night Court* bailiff, Bull).

This *Night Court* episode revealed that organizational rules — such as the instruction to directly return an escapee to prison — and organizational and cultural norms—such as empathizing with and honoring a dying man's request — are sometimes opposed to each other. In this case, the organizational members essentially blackmailed Gerard with an overly strict interpretation of the law in order to get him to bend his own overly strict interpretation of the law. In other cases, organizational members simply deviated from and defied such rules and laws in order to conform to those higher organizational and cultural norms. In so doing, the "norm"al relationship between deviance and conformity was inverted so that a higher set of values was affirmed.

The blurred lines between heroes and villains. A final way in which the values of conformity and deviance were integrated in prime time organizations was in the blurring of the distinction between heroic and villainous characters, especially in law enforcement and public administration organizations. Although we agree with Marc (1984) and others that most of these police shows revealed the differences between heroes and villains in clear (sometimes overly obvious) ways, shows such as *Miami Vice* and *Hill Street Blues* clouded many of these traditional distinctions.

The 1986 episode of *Miami Vice* was especially eloquent in its blurring of heroes and villains in prime time police work. The episode, titled "Payback," began as undercover vice officer Sonny Crockett was summoned to prison by a criminal whom Sonny had arrested several months earlier for selling cocaine. This criminal, as we discovered later, had taken off with $3 million that belonged to his supplier, before he was arrested by Crockett, although he did not actually have the money or know where this money was. In a powerful opening scene, this criminal pulled out a self-made gun and shot — not Sonny but himself—thus setting Sonny up as the person who knew where the missing $3 million was located. Indeed, this subtle payback worked as Sonny's boat was ransacked and the message "Where's the money, Crockett" was left.

The plot became more complex when Sonny and his partner Tubbs went undercover to purchase cocaine from (and then arrest) a major drug supplier named Fuente. Fuente — who turned out to be the same supplier who was missing the $3 million dollars and who wanted it returned — only did business aboard his yacht but would not even meet with Crockett and Tubbs. Enter the main antagonist in the program: Cates, a federal undercover agent. Cates was initially introduced to Crockett and Tubbs as a vice cop from New Orleans, but he was really a federal undercover agent who had been investigating this major drug supplier for several years. Cates became involved with Crockett and Tubbs in an apparent effort to help them arrest Fuente; in fact, Cates arranged for them to meet Fuente aboard his yacht. But when Crockett and Tubbs met Fuente on his ship, they discovered that Fuente knew that Crockett was a cop and that he thought Crockett had his $3 million.

Crockett and Tubbs managed to escape the ship with their lives, but they did not know how to resolve Sonny's dilemma — his cover had been blown and this dangerous drug supplier believed that Sonny had his $3 million. Cates, his identity as a federal agent now known to Crockett and Tubbs, offered a solution: tell Fuente that Sonny did have the money and that he would return it for a small "finder's fee" of several kilos of cocaine and Fuente's face-to-face word that he would not have him killed. Sonny — with the approval of his boss Lt. Castillo — agreed to try the plan, even though his partner Tubbs called it "suicidal." Not surprisingly, Cates had a different plan in mind: to set Sonny up to be killed by Fuente as the fall guy so that Cates could selfishly enjoy the $3 million that he had actually stolen and never be suspected of taking the money.

Crockett, of course, was not killed, but Cates was shot in an action-packed struggle with Crockett on a speeding boat in the final scene. Before Cates died, however, he and Crockett exchanged the following dialogue about what the stress of police life can do to a cop:

Sonny: You know what you did to me? You know what you put me through?

Cates: Do you know what this job did to me?

Sonny: [After long pause] Yeah. Yeah, I do.

Cates: I just wanted to sit and rest, Crockett. That's all I wanted. [long pause] I'm sorry, Sonny. [Cates fell over dead]

As this episode powerfully illustrated, the values of deviance and conformity and the lines between heroes and villains can become very blurred for some organizations and their members. In particular, the line between the heroic organizational member and the villainous outsider was blurred in *Miami Vice* through the actions of Cates, an officer who was just as bad as (or even worse than) the criminals he dealt with. Cates was a cop turned bad, the worst kind of cop, who was willing to have another cop killed so that he could selfishly enjoy $3 million and never be suspected. So, too, we saw Sonny Crockett transformed from a heroic law enforcer into a victim who suffered from paranoia and self-doubt because he was suspected — briefly by his own colleagues and permanently by Fuente — of violating the laws he was supposed to enforce. Finally, and most subtly, the lines between Cates as organizational villain and Sonny as organizational hero were blurred when, after all the terrible things Cates did to him, Sonny empathized with and forgave Cates. Sonny understood that the lines between deviance and conformity to the law could become blurred for cops — the injustice of a criminal justice system in which all cops work hard and stay poor; while some drug dealers, like Fuente, get rich and stay free can lead one to question what justice is. Sonny understood why this once good cop did this very bad thing. Thus, the usually clear opposition between the hero and the villain and between conformity and deviance blurred for members of this law enforcement organization.

CONCLUDING OBSERVATIONS

We conclude from our analysis of these sample weeks that prime time television generally portrays organizations and organizational members positively and in compliance with normative values of American society. We see a plethora of professionals, managers, and ordinary employees working in organizations which value people as individuals, which value superior quality and service, which value open communication and organizational equality. In short, many of our prime time organizations represent fictional enactments of what Peters and Waterman (1982) identified as "excellent companies." Admittedly, such prime time organizations represent a reification of the status quo; however, they also offer an affirmation of the positive values of organizational America.

Indeed, prime time television does not only provide morally heroic or ideologically conservative visions of organizational life. Prime time organizations were populated as well by rude, selfish, ruthless individuals hungry purely for economic success, who were either determined to climb the organizational status ladder or who merely put in time until payday. We saw workaholics busy sacrificing their health and their families' happiness to achieve personal and organizational goals. We saw cynical organizational veterans, burned out after years of hard work, who realized that profit is not always the "natural by-product of doing something well" (Peters & Waterman, 1982, p. 284).

Much of the time, prime time organizations and organizational members were able to resolve and balance the tensions among apparently antithetical characters or values in a constructive manner. One administrator (Dr. Trapper John McIntyre) arranged for an (overly) enthusiastic young neurosurgeon to seek advice from an older (and somewhat callous) experienced surgeon, thereby integrating efficiently and humanely the values of youth and experience to the benefit of these two individuals, the hospital, and the patients. One judge (Harry Stone) mediated an excessively strict adherence to rules and an intentional deviation from rules in order to honor the request of a dying man and thereby uphold a higher moral ideal. In these and other ways, prime time organizations integrate opposing forces and tensions and, thus, provide lessons on how organizational value conflicts can be resolved in positive ways.

Unfortunately, not all value conflicts were integrated so constructively. In particular, the oppositional values of economic success and human success — arguably the two most important organizational values — remained in opposition on prime time despite the potential for integration. As noted earlier, for example, the human success of the St. Gregory Hotel (Hotel) seemed to contribute to its economic success — at least as implied by the grandeur and elegance of the hotel — yet we never saw the connection between these two senses of success enacted directly on the program. On the other hand, although St. Eligius Hospital (St. Elsewhere) members displayed a commitment to values of human success which was similar to that displayed by members of the St. Gregory Hotel, St. Eligius seemed to be an economic failure, at least until the "Ecumena" health care corporation purchased it in the 1987 season premiere episode.[1] Whatever the case, the link between human success and

---

[1] At the time this book was prepared, St. Eligius was still a run-down city-operated hospital threatened with destruction. When NBC decided to reprieve the series for one more season (1987–1988), the hospital was partly rebuilt and taken over by the "Ecumena" company. Not surprisingly, the tensions between economic and human success were highlighted during the 1987–1988 season as St. Eligius "went corporate" but kept much of the old "community" and "familial" staff who had difficulty

the economic "bottom lines" of these two "sainted" organizations has been virtually ignored. Consequently, prime time organizations do not teach us a key values lesson: that an excellent company's value set integrates "economic health, serving customers, and making meanings" (Peters & Waterman, 1982, p. 225).

As suggested in the beginning of this chapter, prime time organizations enact a set of broad cultural values of the society of which they are a part. However, while prime time organizations generally may share this broad set of cultural values, individual organizations are unique in their particular value priorities and conflicts. In the next chapter, we focus our attention on seven distinct prime time organizations, examining how these organizations and their members enacted their value priorities and conflicts and created their unique organizational cultures.

---

adjusting to the new ownership and its philosophy. In fact, the paternal, humanistic administrator, Dr. Donald Westphall, resigned his position over this conflict of values.

Chapter 6

Prime Time Organizational Cultures

As we noted in the last chapter and throughout this book, prime time television displays the social and organizational values of American culture. In the last chapter, we examined how some of these broader social and organizational values (and the conflicts and tensions among these values) were dramatically enacted in two sample weeks of prime time programming. However, as we also suggested in the last chapter, individual organizations in American society (and on American television) develop and maintain their own unique sets of values and value priorities which reflect the distinct "cultures" of these organizations. In this chapter, we examine some of American television's prime time organizational cultures.

In recent years, the terms "organizational culture" and "corporate culture" have become management buzzwords which have attracted attention in the academic and popular literature (see *Business Week*, 1980; Deal & Kennedy, 1982; *Fortune*, October 1983; Frost, Moore, Louis, Lundberg, & Martin, 1985; Pacanowsky & O'Donnell-Trujillo, 1983; Pettigrew, 1979). Not surprisingly, different organizational researchers have used the concept of culture in different ways. For example, some researchers have treated culture as one of many "variables" in the organization whereas others have treated culture as a "metaphor" for the organization; stated differently, some have argued that culture is something an organization *has* whereas others have argued that culture is something an organization *is* (Smircich, 1983). In this chapter, we adopt the latter "metaphorical" view, treating our prime time organizations *as* cultures and analyzing them "not mainly in economic or material terms, but in terms of their expressive, ideological, and symbolic aspects" (Smircich, 1983, pp. 347–348).

In the next section, we discuss briefly the methods which guided our analysis of these prime time organizational cultures, summarily noting the cultural indicators and sample of television content which we employed. We then examine seven prime time organizations including the Hill Street Police Station (*Hill Street Blues*), St. Eligius Hospital (*St. Elsewhere*), Ewing Oil Corporation (*Dallas*), New York City Municipal Court (*Night Court*), the Cheers bar (*Cheers*), the St. Gregory Hotel (*Hotel*) and the Los Angeles law firm of McKenzie, Brackman, Chaney, & Kuzak (*L.A. Law*). We conclude with a brief discussion of the similarities and differences among these prime time organizational cultures and with a note on the implications of our analysis.

A METHODOLOGICAL NOTE

Cultural Indicators

In this analysis of the values and unique cultures of individual prime time organizations, we used the same four indicators we employed in Chapter 5, namely: (a) dialogue, (b) character, (c) setting, and (d) plot. We used these indicators to examine the values and describe the cultures of these organizations because, as Deal and Kennedy (1982) have affirmed, "Values are the bedrock of any corporate culture" and "for those who hold them, shared values define the fundamental character of their organization" (pp. 21, 23). Thus, these four "cultural indicators" were used together as a cumulative system by means of which we examined the values of these seven prime time organizational cultures. Here we discuss briefly each of these indicators.

One distinguishing feature of any organizational culture is the *dialogue* that organizational members share with each other. As we noted in Chapter 5, dialogue is the most direct indicator of cultural values since organizational members are presumed to control the language they use. Thus, as Sathe (1983) argued, the "shared sayings" of organizational members reveal some of the "shared understandings" of those members. Indeed, as Peters & Waterman (1982) put it, one of the most striking characteristics of excellent companies was the "dominant use of story, slogan, and legend" and "the common flavor" of the language of organizational members (p. 75).

Character refers to an organizational member's dramatic personae which encompasses particular values, emotions, and styles of action. Especially important for understanding the organizational culture are the historical "founders" and the contemporary "heroes," those characters who build and/or lead organizations by adding "their personal sense of values to the world" (Deal & Kennedy, 1982, p. 43; see also Siehl, 1985). On the other hand, so-called "ordinary employees" also reveal the values of the culture in their everyday organizational actions; these characters, too, are emblematic of the shared values and philosophies of the organizational culture.

A third indicator revelatory of organizational culture is the *setting* — the internal and/or external context which frames the symbolic performances of organizational characters. The setting includes such situational elements as the particular participants involved (e.g., police officer and suspected criminal), the geographical locale where the action takes place (e.g., interrogation room), and the occasion which inspires the action (e.g., officer wishes to question suspect about the murder of a local resident). The setting, thus, shapes the meaning of the characters' actions in different organizational scenes and helps the viewing audience understand how these characters and actions fit into the larger organizational culture.

Finally, the *plot* is perhaps the most powerful indicator of the shared values of an organization. At the surface level of storyline, plots reveal the sequentially ordered patterns of particular actions by particular characters in particular settings which, on prime time, generally come to a climax at the end of the program episode (e.g., when the audience learns who really killed the opera singer). However, at a deeper level of narrative structure, the particular story content is of less importance than the broader cultural values enacted through the narrative form itself. At this level, the particular actions, particular characters, and particular settings represent broader social actions, social types of characters, and social settings which typify the organizational culture. In this way, the plot reveals a social model of organizational action for viewing audiences as they come to understand the broader "moral" or "lesson" of the prime time story of organizational life.

Sample

Our sample consisted of videotaped episodes of the prime time programs which featured the seven organizations in the case studies that follow. In all, this sample included 83 videotaped episodes, including regularly scheduled program episodes as well as relevant specials, such as the two-hour *St. Elsewhere* "prequel" — "Time Heals"—and the two-hour made-for-television movie *Dallas: The Early Years*. Most episodes were taped during 1986 and 1987, though in some cases (e.g., *Hill Street Blues, Hotel, St. Elsewhere*) the videotaped episodes spanned five years. In the case of *L.A. Law*, on the other hand, the episodes spanned only the one year the program had aired at the time of this writing. In most cases, the episodes were videotaped during their original network broadcasts on prime time; in some cases, the episodes videotaped were same-season (first-run) reruns of these prime time network series programs. Finally, and perhaps more importantly, the two authors (combined) had been fans of all of these series and had watched them fairly faithfully during their tenures on prime time television. In sum, we believe the videotaped episodes, coupled with our own familiarity with the histories of the programs, constituted a more than adequate sample for analyzing these prime time organizational cultures.

These particular prime time programs were selected for analysis for several reasons. First, and most importantly, these programs *featured* an organization; that is, most of the scenes in each of these programs either took place in the organization or featured an organizational member. Second, we included both programs which had received critical acclaim (e.g., *Hill Street Blues; St. Elsewhere; L.A. Law*) and those which had enjoyed widespread popularity (e.g., *Cheers, Dallas*). Third, we selected programs which would reflect a variety of organizations — a police precinct, a hospital, a law firm, a city court, a bar, a hotel, and an oil/finance company. Finally, and without apology, we selected programs which were personal favorites that we had followed attentively for much of their (prime time) organizational lives. In this regard, Edward Hall's observations to another group of cultural analysts — anthropologists — provide an apt rejoinder to concerns that may be aroused by our personal "involvement" with the observed organizations:

> I think some anthropologists gave the field a bad name because they thought of their tribes as resources to be exploited. They didn't like the people they studied very much. Now my view is that unless you feel love, have a real emotional attachment, understanding and learning will never take place. I know that's weird for a social scientist to say, because in our tradition it is assumed that love interferes with science, with truth. But without love, you get stereotyping: cold, intellectual appraisal. (Tavris, 1983, p. 15)

Although it would be stretching it to say that we "loved" *all* of these shows, our appreciation for these programs influenced our decision to select them and, we believe, ultimately enhanced our analysis of them.

We now turn our attention to each of the seven prime time organizational cultures in our sample: Hill Street Police Station (*Hill Street Blues*, NBC), Ewing Oil (*Dallas*, CBS), St. Eligius Hospital (*St. Elsewhere*, NBC), New York City Municipal Court (*Night Court*, NBC), Cheers bar (*Cheers*, NBC), the St. Gregory Hotel (*Hotel*, ABC), and the law firm of McKenzie, Brackman, Chaney, and Kuzak (*L.A. Law*, NBC). We begin each section with a brief note on the program itself, since the program features (e.g., genre, production techniques, etc.) influence our "readings" and understandings of the organization. We then describe the organization itself and its members, focusing on the key organizational characters in each organization. Next, we examine one "critical incident" or episode in the life of each organization which was particularly revealing of the values of the organization. We conclude the chapter by summarizing some of the similarities and differences among these seven prime time organizational cultures.

HILL STREET POLICE STATION (*Hill Street Blues*, NBC)

Hill Street Blues (HSB) was one of the most critically acclaimed and innovative police dramas of the 1980s. Beginning January 15, 1981, HSB aired regularly until May 12, 1987. HSB was an MTM production which featured a large cast of major and minor regulars on the Hill Street force including, among others, Captain Frank Furillo (Daniel J. Travanti), Lieutenants Henry Goldblume (Joe Spano), Ray Calletano (Rene Enriquez), and Howard Hunter (James Sikking), Sergeants Phil Esterhaus (Michael Conrad), Stan Jablonski (Robert Prosky), and Lucy Bates (Betty Thomas), Detectives Mick Belker (Bruce Weitz), John LaRue (Kiel Martin), and Neal Washington (Taurean Blacque), and Patrol Officers Andy Renko (Charles Haid), Bobby Hill (Michael Warren), and Joe Coffey (Ed Marinaro). Joyce Davenport (Veronica Hamel) was one of the public defenders on the Hill who was in constant conflict with Furillo, her lover (and later husband). Frank's ex-wife Fay Furillo (Barbara Bossom) also dropped by the Hill in the early years of the program to consult with Frank about their son.

Hill Street Blues' noteworthy aesthetic innovations contributed to the unusual character of this prime time organization. The program's "quick cuts, a furious pace, [and] nervous camera made for complexity and congestion, a sense of entanglement and continuing crisis that matched the actual density and convolution of city life, of life in a ghetto police precinct in particular"; these production techniques, mixing episodic and serial format, were designed to "make it look messy," and created a more textured and realistic view of organization life on the Hill (Gitlin, 1983, p. 274).[1]

The Station House and Its Characters

Hill St. station, as indicated above, housed a large number of major and minor regular characters as well as visiting cops and criminals. The force was a fairly integrated lot which crossed gender, racial, and religious lines — an Italian-Catholic captain, an Hispanic (Columbian) lieutenant, a Jewish lieutenant, a white female sergeant, and black and white, male and female detectives and officers.

Captain Furillo, the central dramatic character and primary organizational leader, was an unusual authority figure and an enigmatic heroic character. Gitlin (1983) succinctly characterized Frank's qualities: "Furillo stands for commanding patience, wry humor, self-control under fire. He manages his men without judging them. He listens to everyone and understands everyone's frailties. . . . He plays his emotions with a soft pedal; his voice usually stays in the same muted register" (p. 311). In this sense, Furillo epitomized a strong but not stale or sterile "administrative" style of management (see Chapter 5).

Of the three lieutenants, Henry Goldblume was perhaps the most compelling. Goldblume was an especially sensitive and idealistic cop who "believed in talking criminals into surrender whenever possible" and who "always tested his beliefs in the crucible of the streets, unlike the pompous, puffy-faced liberal Chief Daniels, whose 'concern' for the community, one gathered, was less a matter of principle than a response to political pressures" (Gitlin, 1983, p. 309). Although Goldblume's idealism and sensitivity were challenged and strained over the years, he managed to maintain them relatively intact.

Phil Esterhaus was the mild-mannered sergeant who began every day at the station (and every episode) with "roll call," until his death in the middle of the 1983–1984 season (following the death of actor Michael Conrad). Esterhaus' roll call served an integrating function at the station as he merged the presumably "informational"

---

[1] This form violated most conventions of network television at the time and led producers to wonder whether or not audiences could follow the program's action. And indeed, as Jenkins (1984) noted, "This mix, according to the gulf between Emmy nominations and 'abysmal ratings' suggests that the format appeals more to critics than it does viewers" (p. 186).

roll call into an important interpersonal ritual for the Hill St. officers. His eloquent and witty delivery of the daily information was ex-emplified in this passage from an early episode about an item from headquarters:

> Item nine is a memo from Chief Daniels (officers groan) regarding profanity in our dealings with the civilian populace . . . People, I recognize downtown's tendency to be unrealistic in these matters, but consider a complaint I took yesterday from an elderly woman who took assistance with a stalled vehicle by one of our uniforms. Now here was one of our own, going the extra mile in the performance of his duty. Yet [he] was so accustomed to certain patterns of speech that, when arriving at the scene, he cheerfully responded, 'So what the bleep's wrong with your car ma'am (officers laugh), said bleep allegedly causing the complaint a severe migraine. Now there are some terms that you might try substituting for the swear words in question as you move through your daily routine [he points to the blackboard filled with such words as fudge, golly, heck, etc.]. Now they won't come trippingly to your tongue at first, but with time and usage you could find them becoming second nature. Your recourse to obscenity will then be fresh and vital when you encounter those situations and individuals for whom only obscenity will suffice. Now the officer in question could have used the word 'heck,' or the equally suitable 'drat,' 'shoot,' or 'fudge' (more howls from the officers) instead of the more common expletives usually associated with your street patois. (Hill Street Blues, "Trial by Fury," 9/30/82)

Phil, indeed, was not your everyday cop, and his organizational performances added concern for work relations and a bit of good-natured humor to Hill Street station life.

The remaining detectives and officers were as diverse as they were many. Johnny (J.D.) LaRue was a rather sleezy detective with a drinking problem; Andy Renko was a white redneck who expressed ongoing disdain with the inner city to his black and generally sensitive partner, Bobby Hill; Mick Belker was a dedicated but somewhat overzealous detective who was known to have bitten suspects who resisted arrest; Lucy Bates was a strong female patrol cop whose hard work and persistence were rewarded by a promotion to sergeant. As Deming (1985) concluded about the members of the Hill:

> The fourteen main characters are essentially good people — albeit consistently flawed and morally vulnerable — seeking to be better in the face of vital challenges. In contrast to heroes of romantic crime dramas, whose moral and physical superiority are beyond question,

the main characters of *Hill Street Blues* are more ironic. They face ambiguous moral problems; and they sometimes weaken in the face of adversity. The struggle for order and sanity occurs therefore, within and among them as well as between them and the chaotic world of the streets. Yet despite apparently overwhelming odds, they never lose their essential goodness. They are trying, and that makes them heroic (pp. 14–15).

Hill Street Police Station was a study in paradox. Hope and despair coexisted in officers, in the organization, and in the society the organization defended, deflected, and, yes, reflected. Hill Street was characterized by a constant struggle between powerful, opposing values. The lines between deviance and conformity, rationality and emotion, and justice and the law were blurred in this organization. And understandably so. They were blurred as well in the larger culture in which members of the organization worked and with which they struggled. As the incident that follows revealed so powerfully, there were no real heroes and no real winners at Hill Street. Steven Bochco (cocreator of the program, along with Michael Kozoll, and executive producer for six of the series' seven years) described the program *Hill Street Blues* as "dark" in both lighting and content. His comments about the program also typified the culture of this organization quite cogently: "It was a show quite literally about life and death, about a beleaguered group of men and women laboring to keep despair at arm's length . . . about people with much responsibility and no real authority" (Shaw, 1986, p. 35).

The selection of a single emblematic incident for case analysis was particularly difficult for *Hill Street Blues*. As admitted fans of the show ourselves, so many episodes were worthy candidates for closer consideration. We ultimately selected the award-winning episode "Trial by Fury" (9/30/82) as one powerful critical incident in the organizational life of the Hill St. station.

"Trial By Fury"

Of all the crimes committed by the civilian "dirtbags" of the Hill, one of the most heinous was the brutal rape and murder of a Catholic nun in connection with the burglary of a church and convent which occurred in the 1982–83 season opener. Lt. Goldblume, at the scene of the crime, reported the ugly details to Furillo: "Rosa Lombardi, her name in Christ is Sister Anna Carmella. Thirty-eight, raped, beaten with fists and blunt instrument, mutilated. They engraved crosses in her torso and thighs with a knife. Multiple internal injuries, shock and severe hemorrhaging, multiple skull fractures."

Furillo, himself a devout Catholic, was incensed by the heinous nature of the crime and immediately directed most of the manpower of the Hill toward solving this case. In a chillingly neutral tone, he issued a series of directives to Lts. Goldblume and Calletano, warning that "this crime is going to make them [the citizens] ugly and we'll need all the help we can get keeping the hysteria at a manageable level."

Not surprisingly, the Hill St. station became a madhouse, with reporters and outraged citizens demanding information about leads. But there were none. The only eye witness — another nun at the convent — could not identify any mug shots at the station. Nonetheless, Furillo personally promised that "we'll find these men and I swear to you they'll be punished."

The suspects were found, thanks to a call from a pawn shop owner to whom the suspects tried to sell the stolen artifacts. Their interrogation at the station was intense. LaRue interviewed suspect Celestine Grey while Washington interviewed the other, Gerald Chapman, in another room. Furillo watched as J.D., blowing cigarette smoke in Grey's face, conducted the more revealing of the two interviews. When the suspect, apparently loaded and jumpy from drugs, let slip a telling detail that only the perpetrators would have known, Furillo interpreted this slip as a convincing display of guilt, and as he described it later to D.A. Irwin Bernstein, "the hairs on the back of my head stood up."

Even though Furillo and the other cops at the Hill were convinced that they had the guilty parties, the eyewitness could not identify them in the lineup, no prints were found in the church, nothing was found in their apartment, and the lab report provided no meaningful information other than the blood type of the assailants. When the hospital call came informing them that Sister Anna had died, Belker expressed to Frank the concern of the men on the Hill that they "might lose these guys," a concern they shared often, though perhaps not with the same intensity as in this situation.

Meanwhile, the crowd inside the station had turned even more violent as one civilian jumped on a desk and fired several rounds into the station. Forced outside, they were an angry mob. And Howard Hunter, who had just been pelted with rotten fruit in his attempt to control the outside mob, waxed philosophic in a brief bathroom conversation with Furillo: "It's blasphemy, but dog-gonnit, Frank, when I think of that poor nun, when I think of these miscreants, when I contemplate their endless sojourn through the futility of that judicial process. Frank, I think to myself, let us provide that mob with the lumber and the tools and a picture of the scaffold, and then we'll throw open the prison gates and let those two subhuman savages be consumed by the monster they have created." He looked up at Frank and concluded, "One man's opinion, without tears."

Frank never paid much attention to Howard's philosophical grumblings, but this time he listened and used Howard's suggestion, as was revealed in the subsequent scene between Frank and D.A. Irwin Bernstein. Irwin promised Frank that they could have an indictment by 6:00, but Frank refused, saying "I know you can get an indictment now, but what about down the road? We have no weapon, no forensics, no one to place them at St. Mary's, and all they have for priors are low rent B-and-Es." When Irwin protested to Frank that there was a whole city screaming for action, the pragmatic administrator, Furillo, rationally yet metaphorically summarized the situation: "Irwin, I have a lot of wrapping with nothing in the package. You know as well as I do what we don't have today isn't going to get any better tomorrow." Frank conveyed his certainty that the suspects were guilty but reminded Irwin: "I need a confession, now. If we indict for murder without it, they go right into protective, their lawyers around them like armor plating, and six months from now we don't have a confession or a case. But consider the alternative." Frank then advanced the spirit of Howard's suggestion as the alternative: "We charge them with what we have, stolen property. We set the bail accordingly and they'll have an interesting choice, won't they?" A flabbergasted Irwin reminded Furillo that there was a lynch mob out there, that Frank's plan would be "signing a death warrant." But Frank insisted that he could use that lynch mob to effect a confession and, ultimately justice. Irwin went along with Furillo and telephoned the judge.

Bernstein told the judge in the subsequent courtroom scene that "in view of the relative lack of seriousness of the crimes charged [possession of stolen property], the people are not asking for bail and we ask that they be released on their own recognizance." The outraged public defender, Joyce Davenport, protested vehemently: "Judge, my client was shot at this afternoon. My client's name is in every newspaper connected to a heinous crime. Look at this courtroom infested with vultures. I demand protective incarceration for my client!" However, the judge agreed with the D.A. and explained to Joyce that he was merely following the [letter of the] law: "Ms. Davenport, this is a tribunal with rules and procedures.

If your client was charged with a felony, he could elect to remain in custody under CCP 3606, but since we only have a misdemeanor. . . ." Despite Joyce's objection that "the items taken from the church are very possibly of felony value," the judge maintained his position. A morally outraged Joyce offered this closing monologue which netted her a judicial reprimand: "For the record, *for the record!* The district attorney and the police department have clearly conspired to dismiss the charges in this case in order to force a confession of murder by my client or his codefendant. So what we have here is a neat little exercise in legal vigilanteism. What got you into their bed, your Honor? A little letter of the law in one ear, a little good of the community in another?"

Not surprisingly, suspect Gerald Chapman immediately tried to plea bargain. In exchange for a confession, Furillo offered "no leniency" though Bernstein promised that Chapman would receive the "standard change of identity" and would serve his time in a "maximum security federal penitentiary." Chapman subsequently confessed that it was his partner "who said to do it."

As the day shift ended on the Hill, Davenport marched into Furillo's office. Joyce accused Frank of throwing legal procedure out the window; Frank responded that he had "pushed a little hard at the bindings," doing for the city only what Joyce always did for her clients — using every resource. Joyce rejected Frank's claim, and they exchanged the following closing words:

Joyce: Furillo, I'm a public defender. I play a role in a system of checks and balances. And other people are supposed to play theirs with the same kind of energy. You with your jungle justice threw that all out of whack today. Gerald Chapman would have confessed to killing Abraham Lincoln to avoid that mob tonight.

Frank: I can live with what I did, Joyce. I went by my instincts and they were right. Under these circumstances, I'd do it again.

Joyce: You can trust your instincts, Frank. Maybe even I can trust your instincts. But I don't want to trust everybody's instincts. I want there to be rules and I want them followed, especially by people who wear badges and guns. You perverted the law tonight and you're so damn happy about snagging your confession that you don't even begin to see it yet. Please see it Frank. . . . Frank, I don't think I want to be with you tonight.

Frank: I understand. [pause] Gerald not only gave us a confession, he gave us the location of the murder weapon. There's no mistake here. These are the killers.

Joyce: Is that where you make your stand finally, Frank? With the oldest excuse in the world, the end justifies the means? (She leaves).

As Joyce exited, Lt. Calletano entered and told Furillo "the men are proud of what you did today, Frank." Furillo, however, was not entirely proud. And in a compelling final scene in a church confessional, he asked an anonymous priest to "Bless me Father, for I have sinned."

The rape and murder of Sister Anna was a powerful event in the organizational life of the Hill, one which revealed the mettle of the Hill Street organization and its leader. This particular crime challenged Furillo's deep-rooted religious and moral convictions, and he was unwilling to let these "miscreants" escape through the tangled legal webs of the criminal justice system. On the one hand, then, he did manipulate the law to accomplish his ends, as Joyce pointed out to him in their last scene. On the other hand, Frank conformed to a higher order inasmuch as the suspects were indeed guilty and deserved to go to prison; thus, "justice" had been done. In "bending" the law, however, Frank violated his own sense of ethics. Yet, we remain unsure in the end, whether Frank confessed regret for what he did, or whether he sought forgiveness because he did not regret his actions and would "do it again" under similar circumstances. The values of deviance and conformity, indeed, right and wrong, remained blurred on the Hill.

The enactment of these values was more focused from Joyce's perspective as an idealized public defender. "Jungle justice," as she called it, violated her sense of ethics. Joyce found the threatened release of the suspects in the face a lynch mob a violation of moral values and of the spirit of the law, and she publically insulated the police department, the D.A.'s office, and a judge to make her point. The American Civil Liberty Union must have been proud of her.

In summary, this incident revealed, in the most dramatic of ways, that the Hill was sometimes a very ugly place. This was a most villainous crime, one that struck at the heart of officers and the community alike. Yet, the cops on the Hill had to protect these suspects from the angry, emotional citizenry with whom the officers themselves could most identify. Justice won out, ironically not because of the proper enactment of the system but because of the manipulation of it. Such irony describes the essence of the Hill Street organizational culture, and perhaps of American society as well. Indeed, as Gitlin (1983) concluded: "*Hill Street* speaks to a larger cultural sense, stretching across political positions, that the major government institutions . . . and the cities as a whole simply do not work. Like *M*A*S*H* and *Barney Miller*, it shows the state to be inept; the best that can be said for top authority is that, quaintly, it tries to keep order. People suffer, and the institutions authorized to redress that suffering fail in their stated purpose" (pp.

312–313). Nevertheless, officers on the Hill kept trying, and organizational life in the Hill St. station house went on.

ST. ELIGIUS HOSPITAL (*St. Elsewhere*, NBC)

Outside St. Eligius Hospital, post WWII 1940s. Father McCabe, founding father of St. Eligius Hospital, has just informed Dr. Daniel Auschlander that the city has purchased the hospital from the church and that he is being reassigned to New Mexico. McCabe turns to the statue of St. Eligius: "Hardly anyone has heard of St. Eligius, the patron saint of artisans and craftsmen. My father was a cabinet-maker. He always like to pray to St. Eligius. I figured he'd show us special attention. But judging from the way the roof is built, I'd say he was out to lunch a good deal of the time." He closes by turning to Daniel and saying: "Take care of my hospital, Daniel. It's been good to me."

("Time Heals," 2/19/86, 2/26/86)

"St. Elsewhere" was the nickname of St. Eligius Hospital, the Catholic-founded, later city-run, and finally corporate-owned Boston hospital featured in NBC's one-hour serial medical drama. *St. Elsewhere* (created by Joshua Brand and John Falsey; Bruce Paltrow, executive producer) was another MTM "ensemble series" which featured a large cast of major and minor regular characters including (for its first five seasons) two highly visible administrators, chief of medicine, Dr. Donald Westphall (Ed Flanders) and chief of hospital services, Dr. Daniel Auschlander (Norman Lloyd), as well as the ascerbic chief of surgery, Dr. Mark Craig (William Daniels), resident doctors Jack Morrison (David Morse), Victor Erlich (Ed Begley, Jr.), Wayne Fiskus (Howie Mandell), and Phillip Chandler (Denzel Washington), head nurse Helen Rosenthal (Christina Pickles), and orderly Luther Hawkins (Eric Laneuville).

Several aesthetic features of the program *St. Elsewhere* made St. Eligius, the hospital, an interesting organization for analysis. First, the large ensemble of characters represented a diverse group of organizational members and, thus, presented a more complete portrait of hospital staffs than has been seen on most hospital dramas. Second, like *Hill Street Blues*, *St. Elsewhere* combined episodic and serial formats such that some stories were presented in their entirety during a single episode whereas other plots overlapped across multiple (normally three or four) programs. This combined format forced viewers to pay closer attention to the temporality of the organization and its members.

Action occurred in a variety of formal and informal organizational settings — in patient rooms and surgical areas as we expect of hospital dramas, but also in elevators, stairwells, morgues, bathrooms, and resident locker rooms (see Barker, 1985, for a discussion of production techniques). As Schatz (1987) observed: "The camerawork and editing provided a means of weaving the various plot threads together into an integrated, apparently seamless narrative. These techniques also situated the viewer as a sort of participant-observer, drawing the audience "into" the drama without binding them to any single character or plot line, as most dramatic series tend to do." (p. 89). Thus, the production techniques of the program helped create a chaotic workplace with "much of the same gritty reality and cinema-verite technique" as *Hill Street Blues* (Brooks & Marsh, 1985, p. 733) and contributed to the overall complexity of St. Eligius, the organization.[2]

The Hospital and Its Characters

St. Eligius hospital was founded by the Catholic Church in 1935, as we learned in the "Time Heals" prequel episode — though viewers did not have access to the hospital until it aired on NBC beginning in October, 1982. As Brooks and Marsh (1985) described it, "St. Eligius was one of the seedier hospitals on TV, a big-city dumping ground for patients not wanted by the higher-class (and more expensive) medical facilities in Boston" (p. 733). Certainly this was one probable reason why quality service did not produce staggering profits for this organization while it was run by the city.

The doctors of St. Eligius. Not surprisingly, most of the action in St. Eligius, as in most prime time hospitals, focused on patient care by doctors (see Turow & Coe, 1985). At St. Eligius, these doctors included veteran physicians like Westphall, Auschlander, and Craig who also held administrative positions in the hospital, as well as young residents such as Morrison, Erlich, and Fiscus. For the most part, these doctors were not unlike most prime time doctors — they were highly competent and caring professionals who usually, but not always, saved their patients' lives. Although most of the major regular doctors were white males, St. Eligius, unlike many other

---

[2] As an aside, shows like *St. Elsewhere* (as well as others like *Hill Street Blues*, *Lou Grant*, etc.) survive despite periods lower ratings than competing shows because of their "quality demographics" — that is, upscale young urban consumers who are an especially desirable target market because of their buying power (see Feuer et al., 1984).

prime time hospitals, also had several minority physicians including a black male resident, two white female residents, one Asian female resident, one black female staff physician, and one Asian female staff physician as minor but regular professional staff members over the years.[3]

St. Eligius' doctor administrators were also competent and caring. As noted in Chapter 4, Dr. Donald Westphall was a very compassionate manager who was passionately committed to quality patient care and quality employee relationships. Dr. Daniel Auschlander, too, generally was portrayed as a heroic professional. In one episode, for example, Daniel recorded himself as the physician in charge of a very risky transfusion procedure performed as a last-ditch effort to save a child's life even though resident Jack Morrison was operationally in charge of the case. Auschlander did this because he feared that if the transfusion procedure failed, the ensuing lawsuit could ruin the younger doctor's budding career whereas his career was already established. On another episode, Auschlander displayed his moral courage and integrity when he accepted responsibility for the asbestosis that a lifelong hospital maintenance worker developed. He advised the worker that he was entitled to compensation, promised to testify on his behalf if the worker sued the hospital, and even gave the worker the name of the best lawyer in town whom Auschlander had already convinced to take the case. In short, St. Eligius doctors were capable and compassionate physicians and managers.

Unlike the prime time doctors of past hospital dramas, however, the doctors at St. Eligius did not really have the so-called cushy "top jobs" of prime time (see Gerbner, Morgan, & Signorielli, 1982b). St. Eligius' young residents, in particular, led very harried organizational lives and often paid a high price for their concern for patients. In one episode, Fiscus was shot by the wife of an emergency room patient as he attempted frantically to attend to the patient. In another episode, Jack Morrison, a particularly tragic figure, lost his son to a kidnapper as Jack completed his rounds with a broken leg (though his son was found on the next episode). Despite the frenetic and less than glamorous nature of their work, however, these residents also almost always served patients in a compassionate and caring manner.

The lives of these doctors outside the hospital, though presented

---

[3] It should be noted, too, that these minority doctors were not portrayed as weak or submissive physicians, but rather were cast as fairly assertive characters with strong convictions.

infrequently, were not glamorous either. Apart from the arrogant Dr. Craig who seemed moderately affluent, most doctors, even top administrator Westphall, led pretty modest lives. Indeed, Westphall, a widower who never remarried, spent most of his time at home struggling to raise his two kids, including his autistic son. Westphall's minimal leisure time consisted primarily of drinking a beer while reading a medical journal on his couch, television on in the background. Resident Jack Morrison's private life was nothing short of a tragedy — his wife was killed early in the series in an accidental fall; later in the series he was beaten and raped by a prisoner when he volunteered to help the doctors at a local prison, and then, one year later, he and his new girlfriend were held prisoner and were about to be raped by the same prisoner until Jack's very young son shot and killed the prisoner with the gun Jack had purchased to protect his family from that very prisoner. Not quite the Dr. Kildare of old.

The other organizational members at St. Eligius. Nurses and other staff members (i.e., orderlies) had relatively minor, though not unimportant, roles in the hospital. Although the personal life of Helen Rosenthal was something of a mess (she had been married four or five times), she was a strong lower level manager who kept things running at St. Eligius, serving as a competent and caring head nurse as well as an assertive negotiator for the nurses union, as will be seen shortly.

Although we saw many background characters at St. Eligius who served as orderlies, Luther Hawkins was one foreground character in this position. Luther was an "ordinary" nonprofessional staff member who showed a not-so-ordinary interest in the patients who came to St. Eligius. In one episode, for example, Luther noticed that one of the young patients on the burn unit (a fireman named Michael) was not responding well to treatments. Luther displayed his concern for this patient not only through the performance of his operational actions — lifting the patient ever-so-gently when he took Michael for his special skin treatments — but also through the special efforts Luther took to check periodically on Michael's progress as he walked by the burn unit. In fact, it was during the course of one of these visits that Luther made the connection between Michael's lack of progress and a visitor of Michael's who Luther discovered was bringing Michael drugs which were inhibiting the effects of his prescribed medication and therapy. Luther's concern for the patient — above and beyond the job description of an orderly — were instrumental in enabling other organizational members to provide additional treatment to help the patient. Indeed,

such special efforts led Drs. Westphall and Auschlander to rec-
ommend that Luther study to become a paramedic (a position he
attained) and then a physician's assistant — a position for which he
was taking classes while working as a paramedic at St. Eligius late
in the series' history.

The doctors, nurses, and orderlies at St. Eligius were generally
a competent, professional lot. While we did not see a particularly
glorified treatment of health care, these folks did their jobs well.
Indeed, it was through their performances in trying times that the
true character of St. Eligius hospital was revealed.

Throughout its entire existence, St. Eligius was an organization
in transition. Like many urban service organizations, right and wrong
were not always easily distinguishable and change was something
the organization had good reason to fear as well as welcome. From
its early days as a religious hospital with a deep commitment to
community, to people above all, and with an irrepressible idealism,
St. Eligius evolved into an ever more fragmented, ever more formal
collectivity of eccentric independent professionals. Such changes
were felt by many experienced and veteran members of this culture
to be a very sad and frustrating loss. For others, these changes were
unavoidable. And for some, like the nurses who felt singularly
unappreciated, change was welcomed. In the incident described in
the next section, we saw the difficulty — indeed the impossibility—
of an organization remaining unchanged over time, the need for
growth and change, and the human cost of change for this organization and for some of its members.

The Nurses Strike

While many organizational crises could have been selected to display
the culture of this organization, we have selected the nurses' union
strike that occurred over several episodes during the 1984–1985
season, a strike which seriously disrupted the everyday organizational life of St. Eligius. The key players in the strike were Helen
Rosenthal, head nurse and chief negotiator for the nurses' union,
Dr. Daniel Auschlander, chief of hospital services and chief negotiator for hospital management, and Richard Carrington, a federal
mediator who was called in by the hospital board of trustees after
Helen and Daniel failed to resolve their impasse.

The possibility of a strike was put forth by Rosenthal in one of
the early negotiating sessions when Daniel rejected the union's
counter proposal to management's final offer and threw in some

insults at Helen along the way, which she wisely ignored. The next negotiating session proved fruitless. As Helen began to issue the ultimatum that "until nurses are recognized as professionals," Daniel interrupted with "a professional doesn't abandon those who need help." As a result of Daniel's intransigent refusal to consider contractual changes, the nurses union went on strike at 6:00 a.m. the next rainy morning and began to picket the hospital's front doors.

Tensions between Auschlander and Rosenthal remained high during the strike. At one point, Daniel brought his longtime friend and colleague Helen some hot chocolate as she picketed in the rain. But what started out as a friendly interaction deteriorated quickly:

Daniel: How could this thing get so out of hand? We used to be able to settle our differences so easily.

Helen: You know, Daniel, when I first came to work at St. Eligius, it *was* like a family and you didn't mind working hard and doing all kinds of extra things because everybody else was doing the same thing, sharing. But now, it's — for instance, you know doctors sometimes stroll out of here at 5:01 and it kind of makes you feel like maybe you're being taken advantage of.

D: That's the crime I'm being charged with?

H: The nurses just feel that they should get the rules down in black and white so there's no misunderstanding.

D: St. Eligius is more vital to this community than ever. And it's because we're still a family that we can pull together and overcome our differences.

H: Daniel, If you really think that's true, why do you think I'm out here in the rain?

D: I'm not going to allow you to turn this into a sterile hospital with nameless patients and faceless employees. I've worked too hard to allow that to happen. (Daniel stormed off and Helen resumed picketing).

As the strike continued, rumors about the status of the bargaining talks filled the small talk of other hospital members in stairwells and other settings. More importantly, however, the strike jeopardized the successful performance of health care in the hospital. In one instance, resident physician Victor Erlich was forced to perform an emergency surgical operation that he had never done before. Since there were no nurses available, resident physician Elliot Axelrod prepared to assist; however, Elliot realized the futility of this when he could not even find the surgical equipment. In a panic, Elliot rushed out to the striking nurses for assistance. Even though the nurses were officially on strike, Lucy, a surgical nurse, responded to Elliot's call for assistance by dropping her placard, crossing the picket line, and scrubbing up. Later, when one of the very few nonstriking nurses caustically queried Lucy about her "scabbing," Lucy retorted: "I'm on strike, but if somebody's dying I'm not on strike. It's that simple." In short, Lucy cared too much about patient care to neglect emergency situations.

The strike and the bargaining sessions continued to be unproductive until Carrington arrived one morning with the news that the mayor and comptroller's office had given them 48 hours to settle the strike before they shut the hospital down. Carrington noted that given the $260,000 a day the city was losing during the strike, "If you let that happen, there may not be much of a hospital left to reopen. . . . Does anyone *not* understand the subtext of my statement?" Not surprisingly, from that moment on, the negotiations took a turn for the better as Daniel and Helen suddenly agreed on matters of salary, health benefits, longevity bonuses, and flextime call-in. But Auschlander resisted discussing one item, the establishment of a formal grievance procedure.

Auschlander left the bargaining table for a recess and went to his office where Donald Westphall found him and once again helped his friend and fellow manager with gentle, leading advice. Westphall realized that Daniel had taken the grievance procedure demand personally. Indeed, as Daniel put it, "Why on earth do the nurses need a grievance system? My door has always been open." Westphall gently reassured Daniel that he could be proud that the system he had established decades ago had lasted this long, and then explained that the time had come to improve that system: "Daniel, as physicians, we've always believed that in order to improve the quality of medicine our work had to be critically examined and eventually replaced by better theories. I think that applies to running a hospital as well."

By using a medical analogy for this management problem, Westphall appealed to Daniel's positive valuation of medical changes. This defused Daniel's defensiveness and allowed him to confront his fear that he had become the same sort of managerial tyrant for whom his parents had worked in the sweat shops and that the informal family system he had developed had become unfair and exploitative of nurses. As Daniel admitted to Donald: "My parents met while they were both working in the garment district. My mother was in a sweat shop and my father pushed a clothing rack down Seventh Avenue. We were worse than poor. Unions changed the quality of our lives. And I marveled at the men who risked everything in order to form them. . . . And I vowed that should I ever get into a position of power, I wouldn't misuse it. (He looks up at Westphall) Have I become in age, something that I despised in youth?" Westphall's assurance helped Daniel put his concerns into perspective and to understand his opposition to these changes.

The strike ended officially in the next bargaining scene as Daniel agreed to the formal grievance procedure demanded by the Helen while Helen agreed to amnesty for all nurses hired during the strike. As they began to leave the room, Helen made the first move to repair her damaged relationship with Daniel as she offered her hand to him and said: "I think we reached a fair agreement. I hope in the long run this doesn't come between the two of us." Auschlander initially refused the handshake, retorting "I don't know if I'm that good a person," but ultimately extended his hand and promised, "But I'll give it a try." And so ended the nurses strike of 1984.

The nurses strike was a dramatic event in the history of St. Eligius hospital. Its most obvious and most powerful impact was on Daniel Auschlander, who was forced to realize that the rather informal policies he had designed in the early development of the hospital "family" were no longer adequate for the modern political era of St. Eligius. It was a very hard lesson for the stubborn administrator to learn, and it took the helpful advice and understanding words of his friend and colleague Donald Westphall for Auschlander to understand that these changes in the rules and policies of the organization did not necessarily change the caring values of the organizational culture itself.

It was also a very powerful event for Helen Rosenthal, who had represented the nurses union in a very assertive, courageous, and sensitive manner. She won almost all of the demands of her union, but we also saw the pain this hard work and success had caused her personally when she tried to repair damage that her relationship with her longtime friend and colleague, Daniel Auschlander, had suffered.

Finally, we saw the disruptive power that a social drama such as a strike can have on an organization (see V. Turner, 1977). It generated rumors in stairwells and jeopardized the main function of the hospital itself — providing quality health care to patients; though it did result in more equitable working conditions for one group of professional employees. Ultimately the strike was resolved only when the threat of shutting the hospital itself down was presented as a real possibility. Even two hard-headed and very stubborn negotiators were not willing to pay this price. The organization emerged from the negotiations a little battered, but reconciliation was the ultimate outcome; and this work community, though changed, remained intact.

In summary, St. Eligius Hospital was a place where organizational members practiced a generally professional and competent form of medicine which usually (but not always) resulted in success; where members at all organizational levels exhibited care and compassion; where organizational members engaged in hard work and sacrifice, especially in a time of crisis; and where organizational members developed and cherished a sense of community and personal history. On the negative side, it was a place where the political realities of high costs, outdated policies, and understaffed facilities resulted in occasional episodes of less than quality care and employee dissatisfaction; where the professional (over)intensity of members had important personal costs including violence, marital problems, and personality disorders. In short, St. Eligius provided a richly textured view of organizational life and an organization in transition.

EWING OIL (*Dallas*, CBS)

Ewing Oil was the family-owned corporation which served as the organizational centerpiece for *Dallas* (CBS). A Lorimar production (created by David Jacobs; with Philip Capice, for eight seasons, and more recently, Leonard Katzman as executive producer) *Dallas* first aired on CBS on April 12, 1978. *Dallas* was a prime time "soap opera" with a long and ever-changing list of regulars including the Ewing clan of John Ross (J.R.) Ewing, Jr. (Larry Hagman), Bobby Ewing (Patrick Duffy), Eleanor (Miss Ellie) Southworth Ewing Farlow (Barbara Bel Geddes and, for a short time, Donna Reed), John Ross (Jock) Ewing, Sr. (Jim Davis), Sue Ellen Ewing (Linda Gray), Pamela Barnes Ewing (Victoria Principal), Ray Krebs (Steve Kanaly), Clayton Farlow (Howard Keel), and a variety of other relatives as well as a group of Ewing outsiders who were in regular conflict with them including, among others, Willard "Digger" Barnes (David Wayne and Keenan Wynn), Cliff Barnes (Ken Kercheval), and Jeremy Wendell (William Smithers). *Dallas* was one of the most successful of prime time soaps in the history of television. Indeed, the popularity of *Dallas* extended worldwide: "In over ninety countries, ranging from Turkey to Australia, from Hong Kong to Great Britain, *Dallas* has become a national craze, with the proverbial empty streets and a dramatic drop in water consumption when an episode of the serial is going out" (Ang, 1985, p. 1).

From an aesthetic and production perspective, *Dallas* used conventional production techniques to provide "an expertly made sample of mainstream Hollywood television" (Ang, 1985, p. 9). However, from a dramatic perspective, *Dallas* was innovative. First, *Dallas* was a soap with "characters that were larger than life, conflicts based on the struggle for money and power, and lots and lots of sex" (Brooks & Marsh 1985, p. 195). Indeed, *Dallas* was a uniquely "melodramatic soap opera" with its endless serial structure, large cast of characters, limited development of themes apart from personal relationships, and grotesque personal conflicts and catastrophes (Ang, 1985, pp. 56–60). However, *Dallas* was not merely another daytime soap which aired at night. Newcomb (1982b) has pointed out that *Dallas* resembled the "westerns" of old: "What *Dallas* has done — and it counts in large measure for the show's success — is to transfer these old western meanings to a new and different world, to the Dallas express highways and sunny skyscrapers. . . . The shootouts have merely been transfered to the boardrooms" (pp. 170–171). This fusion of generic elements made Dallas a somewhat unusual dramatic context for an unusually political prime time family organization.

The Company and Its Characters

As we heard often during the series and watched in the prequel movie *Dallas: The Early Years*, Ewing Oil was founded by Jock Ewing who struck it rich in the 1930s as an oil wildcatter with his then-partner Digger Barnes. Digger was an alcoholic, a gambler, a generally irresponsible and pathetic character with a "nose" for oil. Jock, on the other hand, was a clean-cut, hard-working young man with an unusual sense of honor — indeed, Jock once gave a prostitute the $10,000 Digger had won in a poker game that they were to use to build their first oil rig because she told Jock that a drunken Digger had promised she could have it all; later, Jock endangered his own life to protect a black sharecropper and his family (upon whose subleased land they were drilling for oil) from Klu Klux Klan members. In the end, of course, Jock and Digger went their separate ways — the honorable Jock with Digger's true love Ellie Southworth—and thus began a feud which continued into the next generation.

Honorable would not be a term many would use to describe J.R. Ewing, the eldest son of Jock and Ellie and the modern day leader of Ewing Oil. Although he temporarily lost control of the company several times, most recently in fall 1987, J.R. has always managed eventually to regain control. Thus, while J.R. valued the economic success of the family business tradition, he did not share the business ethics and honorable values of his father. Indeed, as we noted in

Chapter 5, J.R. was the quintessential negative political manager. As Ang (1985) described, "J.R. runs the family concern, Ewing Oil, in a villainous manner, treats his wife like dirt, and only shows respect for his parents when it suits him" (p. 6).

J.R.'s brother Bobby, on the other hand, did share the more honorable business values of his father. Bobby was a fairly compassionate manager and husband, even in times of trouble. As an executive and a shareholder of Ewing Oil, he attempted to make decisions that both benefitted the corporation and that did not hurt other individuals. In this sense, Bobby served as a constant organizational challenge to J.R. throughout the corporate history of Ewing Oil. Although Bobby apparently died in the 1986 season, resulting in J.R.'s complete control of Ewing Oil, he returned in 1987 (as we were told that the entire 1986 season was merely Pam Ewing's (and our own?) bad dream) — so much for organizational "reality" on prime time soaps).

A large cast of family members, most notably Miss Ellie Southworth Ewing Farlow, Sue Ellen Ewing, Ray Krebs, and Pamela Barnes Ewing owned stock in Ewing Oil but had little impact on the organizational life of the corporation. Several organizational outsiders, most notably J.R.'s main nemesis Cliff Barnes, tried to destroy Ewing Oil but have never really succeeded in doing so. Cliff Barnes initially appeared as a morally righteous assistant district attorney who sought to legally dethrone J.R. and dismantle Ewing Oil, but power corrupted Cliff, too, and he became as sleezy as J.R. — though not as effective—when he inherited the position of president of Barnes-Wentworth Oil.

Although Ewing Oil served as the corporate context for many characters, we did not see much of Ewing Oil's members, except for those stockholders and executive managers who were members of the Ewing family. This was a family business and we were limited (with very few exceptions) to displays of how this organization affected members of the Ewing family and its close business and personal associates. This, of course, was in keeping with the soap opera genre, as Ang (1985) observed: "In *Dallas*, the business imbroglios to do with Ewing Oil are always shown with an eye to their consequences for the mutual relations of the family members . . . in the world of the soap opera all sorts of events and situations from the public sphere occur only insofar as they lead to problems and complications in the private sphere" (p. 60). In short, Ewing Oil and the Ewing family, then, were indistinguishable and both were constantly torn by a raging battle between competing values —

the ruthless economic vision of success epitomized by J.R. and the human, family-oriented vision of success epitomized by Bobby.

The More Things Change, The More They Stay The Same

In a sense, we could have selected almost any of J.R.'s transactions to illustrate the organizational life of the Ewing Oil family corporation. We selected one "deal" which dramatized the inseparability of J.R. and the Ewing Oil organization and the impact of J.R.'s values on the Ewing family and Ewing business associates. As part of a complex deal, J.R. had hired a suspected terrorist to blow up foreign oil fields. The Ewing family learned the full extent of the deal not from J.R., but from a newspaper article read to them at breakfast one morning by their attorney. As Harvey, the Ewing's attorney summarized, the headline story in the Dallas papers (based on a story published in a little paper in Navarro County) reported that "secret documents made available to this paper show conclusively that Ewing Oil company was involved with terrorist B.D. Calhoun in a terrorist-for-hire scheme to blow up foreign oil fields." Harvey, not surprisingly, returned to his office to draw up libel lawsuit papers while Bobby and J.R. flew to talk to the editor of the Navarro County newspaper.

When Bobby and J.R. confronted Mr. Harrigan, the editor of the small paper, Harrigan defended his story saying that "every word we printed was true." He added, though, that the CIA had refused to confirm the secret documents he had been given and "since I'm not some powerful Eastern newspaper to go around spending lots of time and money finding out what really happened, I guess the story will die right here." However, Harrington used the opportunity to castigate these Ewing Oil executives for being concerned solely with profits and not at all with the people in that county: "I lived all my life in Navarro County. People treated Ewing Oil fair and square. Course one hand washed the other, I'm not denying that. But the minute there was trouble, you shut down the oil wells. You turned this place into a ghost town practically overnight." And when Bobby responded that "we didn't have any choice," Harrigan concluded: "No, we didn't have any choice."

What made J.R.'s deal so problematic this time was that it was not just a private organizational matter between J.R. and the Ewing family. This time J.R.'s deviance made the front pages of the newspaper as well as the evening news. His lack of concern about the impact of his actions caused public embarrassment to Miss Ellie

and her husband Clayton Farlow. At dinner that evening in a
restaurant, some sotto voice insults by other oil executives led
Clayton to demand that they express their complaints directly to
Clayton and Miss Ellie or leave. One of the oilmen did, saying: "All
right, if you really want to know. We think it's pretty damned
arrogant of ya'll to show your face in here after the way the Ewings
have disgraced the good name of Texas oilmen."

Miss Ellie was visibly hurt by this insult and admitted to Clayton
that "this time J.R.'s gone too far — and Bobby too." Indeed, we
saw just how upset Miss Ellie was when she made a rare trip to
the Ewing Oil corporate offices the next day and confronted J.R.
and Bobby:

> "I always thought that no matter what happened, I'd always stand by
> my family. It was always that way with the Ewings. It was always
> the family against all outsiders. We always stuck up for each other,
> even when we knew we were wrong. But no more. It's gone too far.
> And I won't defend either of you any longer. I can't. . . . I've thought
> about this a lot. And believe me this is one of the hardest things I've
> ever had to say. But as far as I'm concerned, you two don't deserve
> to own Ewing Oil."

When J.R. interjected a reminder that this was "daddy's company
you're talking about," Miss Ellie replied:

> "Don't you ever, ever speak his name in front of me again! You
> dishonored his name and his company. And I guess that's what hurts
> me the most because your daddy would have been so ashamed of
> you. I know he would because I sure as hell am. . . . I have nothing
> more to say. You're both on your own now. And as far as Ewing Oil
> goes, it should have died with your daddy. It would have saved us
> all a lot of trouble."

This reprimand from "momma" was most surprising because
Bobby did not usually bear the brunt of her attacks — they were
usually reserved for J.R. However, this time the entire family and
the organization were inseparably linked in the public perceptions
with J.R.'s unpatriotic and illegal activity. For Miss Ellie, that was
too much. Bobby came to the realization that his "momma" was
right, that he had dishonored the good name of the family and the
organization. As he and his wife Pam watched J.R.'s public antics
on the evening news, Bobby expressed disgust with J.R.'s deviance
and ruthlessness and promised to distance himself from his pervasively corrupt brother and family organization: "What have we

turned into? All this deception and lies and then more lies to cover everything up. It just doesn't stop. I've had it, Pam. I've had it up to my ears with J.R. and the whole way he does things. I'm getting out. . . . J.R. has disgraced the name of Ewing Oil, every last one of them." (And if you believe that . . .).

J.R., too, realized he had gone too far this time. However, he did not admit nor feel that his illegal activities had been wrong, but rather, merely unsuccessful strategies which he would not use again. The inseparability of family and business (of J.R. and Ewing Oil) was affirmed in the final scene of this episode. There J.R., head of Ewing Oil, sat on the back porch of Southfork ranch with his son John Ross III on his knee and rationalized the situation to his son: "I tried to do something and it just didn't work out. And your grandma's not the only person who's mad at me. You might be hearing some bad things about your daddy at school too. I just want you to know the truth before that happens. . . . You see, what I did, deep down in my heart I did because I thought it'd be good for Ewing Oil and the independent Texas oilman. But it just didn't work out the way I planned and a lot of people think I'm wrong." As John Ross III looked up at his daddy and told him, "You're the best daddy in the world," so the value of and link between the family and the corporation was affirmed for the next generation.

NEW YORK CITY MUNICIPAL COURT (*Night Court*, NBC)

Night Court was an NBC situation comedy that centered around life in an after-dark New York City municipal courtroom. The show (Reinhold Weege, creator and executive producer) first aired on January 4, 1984, and was still being broadcast at the time of this printing. Not surprisingly, most of the action in the courtroom involved the rather bizarre caseload of the court which included such characters as the man in a Santa suit who tried to convince the court that he was indeed the real Santa Claus, the disorderly ventriloquists who totally disrupted courtroom proceedings, and the residents of a clothing-optional apartment building. More notable courtroom guest characters included Mel Torme, who played the Judge's favorite singer, and Grant Tinker, the NBC executive who appeared as himself in defense of a case involving a Nielson family accused of cheating.

The Courtroom and Its Characters

Most of the comedies of this courtroom centered around Judge Harry Stone, played by comedian-magician Harry Anderson. The judge was an amateur magician who relaxed in his chambers by playing card tricks and by playing practical jokes on the rest of the courtroom staff. He often appeared wearing blue jeans and a tee-shirt under his robes, not exactly the somber judicial image seen on most courtroom dramas. In fact, Judge Harry evoked, as Martinez wrote in *TV Guide*, "the image of a little boy all dressed up in his daddy's black judicial robe" (February 9-15, 1985, p. 11).

Judge Harry was the social leader who helped maintain familial relationships among courtroom workers by organizing birthday and Halloween parties for the staff and, more importantly, by counseling these workers in times of despair. He served as the foster parent of the young black boy who shined shoes in the court building when the boy was unable to be placed in a stable foster home environment. Most notably, Harry was *always* willing to bend the laws and rules of the court in order to assist the workers or clients of the court. Indeed, his rather deviant and eccentric enactments of the law prompted a judicial review board to evaluate his fitness as a judge in one episode. In short, Harry placed people over procedures and showed us that often rules can be best used when they are abused.

Dan Fielding, the night court's prosecuting attorney (played brilliantly by Emmy-winning actor John Larroquette) was an expensively dressed, political, self-centered "slime," as one of the bailiffs aptly labeled him. Over the years we saw Dan's selfishness when he moonlighted as an escort for wealthy widows, when he proposed to one homely heiress soley for her $40 million, and when he demanded (but did not receive) sexual favors from Christine Sullivan, the attractive defense lawyer, for saving her life.

During the court's prime time history, there were three different female defense attorneys including, Liz Williams (Paula Kelly), Billie Young (Ellen Foley), and, most recently Christine Sullivan (Markie Post). These female lawyers were all portrayed as competent and idealistic young public defenders who sometimes stubbornly held to their ideals. Indeed, both Billie Young and Christine Sullivan spent time in jail for their convictions, the former for not revealing the whereabouts of a cat her client was accused of stealing, the latter for not apologizing after she publicly challenged as unfair the ruling of an insensitive visiting judge.

Other organizational members of the court included Bull Shannon

(Richard Noll), the hulk-like uniformed bailiff who once quit his job temporarily to become a pro wrestler, and Mac MacGregor (Charlie Robinson), the friendly court clerk. During its prime time history *Night Court* also has had three uniformed female bailiffs, including Selma Hacker (Selma Diamond), Florence Kleiner (Florence Halop) and more recently, Roz (Marsha Warfield), all of whom were portrayed as crusty and caustic matrons of the court.

The core of *Night Court's* unique organizational culture was its rule-breaking characters who constantly performed acts of organizational and civil disobedience. Members of this organization — even insulting D.A. Dan—cared about other people, about the larger society, and about broad social values like justice, fairness, and equality. The organization epitomized our cultural tradition of informed dissent and the obligation of responsible citizens to deviate from laws (including rules and policies) felt to be immoral or unjust. However, precisely because this was a public administration organization, the opposing value of conformity to the law was also affirmed. The humorous tension arising from these law-enforcing public administrators and their incessant deviance from laws and policies in the larger interests of justice was what characterized this organization. The incident below, from 1986, illustrates this characteristic and the culture.

Flo's (near) Retirement

The situation unfolded as Judge Harry, Dan, Christine, Mac, and Bull gathered in Harry's chambers for Flo's surprise birthday party. But when Flo arrived, she did not celebrate; instead, she stalked in, swept up her gifts, said "It's been fun," and walked away. Flo's reaction astonished the group until they discovered that Flo had just turned 65, the mandatory retirement age for bailiffs in the New York City public administration sector.

Flo did not want to retire and the rest of the night court regulars did not want to see her forced into retirement. Thus, the mandatory retirement age rule was interpreted by the group as a cultural injustice. As Flo poignantly protested to Harry: "All I've done is had another birthday and I feel like I committed a crime. . . . They're punishing me because I survived." But rules were rules and so when an insensitive bureaucrat from the city came to the office to give Flo her last paycheck, it appeared that Flo would indeed be forced to leave the job despite her ableness and willingness to keep working.

However, rules in Harry's court, especially unjust ones, were made to be broken. In this case, Bull took matters into his hands by driving to Albany (the state capital) to steal Flo's birth certificate, the only legal proof of her age. However, when Bull returned and presented his plan to the group in Harry's chambers, Flo herself explained that while she appreciated the familial concern, "nobody is going to break any rules around here for me." She convinced Bull to return the birth certificate to the relieved bureaucrat. However, just as the bureaucrat attempted to put the birth certificate in his pocket, the document mysteriously burned up. Although everyone suspected that Judge Harry had caused the certificate to incinerate — since he was known around the court for his magic tricks — no one really knew how the document burst into flames. When Flo realized that the only legal proof of her age was gone, she announced she then would do what any self-respecting woman would do — "lie like a cheap rug" and remain at work as a court bailiff.

This incident and much of *Night Court* displayed the organizational philosophy that institutional rules — such as mandatory retirement — were sometimes opposed. In such cases, Harry and his court broke unjust and unfair rules to conform to those higher cultural norms (see Chapter 5). Thus, Flo's concerned colleagues — or "family" as Flo referred to them—were willing to break the rules to enable her to keep her position and remain in the work family. Although they themselves believed in the general principle that rules should not be broken, they regularly broke unjust rules. In the case of Flo's retirement, Bull stole the birth certificate, Christine Sullivan (affectionately known as "Miss Goodie-Two-Shoes) actually incinerated the document (by means that were never made clear), and Flo lied about her age. But in this and other instances of rule breaking, Harry's night court maintained a higher set of cultural values and norms.

CHEERS BAR (*Cheers*, NBC)

Cheers, a fictional Boston bar established in 1895, opened for business on prime time television on September 30, 1982, on the NBC comedy *Cheers* (produced by Les Charles, Glen Charles, and James Burrows). Cheers was a small, intimate neighborhood pub — one main room with an open freestanding bar in the room's center, the manager's office, and another (rarely seen) game room in the back. Cheers had a small staff, a small coterie of regular clients, and many drop-in clients who quickly learned that Cheers was indeed one place where everybody not only knew your name, but also knew about your personal life, especially your romantic exploits.

The Bar and Its Characters

For the first five seasons Cheers appeared on prime time television, its regular staff members consisted of two waitresses, one bartender, and the owner/manager who also acted as bartender. Equally important, however, were a group of regular clients — all male. Organizational members and regular clients were on a first name basis — with the exception of Cheers newest employee, Woody Boyd, who only referred to waitress Diane Chambers as "Miss Chambers." But then Woody had a bit of a crush on schoolmarmish Diane; indeed, as "Diane" herself noted in her diary, "If Cheers were the land of Oz, then Woody would be scarecrow to my Dorothy" (Chambers, 1987).

Cheers first regular bartender was Sam Malone's old baseball coach and former manager Ernie Pantusso, whom everyone just called "Coach" (played by Nicholas Colasanto). An absent-minded kindly older gentleman, Coach was fond of telling stories (although he usually only remembered part of them). Coach died (when actor Nicholas Colasanto died), and he was replaced (in September 1985) by the youthful and kind but equally flaky Woody. Woody just wandered into the bar one day and never returned to his home of Posey County, Indiana. For all his naive, good-hearted country bumpkin ways, Woody had a country shrewdness as well. He demonstrated this, for example, when he declined to invest in Norm's combination tanning salon and laundromat, saying "When I left home my father gave me some very sound advice: Never trust a man who can't look you in the eye. Never talk when you can listen. And never spend venture capital on a limited partnership without a detailed, analytical, fiduciary prospectus." And although we doubted whether Woody knew what a "detailed, analytical, fiduciary prospectus" was, he was smart enough to know that Norm didn't have one.

Waitress Diane Chambers, a well-bred perpetual graduate student and erstwhile writer, also wandered into the bar one day and stayed for five years. She finally left Cheers and Sam, her boss and fiánce, at the end of the 1986 television season when she received a book contract. Diane's presence was a source of constant chagrin for Cheer's other waitress, Carla Tortelli. This brash, mouthy, and rough-edged (often) single working-class mother of a tribe of kids found Diane's condescension irritating, but her main objection to Diane was Diane's on-again-off-again romance with bar owner/ manager Sam Malone. Carla was not exactly jealous, but she feared a lifetime of unhappiness was in store for her macho jock friend and boss if he married the cultured and snobbish Diane. Carla's verbal antagonism toward Diane was unrelenting; however, Carla's churlishness was as much a part of the bar's charm as were Diane's pompous lectures and the ever-present sports programming emanating from the television screen mounted on the wall.

Sam Malone, the on-site owner/manager of Cheers bar (until fall 1987), spent most of his time behind the bar serving drinks and getting back with (or at) Diane. A former major league baseball relief pitcher and a recovered alcoholic, Sam was an easy-going-lothario who most of the time was just "one of the guys." Sam rarely "managed" the bar inasmuch as he did not do much except exchange small talk with customers and damage or repair relations with women. Indeed, Sam mixed freely his occupational and personal life and his roller coaster involvement with waitress Diane Chambers dominated the activities at the bar for five years, providing conversational grist for Cheers staff and regular customers who took considerable delight in offering Sam advice and suggestions.

Three regular customers of Cheers were an integral part of the life of this organization and functioned almost as adjunct organizational members. One of these was Norm Peterson, "the wiseacre barroom regular with a body that makes Nautilus instructors tremble, who hasn't had a steady job since the Red Sox won the pennant, whose marriage to the ever-absent Vera started off in a honeymoon suite he calls The Dead Zone" (Turnan, *TV Guide*, July 6, 1985). Another Cheers regular was U.S. postal service employee Cliff Claven whose tendency to opine about everything (especially topics about which he knew little or nothing) and whose reliance on the *National Enquirer* for news and information didn't prevent the staff and other regulars from generally liking him. However, Cliff was usually the last one to catch on; thus, being "the Claven" became a Cheers inside joke. During the 1984 season, Dr. Frazier Crane (formerly Diane's psychiatrist and lover and later Sam's counselor) became a third regular customer of the Cheers bar. Frazier provided occasional advice and regular pontifications from his bar stool, blissfully unaware that the Cheers staff and regular clients found him a pompous bore.

Cheers was, as Deming and Jenkins (1983) characterized it, a "man's world." It was an essentially sportive, antifeminist neighborhood drinking establishment. Woody and Sam armwrestled friendly newcomers for a brew, and the television set on the wall was always tuned to sporting events, on which Cheers employees (except Diane) and regular customers placed bets. And (except for Diane) most of the staff and customers regularly got out their "scorecards" and tallied up Sam's latest romantic exploits. In short, Cheers was a genial, nonintellectual haven of male comaraderie whose most pervasive topic of conversation was the romantic life of Sam and Diane. Not surprisingly, organizational romance was, in some ways, the essence of this organizational culture. The incident described below, while not particularly dramatic, reflects the playful culture of this organization, its primary focus on Sam's (organizational) romances, and the advisory role the staff and regular customers played in Sam (and Diane's) romantic dueling.

Advice But No Consent

On September 26, 1986, regular customer Norm Peterson jauntily stepped down the Cheers stairs and hollered "Afternoon, everybody!" as he headed toward his bar stool. With one voice this pub version of a Greek Chorus shouted back, "Norm!" Bartender Woody looked up and also greeted Norm, "Afternoon, Mr. Peterson. What's the story?" to which Norm responded "Boy meets beer. Boy drinks beer. Boy gets another beer." And by the time Norm arrived at his stool, a cool draught was waiting for him. So far, it was life as usual at Cheers bar.

Norm sat down and chatted with Cheers other regulars Cliff and Frazier and watched as Sam emerged from his office and stepped behind the bar, holding a telephone book. The afternoon's main business began — finding an "out of the ordinary and classy" place where Sam could take a "special lady" for dinner that evening. As usual, everyone joined in and their helpful suggestions both reinforced the sociable atmosphere of this organization and revealed something about the character of the individuals who made up the organization. Carla, for instance, suggested a nude barbeque, an idea that was rejected because sparks could be dangerous. Cliff, Norm, and Frazier interrupted the search for a brief 21-peanut salute (spitting peanuts like rifle bullets in unison into the air) when they heard that Sam's "special lady" was not city councilor Eldridge whom Sam had been dating. Indeed, when Carla heard that Councilor Eldridge was "in the dumper" and that Sam had yet again avoided the pitfall of matrimony, she advised Cheers staff and regulars to "Get out the scorecards, boys. Sammy's back in action."

It was Cliff, however, who finally came up with the winning idea: "Well, all right, Sam. I got something I think is just the ticket for you. How about this: Sailboat anchored off the shore. Chilled champagne. Candlelit dinner under the stars, heh? Worked great for Sean and Madonna." Sam agreed and retreated to his office to arrange for this romantic evening. Everyone relaxed — until Woody came back from a confidential chat which he immediately spilled to everyone in the bar (as Sam knew he would). The romantic setting, it seemed, was needed because Sam was going to propose. This news sent the bar staff and customers into a tailspin, especially after they concluded that Sam must be proposing to Diane.

The next day when Sam walked into the bar, Carla and Woody stopped working and all conversation ceased until Sam disclosed that he had proposed and had been rejected. Sam took Frazier's advice to take the boat out by himself to reflect on Diane's rejection. Meanwhile, Diane, on the other hand, had changed her mind and wanted to find Sam. She ultimately found the boat, but Sam had already loaned it to a priest and had returned to the bar. And so continued the (non)romance of Sam and Diane.

In sum, while interpersonal actions were fairly common across all organizations on prime time, they dominated organizational life in the Cheers bar. As a retail eating and drinking establishment, customers came as much for the friendly intimate atmosphere of the organization as for the food and drink. And the very (inter)personal relations of the bar manager Sam and the subordinate waitress Diane constituted the key area of interpersonal life (and the key topic of interpersonal conversation) at the bar. In this way, Sam spent more time managing his romance than managing his investment. Perhaps not surprisingly, in the fall of 1987 after Diane's departure, Sam sold the bar and when the boat he bought to sail around the world sunk, so did his ability to recover his ownership in the bar. Even less surprisingly, however, when he returned to Cheers as a bartender, a new sparring romantic interest sprang up between Sam and the new female bar manager of Cheers. The romance-driven culture of Cheers continued only slightly changed.

THE ST. GREGORY HOTEL (*Hotel*, ABC)

The elegant San Francisco luxury hotel, the St. Gregory, was the organizational setting for the ABC episodic television drama, *Hotel*

(Aaron Spelling, executive producer). Most of the episodes which have aired since the program's debut September 21, 1983, have concluded happily, although not all the issues, problems, and experiences portrayed in the three or four dramatic, comedic, and romantic vignettes we saw each week were happily resolved.

Like many older luxury hotels in the heart of large metropolitan cities, the St. Gregory had a spacious lobby in which people gathered and through which people passed on their way to check in or out of the hotel, to attend conferences and meetings, and to go to the hotel's restaurant, bar and lower arcade level. The St. Gregory's imposing facade conveyed a sense of spacious and dignified elegance, an impression that was reiterated in the hotel lobby, where sonorous tradition merged with computer age technology at the gleaming walnut information and reservation desks.[4]

The Hotel and Its Characters

In the premiere episode, Bette Davis appeared as hotel owner, Laura Trent; however, as a result of Ms. Davis' illness, her character Laura Trent departed on an extended trip and left the hotel under the supervision of her sister-in-law Victoria Cabot (Anne Baxter). Subsequently, Mrs. Cabot inherited the ownership of the St. Gregory; then she later died, leaving one-half of the hotel to suave, dedicated manager Peter McDermott because, as her will noted, he cared about

---

[4] The lobby set of the St. Gregory Hotel was a recreation of the lobby of the real San Francisco luxury hotel, the Fairmont, and as noted in *Hotel & Motel Management* (Breen, 1983), the television program set is so realistic that it "causes those familiar with the real thing to mutter to themselves in amazement and suffer eerie attacks of deja vu" (p. 2). According to the Fairmont Hotel's general manager, Herman Wiener, not only do the sets of *Hotel* abound in real-life detail (enhanced by such things as real crystal chandeliers), but so do at least *some* of the dramas. Wiener observed that typical "drama" at the Fairmont runs along the lines of a recent *Hotel* plotline involving a wealthy woman who lost a diamond from an earring while showering. Based on her speculation that the gem had gone down the drain, plumbers tore up the ceiling of the bathroom below only to be disappointed in their search. A crafty plumber then headed back upstairs and finally found the stone — right inside the woman's shower cap" (p. 4). Weiner also noted that the Fairmont's guests, like those of the fictional St. Gregory, have ranged from "kings and queens and presidents to rock stars and sports heroes" (p. 4). However, Weiner observed that there were two aspects in which the fictional St. Gregory did not resemble the Fairmont. First, while some of Hotel's plotlines have reflected his hotel experience, many more have been far more exciting than his everyday working experiences. Additionally, Weiner noted admiringly the very competent but unrealistically small staff with which the large, fictional St. Gregory is apparently run with superb quality and efficient service.

the organization as much as she did. Mrs. Cabot's family was not particularly delighted with her bequest, but their efforts to remove Peter from both his position as executive manager and half-owner failed.

Beside the owners, other administrators at the St. Gregory included assistant manager and then manager Christine Francis (Connie Selleca); director of guest relations, Mark Danning (Shea Farrell, who left after the fourth season); and director of hotel security, Billy Griffin (Nathan Cook). Billy was an ex-con and Christine was an inexperienced small-town native, yet McDermott had hired them because they were eager to work in that organization, had displayed creativity and initiative in gaining his attention, and had expressed the desire to prove that they were eminently capable despite a lack of formal job training and past hotel experience. Needless to say, they more than rewarded management's willingness to take a chance on them with loyalty, dedication, and quality work.

Nonmanagerial members of the St. Gregory hotel included Julie Gillette (Shari Belafonte-Harper) at the Information Center and married workers Megan Kendall (Heidi Bohay) and Dave Kendall (Michael Spound), receptionist and bellhop, respectively. All three employees were dedicated providers of quality service. Dave spent the first four seasons going to law school as well as working as a bellhop. This joint venture was encouraged and supported both in words and actions by the hotel management — sometimes with schedule rearrangements, sometimes with other kinds of support, as when Mrs. Cabot made a "charitable" request that they act as residential caretakers of her hotel penthouse suite while she traveled, a request designed to provide these newlyweds with some time together close to their jobs.

Occasionally, the program featured "guest" organizational members who joined the organization (and the program) for one to six episodes. Such was the case with the St. Gregory's director of hotel operations, Drew Hayward (one episode) and concierge Elizabeth Bradshaw (five episodes during fall, 1986). Most episodes, however, foregrounded the activities of manager Peter McDermott and assistant manager Christine Francis — and often, as their organizational romance blossomed and wilted, their personal and organizational actions were inseparable. The organization's guests and their experiences in the hotel also have been prominently featured in the series' plotlines. Frequently hotel guests have either arrived at the hotel with personal problems or encountered difficulties during their stay in the city. Almost as frequently, they were rescued, renewed, or reconciled through advice and/or concrete help from the members of this prime time caring company.

Caring — about customers and about larger social values—was the essence of this organization. From the owner and executive manager to the bellhops and reservationists, members of this organization consistently exhibited their concern for organizational members and customers in little ways (pleasantries and small talk) as well as in the solution of serious and weighty problems. For members of the St. Gregory organization, the hotel was far more than a place they worked — it was a work family enacted in its ideal form. This organizational value of caring for others, especially customers, was revealed eloquently in the premiere episode of the series, which we now examine.

The Prostitute and the Rich Punk

One of the central plots from the 1983 premiere episode began when several members of a fraternity, which was having its annual gala ball in the St. Gregory ballroom, pooled their resources for a special twenty-first birthday present for one of their exceptionally shy and inexperienced members — an hour with a gorgeous prostitute (Morgan Fairchild) in a room they had rented in the hotel. This charming and gentle young man spent some entrancing moments with Carol Terry, the prostitute, after which he returned to the ball. As Carol readied herself to leave the room, however, she was stopped by an arrogant, wealthy young cad, Eric Seaver. Seaver and several of his not-so-gentle friends had overheard their fraternity "brothers" discussing the gift. They forced their way into the room as Carol was leaving and gang-raped her, leaving her bruised and bleeding. She was discovered by manager Peter McDermott and head of hotel security, Billy Griffin, who were investigating a complaint from a nearby room occupant about noise.

McDermott and Billy called an ambulance, sought out the group of fraternity members who had rented the room, and discovered that Eric Seaver was the ringleader of the rape. McDermott ordered Seaver to leave the hotel. Just before Seaver was physically ejected from the hotel by McDermott, the young punk challenged McDermott's administrative and moral authority: "What're you gonna' do now, man? You gonna' teach me a lesson? Look, you can't be as dumb as you look. What do they pay you here? 40/50 thousand a year? Well, my father drops that much in this hotel's bank account every month on his out-of-town clients, and I don't think he'd appreciate the hired help pushing his son around, do you?"

McDermott accepted the challenge as he visited Carol Terry in the hospital, explained that the hotel would pay for her medical bills, and encouraged her to file an assault charge against Eric Seaver. Initally, Carol thought the idea was absurd and asserted, "I'm not anyone's cause." But when McDermott persisted over the next several days, and she questioned his motives, McDermott explained: "You were raped in my hotel. They took something from both of us and with or without you, I'm going to get it back. . . . Nobody can do that to another human being and get away with it." McDermott was morally outraged; he felt Seaver's actions had sullied the hotel's honorable reputation as a place where civility, safety, and compassion reigned and he was determined to punish the young punk responsible.

McDermott's police administrator friend, Lou, discouraged filing charges because, as he candidly told Peter, "I am warning you, you are going to get your butt nailed to the wall." Not surprisingly, Mrs. Trent told Peter the same thing when she learned from Eric Seaver's father that Carol had finally filed charges at McDermott's urging. "Our name, who we are, doesn't that mean anything to you?" she asked Peter. Despite Peter's reply: "It means everything to me. That's why I did it," Mrs. Trent remained upset about Peter's failure to consult her about something that might involve the hotel in lawsuits (a liability suit from Carol and a libel suit from Eric Seaver's father, whose company was one of the hotel's largest corporate accounts). Thus, when Peter offered to resign if she thought it would help, Mrs. Trent stated directly, "I might take you up on that."

In a subsequent scene, however, we learned that although Mrs. Trent would not have handled the situation as impulsively or as emotionally as Peter had, she did approve of his doing what was right. In this scene, again in the formal organizational context of Mrs. Trent's office suite, Eric Seaver's father visited Mrs. Trent in an effort to settle out of court. But Mr. Seaver received an unexpected welcome when Mrs. Trent told him that his "lawyers would be better served in keeping your son from getting what he so *richly* deserves." Even though she agreed that McDermott had "acted impulsively and without authority," Mrs. Trent pointed out that "he *cares*." Then she challenged Mr. Seaver and asserted the hotel's organizational philosophy in the following interaction:

Mrs. Trent:	. . . What do you care about, Mr. Seaver? Making more money than you can spend? Throwing your money around to get your son off the hook? Or do you care enough to be a *real* father? To teach your son about *honor*? Do you care about *that*?
Mr. Seaver:	I care.
Mrs. Trent:	Well. I'll give you a chance to prove it. (She picked up the phone) Lee, would you send Miss Terry in? (To Peter) I sent a car for her the minute Mr. Seaver phoned. Come in, Carol.
Carol Terry:	Mrs. Trent.
Mrs. Trent:	Carol, this is Eric Seaver's father. (Carol nods.)
Mr. Seaver:	What do you want, Miss Terry?
Carol Terry:	That's what I usually ask my customers. What do you want, Mr. Seaver? You want me to drop the charges, don't you? I was afraid to once. Now I can't. I can't, Mr. Seaver.
Mr. Seaver:	What my son did was wrong, but he is my son. He will face the charges against him, and I will be at his side. I am sorry for all of us. (He left)
Mrs. Trent:	Carol, you came to my hotel. I don't approve of your purpose, but you did come here and you should have been safe. And so, for what it's worth, I offer you my apologies, too. (To Peter) You have to get legal counsel. We may be liable for a law suit.

After Carol left (having first assured Mrs. Trent that she was not going to sue the hotel), Mrs. Trent and Peter discussed the situation. Peter explained why he supported Carol: "You always said that the St. Gregory is a place where everyone who comes here is special. It took some doing to live up to that, but I think we came out of it okay, thanks to you."

In sum, the St. Gregory organization, from owner Mrs. Trent on down, was committed to quality, caring, and compassionate service. And as Mrs. Trent's lecture of Bradford Seaver indicated, the organization (symbolized by the words and actions of its top executives) was deeply committed to doing what was morally right. While Mrs. Trent gave every indication that she would have handled the Terry/Seaver incident differently, she also clearly approved of the values which motivated her manager's actions, especially the value of caring. As this organization illustrated, a company which values people over profits can be, by all appearances, a highly esteemed and highly profitable organization. Indeed, Peter McDermott's St. Gregory *Hotel* may just be the best example of a prime time "excellent company" (Peters & Waterman, 1982).

MCKENZIE, BRACKMAN, CHANEY, AND KUZAK (*L.A. Law*, NBC)

The corporate law firm of McKenzie, Brackman, Chaney, and Kuzak was the setting for the prime time drama *L.A. Law* (created by Steven Bochco and Terry Louise Fisher), which premiered on October 3, 1986. Like *Hill Street Blues* and *St. Elsewhere*, *L.A. Law* was a semi-serial hour-length drama. However, whereas *St. Elsewhere*, and especially *Hill Street Blues* were " 'dark' both in actual lighting and content," Bochco has described the visual ambience and content of *L.A. Law* as "brighter, more colorful;" also in contrast to *Hill Street Blues*, according to Bochco, *L.A. Law* was "about well-educated overachievers who do win, who do have impact" (Shaw, 1986, p. 35).

Such an upbeat show about well-educated, winning overachievers who had an impact would appear to be the perfect show for the 1980s. The essence of this organization's culture was a constant struggle among organizational members (and within individual members) between two opposing sets of values: on the one hand, the "clarion call of 'Enrich thyself' " (evinced in what David Riesman has called a "transaction mentality") and, on the other hand, the social concern for truth, justice, and equality (what Riesman has termed the "endowment mentality") (Shapiro, 1987, p. 15). According to Bochco, a show about the law was the perfect setting for literate, articulate exploration of these important issues within an entertainment medium. "The law," Bochco noted, "has everything — good, bad, right and wrong. . . . The law is human behavior in the crucible of stress — emotional, financial, moral, sometimes even physical stress" (Shaw, p. 35).[5]

The Law Firm and Its Characters

The organization featured in *L.A. Law*, as befitting a program set in 1980s Los Angeles, was a corporate law firm. Two of the four named original partners in the firm of McKenzie, Brackman, Chaney

---

[5] Helping Bochco explore these issues in the context of an organization of corporate lawyers whose business includes tax, insurance, divorce, and criminal law was Bochco's own staff of lawyers: two of the staff writers on the program (Marshall Goldberg and David Kelley) were lawyers as were the associate producer (Bob Breech), the technical advisor (Chuck Rosenberg) and the series cocreator, Terry Louise Fisher. Thus, *L.A. Law* has not presented an uniformed portrait of corporate legal organizations and their members; however, as Bochco has firmly asserted, the program was designed preeminently as entertainment (Shaw, 1986).

and Kuzak — Chaney and Brackman, Sr. — were dead. The most senior member of the firm and one of the founding partners, Leland McKenzie (Richard Dysart) had devoted his career to working in this firm. Leland's role in the firm was that of grand patriarch — a figurehead who symbolized the mixture of idealism and pragmatism that characterized this organization. For instance, Leland was bitterly disgusted when the UCLA law students attending his invited lecture at the law school queried him almost exclusively about starting salaries and monetary matters rather than about cases and points of law. And he grew so exasperated with Douglas Brackman's exclusive concern with paying clients and disdain for pro bono work that Leland ranted at one of the weekly meetings, "I'm sick and tired of this obsession with fees. If Mr. Sifuentes or any other attorney in this firm sees fit to offer his or her services and time for the public good — that's good enough for me!" On the other hand, those rare instances when Leland went out of his way to commend members of the firm for their work typically involved cases in which the firm made a considerable profit and some larger social good was accomplished simultaneously. For example, Ann Kelsey's success, on behalf of a bag lady, in getting the executors of a will leaving money for "the homeless of Los Angeles" to release several million dollars to set up a shelter and a trust fund to administrate it (which McKenzie-Brackman would profitably help to oversee) led Leland to verbally commend Ann and to waive her partnership fee.

Douglas Brackman (Alan Rachins) followed in his father's footsteps in several ways. Not only had Douglas taken his father's place as a senior partner, but like his father he was selfish, critical, negative, and avaricious — at least until a near-mutiny by the younger lawyers and public excoriation by Leland. After that humbling experience, Douglas made a noticeable (and much appreciated) albeit short-lived effort to change his "style."

Michael Kuzak (Harry Hamlin), the youngest full partner in the firm, was bright, witty, and very much a "sixties" person. Whereas Brackman was a balding, early fortyish rule-bound materialist, Kuzak was a playful thirtyish, long-haired idealist. Kuzak was living proof that it was possible to practice trial law with integrity and honor and still make lots of money.

Arnie Becker (Corbin Bensen) was the firm's specialist in divorce law, a specialty he was well suited for since the company of attractive women and the acquisition of money and property were the most important goals and activities in Arnie's personal and professional life. In 1987 both Ann Kelsey (Jill Eikenberry) and Stuart Markowitz

(Michael Tucker) were offered and accepted junior partnerships in the firm. Ann's humanist instincts were often at war with her desire to be a high-powered successful litigator. Stuart, already independently wealthy, was a sweet, gentle, and extraordinarily shrewd tax lawyer who, nonetheless, usually advocated intangible values over dollars and cents. (He, of course, could afford to do so.)

For a time, the firm's affirmative action hire was a young black lawyer fresh out of law school. However, he left bitter and angry — partly because of the insensitivity of the older partners, McKenzie and Brackman, and partly because of his own assumption that lucrative cases would continue to be "handed" to him. Taking his place was the talented Victor Sifuentes (Jimmy Smits) whose mentor and friend in the firm was Michael Kuzak. Indeed, it was largely as a result of Kuzak's assurances and example vis-a-vis integrity, loyalty, and commitment to defending the spirit not just the letter of the law, that Victor joined the firm. Finally, there was Abby Perkins, the firm's legal neophyte, whose excessive emotionality was exacerbated by an alcoholic husband who beat her and who, after she divorced him, kidnapped her son. However, under the gentle encouragement of Kelsey and Sifuentes, Abby regained her confidence and displayed her competence.

In addition, a large support staff included Roxanne (Susan Ruttan), Arnie Becker's loyal Della-Street type secretary whose competence was matched only by her unrequited love of her lothario boss, and Iris, Leland's lifelong secretary/lover who began law school part-time after concluding that there was nothing but a pat on the head in store for her (also unrequited) secretarial devotion.

The organizational culture of this law firm was characterized by value conflicts between firm interests, rational and emotional expressions, autonomy and authority, and economic success and human success. On several occasions, the struggle threatened to tear the organization apart, or at least change it beyond recognition. We have chosen one such situation from the 1986–87 season to illustrate the organizational culture of this unique law firm.

Thirty Pieces of Silver (i.e., "Close to One-Half Million Bucks")

The situation began with a breakfast meeting at which an attorney, representing the New York-based firm of Marshall-Taft, approached Leland, the most senior partner of McKenzie, Brackman, Chaney, and Kuzak [hereafter McKenzie-Brackman], with the informal offer of a merger. Leland refused categorically. But irked and challenged by the intimation that he was afraid to present the proposal to the firm's other partners, Leland raised the issue at the close of the next weekly staff meeting. To Leland's great surprise and disappointment, his announcement yielded the following interchange:

Leland:　Ah, I had breakfast this morning with Raymond Lloyd. He's a senior partner in the firm of Marshall-Taft, which Mr. Lloyd now informs me has over 400 lawyers with offices in New York, Miami, Chicago, San Francisco. They're seeking to establish a beachhead here in L.A. and wondered if we'd be interested in becoming that beachhead. I turned them down.

Arnie:　Why?

Leland:　Well, it was conditional on merging with them.

Ann:　I think they'd have their pick of every law firm in L.A. I mean its a real coup that they want us.

Douglas:　Did Mr. Lloyd per chance mention any figures?

Leland:　Purely speculatively, he threw out something in the neighborhood of $300-400,000 per partner.

Ann:　And you didn't think that was worth putting before the partnership?

Leland:　Well, I felt certain I spoke for us all.

Arnie:　No offense, Leland, but if somebody wants to hand me close to a half million bucks, I don't want anyone speaking for me, *but* me.

Douglas:　I'd have to agree with Arnold.

Leland:　I took it as an article of faith that the firm of McKenzie-Brackman would never cotton to being franchised! I see I was wrong!

Kuzak:　Well, I think that what we are objecting to, is having our opinions preempted, Leland.

Leland:　In that case, Douglas, why don't you and Stuart contact Mr. Lloyd. Get the full proposal, and present it to the partnership at its earliest convenience. (He rose and pointedly left the room.)

Leland's military metaphor — "establish a beachhead" and the machine/factory metaphor "being franchised" — was revealing of the dictatorial (if benevolent) administrative style that Leland occasionally adopted in the firm and that was occasionally challenged by other partners. Although Leland was a founding father, the firm was a community in which all partners shared in decision making about issues that affected the organization as a whole. Indeed, the firm's weekly meeting with its reports on the various cases on which the firm's lawyers were working was just one way of reiterating the interdependency of this collectivity of autonomous professionals. As Kuzak expressed it, Leland's de facto dismissal of a proposal affecting the entire firm smacked of excessive individualism on Leland's part and a denial of the communal decision making that was at the heart of the organization's philosophy.

However, the responses of other members of the firm, both during and after the meeting, indicated that some of them objected to Leland's action, not because of their annoyance at his preemptive paternalism, but because of their own selfish and greedy individualism. Arnie Becker, for instance, rushed out of the meeting and instructed his secretary to call his realtor right away. Victor Sifuentes didn't hear Arnie's instructions to his secretary, Rox, but he accurately interpreted the motive behind both Arnie and Brackman's objection to Leland's categorical action as "the distinctive sound of money talking."

At the next firm meeting, the partners discussed and voted on whether or not to pursue the merger proposal that Brackman and Stuart had begun investigating. Arnie Becker argued for accepting the proposal, explaining his purely selfish reason — he wanted to buy a house (a particular, very expensive house overlooking the ocean) and he could do that only with the $300-400,000 per partner Marshall-Taft was offering. Similarly, Douglas Brackman argued that the organization was "first and foremost a business" and that the first obligation of a business was purely and simply to be as profitable as possible. Accordingly, Brackman voted to pursue the merger on the basis of the purely economic notion that "it's bad business to say no to an offer as potentially lucrative as this one."

Michael Kuzak, on the other hand, argued that to accept the merger offer was to place selfish, material greed over other values — autonomy, integrity, and professional and moral honor. According to Kuzak:

Marshall-Taft is a factory. . . . None of us is exactly starving, here. We already work ten, twelve hours a day. Now, my concern, my *bottom line*, if you will, is quality of life. What happens when we want to tell some client to go to hell? We have to fly all the way back to New York to explain it to some management committee? Half the times you want to tell someone to go to hell, you can't explain it; it's a feeling. So how are we going to talk feelings to New York? I don't know. We're going to wind up representing a lot of folks that we have no business dealing with and that scares me.

Stuart Markowitz also favored rejecting the offer on human and economic grounds. As he explained: "Even speaking strictly from a financial point of view, I think we're being short-sighted. Arnie, their average partner income is less than ours is right now. You understand what that means? It means we'll be making more money for them than they will for us."

These alternative perspectives on the merger pointed out the opposing values that these organizational members constantly struggled to balance. At this meeting the struggle resulted in a 3-3 vote. In the face of this, Leland astonished everyone by changing his vote against the merger to a vote "Yes" to merge. In a speech of considered emotionality (demonstrative of his skill as a trial attorney), Leland explained his concern not only about this particular merger decision, but also about the organization and the appropriate role of organizational leaders. He invoked the family metaphor and compared the role of an organizational leader to that of a parent who must learn "when it's time to let go" and when to heed the wishes of the younger generation. Leland concluded his speech by saying, "Deadlock only exposes our divisiveness. It leaves us vulnerable to raiding. Whereas accepting this offer, by doing that, at least we'll be together." Leland first, and then the other partners, silently filed out.

Once outside the conference room, however, Stuart stormed into Ann's office and confronted her, for Ann's vote had been the third promerger vote. Stuart accused Ann of voting for the merger merely because she wanted to end their office romance. To do so, he asserted was to make a selfish decision on irrational emotional grounds rather than on reasoned, well thought-out solid sentiment and values. Stuart passionately argued that there was a major difference in the corporate philosophies of these two firms. To merge them would make it extremely difficult for Ann to act in accordance with her individual values and would destroy what McKenzie-Brackman represented. As Stuart reasoned: "Marshall-Taft is a factory. It, it's cold, it's impersonal. They go by the numbers, Ann. . . . You think Marshall-Taft is going to look kindly on Ann Kelsey's *humanist* instincts? You think they're going to let your meter run while you represent some *principle* that may or may not have a profitable bottom line? Come on, Ann. Marshall-Taft thinks pro bono is Latin for sucker bet."

Ann denied any romantic motive and argued that she had favored the merger because the "power base" of Marshall-Taft would give her access to clients and cases she did not now have. Stuart, however, did not believe her. He pleaded with her to reconsider and added that he was going to make it easy for her because: "Our relationship is over. I'm not going to bother you any more." Here again, an office romance constitued a complicating factor in organizational life, especially when that romance was torn by conflicting values.

Douglas and Stuart pursued substantive negotiations with Marshall-Taft. As part of these negotiations, Marshall-Taft brought two efficiency experts in to review the McKenzie-Brackman organization.

Their recommendations reflected precisely the cold impersonal philosophy that Stuart and Kuzak had predicted and depressed both Stuart and the secretaries: "You cube the support personnel, you cut down on unnecessary gossip. Get a lot more work done. . . . You make the walls around the secretaries' desks smoked plexiglass. They can't hang anything so they stop bringing in momentoes. It gives the firm a clean, hard-edged look . . . (they can't see out) but you can see in to make sure they're working."

At the next meeting, the merger vote was retaken after Ann reconsidered and changed her vote, explaining that: "The decision was made emotionally and in haste. And I don't think I had the firm's best interest or even my own at heart. So I'm formally changing my vote." Kuzak then inquired if anyone else wanted to "recant." Surprisingly, first Brackman and then Becker expressed reservations and then changed their votes, primarily because Marshall-Taft had misrepresented the upfront cash — they were not going to pay the $300,000 in a lump sum but rather in payments spanning seven years. In a final scene, Leland smiled and changed his vote, noting humorously that he was changing his vote only to go along with the sentiments of all the partners.

For some of the members of the organization, the merger was simply a way to greatly increase their economic cash flow on a short term basis. Neither Arnie Becker nor Douglas Brackman engaged in any serious self-reflection and reexamination of priorities as a result of this merger situation. However, for Leland and Ann, the merger proposal led to serious professional and personal soul-searching, and the result was a clearer understanding of personal and organizational values and goals. For a majority of the members of the firm — Leland, Kuzak, Ann, Stuart, Victor—what made this organization different from other corporate law firms was the feeling of being a team, a familial group of professionals who shared a sense of integrity, community, and a desire to balance individual and group interests, economics and emotions, altruism and opportunism. That they usually juxtaposed these competing values in a profitable manner made this organization something worth keeping. A point on which they all agreed (for very different reasons) in the end.

CONCLUDING REMARKS

The critical incidents featured in these case studies have enhanced our understanding both of these unique organizational cultures and of organizational culture in general. As Anderson (1987) pointed out, such incidents, or "episodes" as he terms them, "are, usually, fully constructed narratives which contain not only the sequence of events and actions but also an extended interpretation of the action in context" (p. 345). We hope that the description and explication of these incidents has yielded a richer understanding of the values of these prime time organizations and of organizational life in American culture.

As these case studies have illustrated, prime time organizational cultures are extremely diverse. Thus, the dark, deviant, and dangerous environs of Hill Street precinct where public administration employees struggled to maintain societal law and order and personal integrity stood in stark contrast with the light, friendly atmosphere of the Cheers neighborhood bar where employees passed cold brews to regular customers and attempted to solve the latest romantic complications in bartender/manager Sam Malone's life. In between was Judge Harry Stone's playfully deviant New York City District Court staff who broke rules in order to uphold moral values and laws of conscience. We saw the ideal of altruistic capitalism enacted by the entire staff of the luxury St. Gregory hotel who provided the highest quality material and moral service to everyone entering the organization's doors. This extraordinarily caring culture of the St. Gregory contrasted sharply with the ruthlessly materialistic and socially irresponsible actions of Ewing Oil executive, J.R. Ewing, and the organizational culture he shaped. Finally, as St. Eligius Hospital struggled to maintain its identity as a community committed to compassionate healing after a forced corporate takeover by a for-profit health care system (in the 1987–88 season), the law firm of McKenzie-Brackman decided against an optional company buyout, choosing instead to retain their history, autonomy, and still healthy salaries.

However, as different as these organizational cultures were in terms of industry, occupation, ownership, and organizational structure, they shared some things in common as well. Most notably they shared a common set of values and value conflicts. Many of the organizations struggled to balance economic success with human success. They struggled over when to deviate and when to conform to rules and policies or higher laws of conscience. They struggled with how to balance the needs and rights of individuals with the needs and responsibilities of the organization. They struggled to meld the energy and idealism of youthful members with the more cautious wisdom of experienced organizational members and to balance solid and true emotions with rationality. They had their share of office romances and had their own peculiar mixtures of hard work and play. And through it all, they all developed a unique sense of the organization as *family*.

In the next chapter, we conclude this book by examining the vision of the organization as family as well as other prime time organizational metaphors. We then discuss some of the lessons about organizational life that were collectively affirmed by the seven organizational cultures examined in this chapter as well as the other organizations we have examined in this book. We conclude with a discussion of the implications of our analysis for television and organizational research and practice.

Chapter 7

Concluding Observations

Although the so-called "family sitcom" remains a vital force on television, prime time dramas increasingly have moved out of the home and have gone to work in various organizations. In some cases, these organizations merely serve as background props for actions that could just as easily occur at home; in other cases, these organizations are themselves important "corporate characters" which frame and shape the actions of prime time programs. Whatever the case, prime time television has featured organizational life with increased regularity in representations of occupations and industries, in presentations of managerial performances, and in enactments of organizational values. Along the way, prime time television has provided viewers with potential lessons about organizational life in American society.

As we noted in Chapter 1 and throughout the book, it is important to study prime time portrayals of organizational life inasmuch as television can both reflect and shape the organizational realities of viewing audiences. Everyday viewers and television researchers alike are quick to point out that prime time does not reflect accurately the demography of organizational or social life in America. We agree. Although prime time does present "real" types of organizations — such as hotels and hospitals and police departments — as well as "real" types of organizational members — such as desk clerks and doctors and detectives—prime time overrepresents some occupations, industries, and activities and underrepresents others. Furthermore, most prime time workers experience more organizational "action" in one television episode than their real-life counterparts experience in a year and sometimes during a career. In this sense, prime time television is hyperbolically "unrealistic."

However, we also believe, as do many television researchers, that prime time television does reflect rather accurately the social and organizational *values* of American culture. Indeed, some critics have argued that prime time television reflects too closely the "mainstream" values of American culture and, thus, reinforces dominant ideologies of American organization and society. In short, while the demographics of prime time organizations are reflected through so-called "funhouse" mirrors which are unmistakably distorted, the ideologies of prime time organizations are presented through mirrors which offer clearer reflections of American culture.

As importantly, however, prime time television also shapes social and organizational reality. Although television's "direct effects" on viewers are (and probably will remain) unclear, most researchers agree that television is one of many socializing agents which teaches viewers about life in American society. As Moses Hadas (1962) admonished a quarter of a century ago, "all who take education seriously in its larger sense — and not the professed critics alone — should talk and write about television" (p. 19). We agree. At the very least, television presents entertaining parodies of familiar organizations and provides vicarious experiences of not-so-familiar organizations which some viewers rarely (if ever) witness firsthand (e.g., criminal justice systems and corporate law firms); at the very most, television presents scripts and dramatic rehearsals of how organizational members can and do act in various organizational contexts. In its most positive sense, television provides constructive models of organizational action which may inform and change our own organizational lives; in its most negative sense, television offers distorted images which create unrealistic (sometimes idealistic, sometimes fatalistic) expectations and visions which may lead us to resist organizational change or to fail to see the possibility of change. In any case, prime time television has the potential to teach us many things about organizational life in America.

In this concluding chapter, we first examine some of the broader visions of organizational life which are presented through prime time organizational metaphors. We then discuss some lessons about organizational life that are presented on prime time as well as some lessons which usually do not (but perhaps should) appear on prime time. We conclude the chapter by discussing some of the implications of this book for the research and practice of television and organizational life.

METAPHORS WE (WATCH) WORK BY: VISIONS OF PRIME TIME ORGANIZATIONS

Metaphors are interpretive language forms which cast one concept (e.g., "world") in terms of another (e.g., "stage"), as in the familiar dramaturgical axiom "All the world's a stage" (see Chapter 4). As many have argued, these language forms reveal much about the ways we think about (and act in) our social world. Indeed, Lakoff and Johnson (1980) have suggested that our conceptions of reality itself are constructed through interlocking sets of metaphors. As they concluded:

> It is as though the ability to comprehend experience through metaphor were a sense, like seeing or touching or hearing, with metaphors providing the only ways to perceive and experience much of the world. Metaphor is as much a part of our functioning as our sense of touch, and as precious. (Lakoff & Johnson, 1980, p. 239).

Organizational researchers of late have also argued that our conceptions of organizational reality are shaped by the metaphors we use (see Bednar & Heinline, 1982; Hirsch & Andrews, 1983; Koch & Deetz, 1981; Morgan, 1986; Ortony, 1975; Smith & Simmons, 1983; Weick, 1979). In *Images of Organization*, Gareth Morgan (1986) argued that "our theories and explanations of organizational life are based on metaphors that lead us to see and understand organizations in distinctive yet partial ways" (p. 12). Metaphors, thus, provide access to aspects of organizational life that are not easily explained and they do so in a compact language form which offers an elegant and vivid vision of the organization. As Morgan (1986) concluded, "By using different metaphors to understand the complexities and paradoxical character of organizational life, we are able to manage and design organizations in ways that we may not have thought possible before" (p. 13).

In a similar way, television critics have also suggested that television uses metaphors explicitly and implicitly in the enactment of prime time drama (see deLaurentis, 1979; Fiske, 1984; Goethals, 1981; Newcomb, 1979b; Real, 1977; Wood, 1976). Inasmuch as metaphors are compact language forms which reveal complexities of social life, they are well-suited tools for packaging television content within the constraints of prime time programming. As Goethals (1981) suggested, such metaphors are powerful images which serve as "icons" through which the belief and value systems of American culture are articulated and shaped.

In sum, both organizational and television researchers have argued that metaphors reflect and shape our understanding of our organizational and social worlds. It comes as no surprise, then, that television presents organizational metaphors which viewers may use to understand organizations (on and off television). We now examine these metaphors of prime time organizational life.

Prime Time Organization as "Families"

> Mrs. Cabot, co-owner of the St. Gregory Hotel, sat in her suite, ready to spend the Thanksgiving holiday by herself. But just as she was about to begin her Thanksgiving dinner, manager Peter McDermott and most of the St. Gregory staff burst into the room.
>
> Mrs. Cabot: Isn't Thanksgiving a time to be with friends?
>
> Peter McDermott: Didn't you know, Victoria, that Thanksgiving is a time to be with family?

By far the dominant vision of organizational life on prime time is revealed in the metaphor of the organization as "family." In some cases, prime time organizations literally were comprised of members from a kinship family. Such family-owned and family-operated businesses in our sample of prime time organizations included such organizations as Ewing Oil (Dallas), Colby Enterprises (The Colbys), Falcon Crest Wineries (Falcon Crest), the Simon and Simon Detective Agency (Simon and Simon), and Ben and daughter Charlene Matlock's law firm (Matlock). Other prime time organizations, however, were presented symbolically as "work families" comprised of members unrelated by kinship but clearly united by shared values, beliefs, and a mutual concern for each other. Such "work families" in our sample included the St. Gregory Hotel (Hotel), the Cheers bar (Cheers), St. Eligius Hospital (St. Elsewhere), NYC Municipal Night Court (Night Court), the law firm of McKenzie, Brackman, Chaney, & Kuzak (L.A. Law), and others (see Chapter 6).

The work families of prime time shared many similarities. First, the formal hierarchy of the organization often resembled the structural properties of a domestic family. As Schatz (1987) observed about ensemble series such as The Mary Tyler Moore Show, Lou Grant, and, from our sample, St. Elsewhere and Hill Street Blues, "the ensemble actually took on the structural features and individual roles of a surrogate family, complete with pater familias, matriarchy, unruly kids, avuncular old pro, and so on" (p. 93). Indeed, older patriarchs and matriarchs in our sample such as LeLand McKenzie (L.A. Law), Daniel Auschlander and Donald Westphall (St. Elsewhere), and Mrs. Cabot and Mrs. Trent (Hotel) were the top managers of their companies as well as symbolic heads of their work families which included a variety of organizational sons and daughters, aunts and uncles, and (future) husbands and wives.

Second, these organizational families spent most of their time and energy engaged in *interpersonal* activities which developed, maintained, and/or repaired their relationships with organizational others. In particular, comforting, counseling, and mentoring dominated much of the action in these organizations — as when attorney Arnie Becker (L.A. Law) gave his shoulder to his crying secretary Roz and promised her that they would always be (working) together, when bar manager Sam Malone (Cheers) advised the naive bartender Woody not to bet his life savings on a set of weekend football games, and when father-figure Dr. Westphall (St. Elsewhere) empathized with and gave encouragement to intern Carol Novino as she agonized over how to tell a patient that he had terminal cancer. Finally, and most importantly, members of these work families shared a willingness to support each other, a sense of belonging, and a commitment to organizational loyalty. In sum, our prime time work families were "united by ties of love, of warmth, and of mutual concern" (Newcomb, 1974, p. 51) and, thus, offered safe, secure, and ultimately caring environments for organizational insiders and outsiders.

Of course, not all domestic families are alike; so, too, our prime time organizational families were rather distinct (see Chapter 6). The St. Gregory Hotel (Hotel) presented the most idealized vision of the organization as family inasmuch as the hotel staff, epitomized by relational manager Peter McDermott, provided unconditional support and compassion to hotel employees and guests. The NYC night court (Night Court) featured the playfulness of work family life as birthday parties and practical jokes punctuated the work activities of the sometimes childlike characters in this organization. The law firm of McKenzie, Brackman, Chaney, & Kuzak in L.A. Law offered a more diverse picture of organizational siblings as patriarch Leland McKenzie dealt with favorite son Michael Kuzak, who could do no wrong, and with spoiled brat Arnie Becker, who always wanted a bigger allowance. Finally, St. Eligius Hospital (St. Elsewhere) highlighted the sufferings and tragedies of family life as members of this rather melodramatic work family helped each other deal with personal problems and organizational catastrophes. Thus, although these prime time work families shared many of the same types of organizational actions and values, they enacted these actions and values in rather distinct ways.

In summary, the family metaphor is a pervasive form through which one broad vision of organizational life is presented on prime time television. Indeed, as many television critics have asserted (see Goethals, 1981; Newcomb, 1974; Schrag, Hudson, & Bernabo, 1981), the family has been an enduring image on prime time television. Goethals (1981) goes so far as to say that the prime time family has become the contemporary electronic version of the Norman Rockwell portrait. As she concluded, "Perhaps because of its power to articulate myths and values that extend beyond its immediate scope, the image of the family has been frequently used as a metaphor for larger communities" (p. 38).

The image of the prime time organization as family can reveal lessons which are relevant and important to our own real-life organizational lives. Indeed, organizational researchers themselves have often used the family metaphor in an effort to explain the importance of certain social values in the organization. The early Hawthorne studies and subsequent human relations movement, for example, first revealed that the care and compassion of formal managers and the development of informal employee relations are key elements for organizational success. Although the overly simplified human relations model of "the happy employee is a productive employee" has been replaced by human resource models which emphasize the fit between human, physical, and technological elements, the idea that employees have *social* needs which must be fulfilled by organizations has become a common assumption. As Peters and Waterman (1982) explained, excellent companies pay close attention to social values such as trust, compassion, and cooperation. In fact, Peters and Waterman (1982) argued that "many of the best companies really do view themselves as an extended family" (p. 261). For millions of viewers, prime time television provides nightly examples of how organizational life can be dramatically enacted and experienced as an extended family.

As noted above, the family metaphor was the most dominant vision of organizational life on prime time television. In fact, in many ways, the family was *the* image of prime time organization. Nevertheless, we now consider less pervasive visions of organizational life that appeared in some of the prime time programs in our sample. Specifically, we examine three secondary metaphors including prime time organizations as "machines," as "organisms," and as "political arenas."

Prime Time Organizations as "Machines"

The metaphor of the organization as "machine" has a rich tradition in the organizational literature, ranging from the early "time and motion" studies and so-called "classical management" of Frederick Taylor (1911) to the rise of the contemporary bureaucratic organization. The machine metaphor places an emphasis on mechanistic ideals such as precision, efficiency, routinization, and the application of technology. As Morgan (1986) pointed out: "Increasingly, we have learned to use the machine as a metaphor for ourselves and our society, and to mold our world in accord with mechanical principles. This is nowhere more evident than in the modern organization" (p. 20).

For better or worse, very few regular or single appearance prime time organizations were cast as machines, and those organizations that were cast as such were usually depicted in a negative light. One regular (though short-lived) organizational machine on prime time was the "Assan Motor Company," a Japanese-owned and-managed auto plant that was located in the United States and which employed American workers (Gung Ho). As prime time is wont to do, these Japanese managers were stereotypically presented as cold and efficient technicians who wore white lab coats whereas the American workers were equally grossly stereotyped as playful and usually lazy or irresponsible employees who cared less about getting the job done and more about their interpersonal exploits. Indeed, the tensions between the narrowly defined rationality of these Japanese managers and the broadly defined emotionality of these American workers served as the grist for most of the storylines on this program, including our sample episode (see Chapter 4). Not surprisingly, these storylines usually revealed the moral lesson that excessive machine-like rationality can be dysfunctional for organizational success.

Although few organizations on prime time were presented as machines, several organizations emphasized machines in their episode-to-episode operations. An emphasis on mechanical technology was prevalent in prime time hospitals such as San Francisco General (Trapper John, M.D.) and St. Eligius (St. Elsewhere), and this health care technology usually (but not always in either hospital, especially St. Eligius) helped caring professionals make successful diagnoses and operations. An emphasis on mechanical technology was also prevalent in military or quasimilitary organizations such as those on Airwolf, MacGyver, The A-Team, and The Wizard. As Goethals (1981) argued, on some programs "it is the machine that frequently becomes the constant against which plot and weekly changing environments are played" (p. 77). Such was definitely the case for Airwolf, a quasimilitary adventure series which was organized around (and named after) the super-machine helicopter known as "Airwolf."

Perhaps the most intriguing use of the machine, however, was seen on the short-lived *Mr. Wizard* wherein the technology of play was juxtaposed with the technology of war as the toys of toymaker Simon *(Mr. Wizard)* were protected by government agents because of their uses as military weapons.

As noted above, the machine as a metaphor for organizational life was usually depicted in a negative manner by the prime time organizations in our sample. Indeed, most prime time organizations resisted any and all attempts to become machine-like. In the case of St. Eligius Hospital, for example, when Helen Rosenthal (the representative of the nurses union) told Daniel Auschlander (the representative of hospital management) that the nurses wanted to "get the rules down in black and white," Daniel responded angrily, "I'm not going to allow you to turn this into a sterile hospital with nameless patients and faceless employees" (see Chapter 6). Similarly, McKenzie, Brackman, Chaney & Kuzak *(L.A. Law)* partners Kuzak and Markowitz recommended against merging with the NYC law firm of Marshall-Taft because it was "cold," "impersonal," and "a factory"; and after the "efficiency experts" from Marshall-Taft came to the L.A. firm and "cubed the support personnel" to give the firm a "clean, hard-edged look," all the partners — even the selfish Brackman and Becker — voted against a merger with this "mechanistic" organization.

In summary, the machine metaphor was an uncommon and rather negative vision of organizational life on prime time television. Prime time organizations generally attempted to maintain a family orientation and to avoid a machine orientation. In this way, prime time illustrated very powerfully the limitations of the mechanistic model of organizational life which "tends to hurt rather than mobilize the development of human capacities" (Morgan, 1986, p. 38). Unfortunately, the consequence was that we saw very few prime time enactments of potential "heroes and heroines of technology" (with the possible exception of *MacGyver*) who "combine reason, strength, intelligence, and a superb command of mathematics and electronics" (Goethals, 1981, p. 84). To the extent that prime time teaches us about organizational life, then, it encourages us to avoid mechanistic thinking in general and mechanistic thinking about organizations in particular.

Prime Time Organizations as "Organisms"

For the past two to three decades, organizational theory has been dominated by the metaphor of the organization as "organism" as articulated in (general) systems theory (see Burns & Stalker, 1961; Emery, 1969; Katz & Kahn, 1966; Lawrence & Lorsch, 1967). Systems researchers have argued that the organization is an *open system* which is composed of interrelated subsystems and which interacts with the larger environment in an effort to survive and grow. The organization is said to regulate itself by importing energy (physical resources, human resources, and information) from the environment, by transforming this energy into a usable form, and by exporting various outputs. In this way, the organization not only maintains a steady state of "homeostasis" but also evolves over time through a continual process of variation, selection, and retention of selected characteristics (Weick, 1979).

Unfortunately, most prime time organizations were presented as self-contained *closed systems* which rarely (if ever) interacted with the larger environment. At the level of the organizational individual, for example, we saw very little of the lives of organizational members outside the physical boundaries of the organization. And on the rare occasions when we did see their outside organizational lives, we only saw their private lives at home — which were often in bad shape because of their single-minded commitment to their organizations. We rarely saw these organizational members interacting *with other organizations in the environment.* Indeed, it was as if these members never needed to interact with any other organizations — not even to cash their payroll checks at their banks, to go grocery shopping at their supermarkets, or to pay utility bills at their gas and electricity companies.

More importantly, at the level of the organization itself, prime time organizations rarely interacted with other organizations in their environments. Indeed, most prime time organizations seemed to exist and flourish on their own. Although we did hear about the relevance of environmental forces such as the pressure from the mayor's and controller's offices and the potential loss of medicare payments during the nurses' strike at St. Eligius Hospital (*St. Elsewhere*), we learned of these outside influences indirectly through the verbal interactions of Rosenthal, Auschlander, and the mediator *within the bounds of St. Eligius itself* (see Chapter 6). In short, the lives of prime time individuals and organizations were essentially self-contained.

This is not to say that interdependence among different organizations was entirely absent from prime time television. Indeed, interrelationships between and among the service industries and public administration industries were common, albeit limited. Such interrelationships commonly were present between private detective

agencies and police forces (Simon and Simon, Mike Hammer), between police forces and district attorneys' offices (Hill Street Blues,
Foley Square), and between law firms and criminal justice court-
rooms (L.A. Law, Matlock). As noted in Chapter 2, these service and
public administration organizations dominate prime time television.
Thus, although we do not see much interdependence among a wide
range of prime time organizations, the two industries that dominate
prime time television (service and public administration) are highly
interrelated.

Prime time television's general omission of visions of organizational interdependence is unfortunate because without such portrayals audiences do not gain a very nuanced picture of broader
organizational systems in America. Every organization in America
is interconnected with many other organizations — such is the sys-
temic nature of American society. In an effort to package prime
time content in closed organizational systems, network television
overly simplifies the nature of organizational openness and, thus,
certainly does not help audiences develop more textured visions of
organizations in American society. Furthermore such presentations
undoubtedly do not help and potentially hinder audiences' understandings of the complex and increasingly interconnected nature of
organizational America.

Prime Time Organizations as "Political Arenas"

In recent years, researchers have begun to recognize, even embrace,
the political nature of organizational life in the organizational literature (see Brown, 1972; Burns, 1961; Conrad and Ryan, 1985;
Mayes & Allen, 1977; Mintzberg, 1983; Pfeffer & Salancik, 1978;
Porter, Allen & Angle, 1981; Tompkins & Cheney, 1985). From a
political perspective, organizations are arenas wherein different
groups and coalitions use various types of power to protect their
diverse and often competing self-interests. Such a political view of
the organization in the scholarly literature is a relatively recent
phenomenon, as Pfeffer (1981a) and Morgan (1986) have argued,
because it violates the longstanding ideal that organizations are
rational enterprises which employ one large collectivity of workers
who share a limited set of common goals. However, as Mintzberg
(1983) has chronicled, conceptions of the organization have pro-
gressed from early visions of the organization as defined by a single
actor with a single goal to more contemporary (and more radical)

visions of the organization as defined by multiple actors with few (if any) common goals.

As we noted in Chapter 4, there was some but not much political action in prime time organizations. Not surprisingly, prime time managers engaged in proportionately more political activity than did other organizational members as these managers conducted their bargaining, grandstanding, and other performances designed to protect their interests and/or enhance their organizational power. Indeed, as discussed in Chapter 4, certain individual managers such as J.R. Ewing (*Dallas*) and Angela Channing (*Falcon Crest*) engaged in so many political actions that they were said to epitomize a "political style" of management.

However, although these and other individual managers engaged in much political behavior, few (if any) organizations themselves were presented *as* political arenas. Even Ewing Oil was not really presented as a political arena composed of multiple coalitions but rather as a monolithic context for the ongoing power battles of two individual members — J.R. and Bobby Ewing. Perhaps the best example of an organization as a political arena itself was St. Eligius Hospital (*St. Elsewhere*) during the nurses strike when several competing groups and cliques developed throughout the hospital in addition to the frontstage conflicts of union and management representatives at the bargaining table. However, as indicated in Chapter 6, this political arena faded after three prime time episodes when union and management representatives reached an agreement and reunited the hospital "family." In other words, while political activities were relatively uncommon in prime time organizations, depictions of prime time organizations as political arenas were downright rare.

In summary, the political activities of prime time organizations displayed the interest-based and power-based nature of organizational life. In this sense, prime time did present to millions of viewers a vision of organizational life that is probably widely known but rarely admitted. As Morgan (1986) has acknowledged, "one of the curious features of organizational life is the fact that though many people know that they are surrounded by organizational politics, they rarely come out and say so" (p. 194). For better or worse, organizational characters such as J.R. Ewing and Angela Channing did indeed come out and say so. Unfortunately, this vision of prime time politics has been individual-centered rather than organization-centered. Thus, although viewers have watched particular organizational actors engage in particular political actions, the broader vision of the organization as a political arena has been virtually absent on prime time television.

The four metaphors presented above — family, machine, organism, and political arena — represent four broad visions of organizational life that have been displayed on prime time television. Not surprisingly, these four metaphors also represent four broad visions of organizational life that have been advanced in the organizational literature. To the extent that television teaches viewers about organizational life, these viewers may be presented with introductory lessons about organizational theory and research while simultaneously being entertained by their favorite prime time organizations. When we realize that literally millions of viewers watch these prime time organizations every night, television's potential for teaching lessons about organizational life is indeed noteworthy. In the next section, we consider some of the specific lessons that viewers may indeed be learning about organizational life. We also discuss some of the lessons that do not (but that we believe should) appear more often on prime time television.

ORGANIZATIONAL LESSONS PRESENTED ON PRIME TIME TELEVISION

We now consider some of the lessons about organizational life which are presented on prime time television. These "lessons," of course, represent our inferences about the "lessons" television teaches through the occupations, industries, performances, values, and cases which appear on prime time and which we have considered throughout this book. These lessons are not necessarily intended by network producers and programmers or received by all prime time audiences. Instead, these lessons represent some of the potential meanings of organizational life which viewers could construct, as we have in this book, by watching prime time television. Further research can and should be conducted to assess the degree to which program creators and network executives intend to teach these lessons and the degree to which audiences actually learn these (and other) lessons.

"In Successful Organizations, People . . ."

"Work hard." Although we do not see a large proportion of work (or "operational") activities compared to other organizational actions,

most members of prime time organizations, especially major regular and minor regular members, are presented as dedicated individuals who are committed to the *value* of hard work. Successful organizational members usually get to their organizations early and stay late, whether they work in prime time bars, hotels, hospitals, police stations, or private investigation agencies. Indeed, most prime time workers spend little if any time away from their organizations. And because of their long hours and organizational persistence, diseases are correctly diagnosed and treated, criminals are caught and brought to justice, clients are heroically defended and protected, and customers get quality service. Not surprisingly, these members are often rewarded for their hard work as well, as vividly illustrated in the case of Benson DuBois *(Benson)*, whose hard work and dedication enabled him to move from butler in the Tate household (in the earlier series *Soap*), to chief housekeeper of a governor's executive mansion, to state budget director, and eventually to lieutenant governor. Although some organizations may get by with lazy managers (e.g., *Cheers*) or lazy employees (e.g., *Gung Ho*), they are not as successful in either an economic or human sense as organizations which employ hardworking managers and employees. As noted later in this chapter, however, hard work has an associated personal cost for the hard worker.

"Cooperate with others." Prime time organizations are successful when hardworking individuals put aside their personal differences and interests and coordinate their activities with others to accomplish the common goals of the organization. On the other hand, organizations are generally *not* successful when individual members act in self-centered ways in pursuit of purely personal goals. Thus, while successful organizations encourage individual self-reliance, initiative, and autonomy, they do so within the context of a community of coordinated and cooperative individuals who complement (and compliment) each other. Indeed, the cooperation in most prime time organizations is so pronounced that these organizations are seen as "teams" and "families" which are united by common values and beliefs.

"Are creative." In successful prime time organizations, individual employees are encouraged to take risks, to act on their trained instincts, and to try innovative solutions to problems. That is, in successful organizations, members and even the organization itself must sometimes go out on a limb. Those who take such creative risks usually prove to be correct and are rewarded handsomely; those who take similar creative risks and fail are usually not punished but rather are encouraged to learn from the temporary setback

and to try harder next time. In short, prime time organizations teach us to "experiment" in organizations, a lesson which excellent companies apply with regularity (Peters & Waterman, 1982, p. 134).

"Pay attention to detail." In prime time organizations, the successful accomplishment of an organizational task or goal sometimes depends on the conscientious attention paid by one or more organizational members to apparently unimportant details. Members who pay attention to such details in informal conversations often learn important information which helps them solve organizational problems. Indeed, for private investigators and police detectives, such details provide essential clues for solving criminal cases and ultimately for saving lives. Those who ignore such details miss potentially important information and, as a result, sometimes suffer organizational failure and frustration. In sum, by paying attention to details, organizational members discover important information which leads to organizational success.

"People are More Important Than Products or Profits"

Prime time organizations are overwhelmingly "people-oriented." They exhibit the importance and centrality of relational styles of management and people-oriented philosophies of organization. As discussed in Chapters 3 and 4, prime time members engage in many interpersonal actions which develop and maintain relations with organizational insiders and outsiders. Through these actions, we learn that values such as concern, compassion, and community are important to prime time organizations (see Chapter 5). Indeed, as we noted earlier in this chapter, the dominant vision of prime time organizational life is the richly person-centered metaphor of the organization as family.

The emphasis on people in prime time organizations generally produces positive benefits for both organization and individual. As mentioned above, when organizational members interact interpersonally, they also often reveal information which helps them later to solve organizational problems. Perhaps more importantly, when customers are treated with care and compassion, they often become regular clients, as in the case of guests who returned to the St. Gregory Hotel (*Hotel*) because the hotel staff "really cared" about them. Finally, and most importantly, when employees are treated with care and compassion, they often respond with their loyalty and dedication, as was the case with the employees of a construction firm who voted to stay and help the owner and manager of the firm when he was beset with sabotage by members of an evil cult who wanted to kidnap his adopted son. The loyal workers stayed on the job because, as they explained to him, "you supported us before when times were tough so it's only fair that we stick with you now" (Knight Rider). In this way, prime time organizations affirm the lesson that human success is far more important than economic success.

"Honesty is the Best Organizational Policy"

Another prime time organizational lesson is that open and honest communication among organizational members benefits both the individual and the organization. Such honest communication helps develop a sense of community and belongingness among organizational members which in turn facilitates employee responsibility for the organization's performance and which ultimately yields quality products and service. Of course, prime time also teaches that such honesty should be tempered judiciously with tact. From watching lawyers on L.A. Law, doctors on St. Elsewhere, and police officers on Hill Street Blues, for example, we learn that devastingly honest and critical feedback can be used to improve job performance only when such critiques are presented in sensitive interpersonal interactions which respect the dignity and feelings of the organizational member being critiqued.

On the other hand, prime time organizations teach us that deceptive communication results in distrust and betrayal and often leads good members of an organization to do inferior work or even quit their jobs. On L.A. Law, for example, when managing partner Leland McKenzie tricked Victor Sifuentes, a talented new attorney in the firm, into examining documents which made it improper for Victor to represent a client who had a conflict of interest with one of the firm's major clients, Victor felt betrayed and decided to resign his position. Ultimately, Victor reconsidered and withdrew his resignation, but only after Leland (having been disparaged by other partners for his inappropriate action) had apologized to Victor and had acknowledged to him that Leland's ethically questionable actions were the result of his momentary forgetting of the organizational policy of honest performances.

"Things Don't Always Go According to Plan"

Prime time television suggests that even the most rational and well-designed plans of organizational members do not always result in the successful accomplishment of intended organizational tasks and goals. Sometimes these plans are disrupted indirectly by good-hearted outsiders, as in the case of *MacGyver*, whose carefully engineered rescue plans often went awry because of the actions of amateurs who tried to help but who just got in the way. At other times, however, these carefully arranged plans are disrupted directly by malevolent or selfish individuals who try, usually unsuccessfully, to sabotage the efforts of organizational members. Finally, on some occasions, organizational plans simply do not work. Indeed, as noted in Chapter 5, prime time organizations are contexts for irrationality and emotion as well as logic and reason. In these and other ways, prime time organizational life is not enacted with the precision of textbook organizational designs.

"Appearances are Deceiving"

A related lesson that can be learned from prime time organizations is that organizational "appearances are deceiving" (see Chapter 5). This lesson suggests that initial judgments based on the surface appearances of organizational members or their actions often are wrong. For example, private investigators (and mystery writers) such as Mike Hammer (*The New Mike Hammer*) and Jessica Fletcher (*Murder She Wrote*) and police detectives such as Cagney and Lacey (*Cagney and Lacey*), and Hunter and McCall (*Hunter*) often encountered suspects who appeared to be guilty but later turned out to be innocent as well as apparently innocent individuals who later turned out to be guilty. If it were not for the willingness of these private and public investigators to suspend judgment until all the facts were uncovered, a lot more innocent one-shot (guest) characters would be regular guests in our prime time jails.

In a similar fashion, some prime time members who did not appear at first glance to be competent organizational members turned out to be quite capable and successful. Thus, on *Riptide* we learned that even "nerds" can be effective organizational performers, as in the case of the nebish Murray "Boz" Bosinsky, whose computer generated information regularly helped his more physically active and attractive partners Nick Ryder and Cody Allen solve their private investigations. And, on *Trapper John M.D.* we learned that older organizational veterans who appeared to be "over the hill" were still capable of professional and personal growth and change, as in the case of the "curmudgeon" Dr. McDuffy who, after suffering a heart attack from overwork, was given a new medical education position in the hospital and who ultimately helped a younger neurosurgeon diagnose a problematic patient case. In these and other ways, prime time teaches us that organizational life is not very predictable.

"Rules Should Be Followed — And Occasionally Broken"

As noted in Chapter 5, prime time television generally endorses a rule-governed approach to organizational life inasmuch as it affirms the dominant American ideology of conformity to social and organizational norms. In general, prime time organizational members do follow most of the rules and procedures of their organizations. Indeed, prime time teaches us that the choice not to follow such rules and procedures can result in organizational failure, as when the rejection of appropriate rules of arrest in law enforcement agencies results in the dismissal of charges against suspects who go free, often to commit more crimes. So, too, the failure to follow organizational rules and procedures can result in personal injury, as Dr. Jack Morrison (*St. Elsewhere*) discovered when he neglected to follow the prison rules for handling prisoner disturbances and found himself (and a prison nurse) taken hostage, beaten, and raped. In this way, prime time organizations teach us to respect the formal rules and procedures of organizational life.

However, as we also discussed in Chapter 5, prime time television also teaches us that it is sometimes appropriate to deviate from organizational rules and procedures, especially when such rules and procedures have unfair or unjust consequences for individuals. Indeed, in these cases, prime time television instructs viewers to bend or break these unfair rules and to do what is morally (not procedurally or legally) right. So, for example, although the acting director of the CIA-front organization on *Spies* declared that he would abide by the official company policy of not negotiating with terrorists, he and his assistant used all their resources to unofficially rescue the chairman of the board who had been kidnapped by terrorists. And on *Night Court*, while members of this public administration organization officially upheld the law, they bent and ultimately broke the law to help a fellow worker keep her job and avoid mandatory retirement, as the official rules required. In sum, prime time organizations teach us that when higher values are at stake, organizational members can (and should) bend, break, and circumvent the formal rules and procedures with impunity.

"Personal and Professional Lives are Difficult (and Sometimes Impossible) to Separate"

Finally, prime time television teaches us that it is extremely difficult to separate one's personal life from one's professional life. After all, most prime time organizational members, including managers, professionals, operatives, and service workers alike treat their work as far more than a mere job — it is an important part of who they are. Moreover, as noted earlier, these prime time members do not have nine-to-five jobs which they leave at the office but rather have jobs which force them to work late into the night and jobs which they often take home with them, physically and/or psychologically. In simple terms, prime time organizations are filled with so-called "workaholics" who are intensely committed to their organizations and who gain a rich sense of self-worth and personal accomplishment from working so hard.

However, prime time workaholics often pay a substantial personal price for their organizational intensity. For example, the romantic and/or family relationships of these workaholics are typically in a state of constant disrepair or disengagement because of their work-related emotional and physical stress. For example, Dr. Mark Craig's hard work and dedication to his job at St. Eligius Hospital (St. Elsewhere) entailed years of long hours at the hospital which prevented him from being at home with his wife, Ellen. One consequence for Ellen Craig, at least in our sample episode, was psychosomatic illness — severe gynecological pain—which she experienced in response to the pain of being neglected by her hard-working physician husband. Similarly, Jason and Maggie Seaver (Growing Pains) revealed to their children that they almost had divorced each other because they had placed their careers — he a psychiatrist in Phoenix and she a reporter for Newsweek in New York — above their personal relationship. Positively, we learned that the Seavers saved their marriage; disappointingly, we learned that they did so because Maggie quit her job and joined Jason in Arizona, a choice which suggested that the tension between personal and professional lives for dual-career couples is particularly problematic and may only be resolved when one party (almost always the female on conservative prime time) terminates her professional life.

For prime time workaholics who do not already have romantic or family relationships outside the workplace, the prospects for developing such outside relationships are especially bleak since these workaholics rarely leave their organizations in the first place.

Perhaps inevitably, then, many prime time workers develop personal relationships with their own organizational colleagues, as witnessed on *Cheers, St. Elsewhere, Hill Street Blues, L.A. Law, Dallas, Head of the Class, Miami Vice,* and *Shellgame,* to name only a few prime time programs in our sample which displayed office romances. Unfortunately, while these office romances make for good prime time drama, they are also rife with problems both for the characters and for their organizations. Office romances create strain and tension among coworkers, especially when two organizational members fall in love with the same third party (as was illustrated on our *Shellgame* episode) or when two members at different hierarchical levels fall in love (as was illustrated on our 1986 *St. Elsewhere* episode). In short, we learned that when the personal and professional lives of members overlap in the same prime time organization, problems inevitably result.

There were, of course, exceptions to this generally bleak pattern of prime time personal and professional lives, including several couples who worked either in the same organization or in the same field and who were able to separate their work from their personal lives and successfully maintain both. In our sample, such exceptions included police captain Frank Furillo and public defender Joyce Davenport *(Hill Street Blues),* corporate attorney Michael Kuzak and public prosecutor Grace Van Owen *(L.A. Law),* and corporate attorneys Stuart Markowitz and Ann Kelsey, both partners in the same law firm. Indeed, the evolution of Furillo and Davenport's relationship offers a particularly interesting lesson on the possibility of hardworking professionals maintaining simultaneously happy personal lives and productive organizational lives. Furillo and Davenport met in the context of their work, developed a passionate romance, and ultimately were married. Surprisingly, neither Furillo nor Davenport allowed their personal relationship to impair their professional performances and neither gave the other softer or more preferential treatment on the job. Indeed, Furillo and Davenport enacted a very adversarial relationship at work, yet managed (with rare exceptions) somehow to leave their working roles at the office and to adopt new roles at home as compassionate and passionate lovers and spouses. For a time, Furillo and Davenport separated, leaving viewers with the predominant prime time lesson about organizational romance — that it is impossible for coworking professionals to maintain healthy personal lives and successful careers. However, they did reconcile and rekindle their romance and their marriage, thereby providing at least one example of the possibility that loving yet dedicated (married) working couples can separate and balance their personal and organizational lives.

ORGANIZATIONAL LESSONS NOT PRESENTED ON PRIME TIME TELEVISION

As noted above, prime time television does indeed present many potential lessons about organizational life. But quite obviously, it does not provide an exhaustive set of lessons about organizations. In this section, we consider some of the lessons about organizational life not offered on prime time television. Stated differently, we consider some of the ways that television limits our understanding of organizational life.

"Organizations Are Economic As Well As Human Institutions"

Prime time television does not give us many presentations of the economic realities of organizational life. At the level of the individual, for example, we rarely see customers pay for products — such as drinks at the Cheers bar or a night at the St. Gregory Hotel — or services—such as health care at St. Eligius hospital or private detective services that are offered by Thomas Magnum or Rick and A.J. Simon. So, too, we rarely see organizational members even charged for their products or services. Sam Malone actually charge Norm for a drink? Magnum actually collect fees for services rendered? Indeed, we more often see organizational members volunteer their services and products to needy (and even unneedy) clients and customers rather than charge and accept money for services and products. Similarly, at the level of the organization itself, we almost never see the broader economic issues and decisions that organizations must deal with in order to stay in business. Payrolls, taxes, investments, and other money matters are just not displayed in our prime time organizations. Quite simply, the economics of prime time organizations are essentially invisible.

Unfortunately, when economic matters are dealt with at all, they are usually presented in a negative light. For example, money itself was presented negatively when organizational administrators expressed concerns for profits over people — as was the case on *Trapper John, M.D.* when the hospital administrator showed more interest in a patient's pocketbook than his health — or, even worse, when shady deals were made by selfish people — as in the case with J.R.

Ewing and Ewing Oil's organizational life *(Dallas)*. Indeed, on prime time it seems that only greedy villains are interested in prime time money whereas corporate heroes do not seem to care much about it. Although many prime time organizations seem to flourish, money itself is an invisible and somewhat seedy resource.

We believe this lack of positive attention to the monies and economies of organizational life is unfortunate. If television does teach us lessons about organizational life, it may be teaching us that money should not be discussed by good, honest, and/or caring organizational members. So, too, we may be learning that customers should not pay for services unless they are asked to pay, and that they will only be asked to pay if the organizational members are greedy selfish people.

At an individual level, then, we simply do not learn how to talk in constructive ways about money from watching prime time portrayals of organizational life. We do not learn that (or how) honorable organizational members should charge for their products and services, especially if those products and services are competently performed. Furthermore, we do not learn how caring organizational members can contribute directly to their organization's bottom lines. At a broader level, we do not learn that organizations need economic resources to provide quality products and services and we do not learn how these organizations can acquire these resources in honorable constructive ways.

In sum, while television does an excellent job of depicting the human successes of organizational life, it fails decidedly in presenting sensitive visions of the economic successes of organizational life. This is unfortunate because both elements of success can, do, and should complement each other in successful organizations. As Peters and Waterman (1982) pointed out, human success contributes to economic success, but without economic success, excellent companies are simply not "excellent" companies. In prime time organizations, however, human success seems unrelated to economic success while economic success is negatively correlated with human success. Prime time television does not yet teach us how these two senses of success can work together.[1]

---

[1] *St. Elsewhere's* 1987–1988 season may, however, be an exception which does deal with economic success as the members of St. Eligius hospital deal with the new for-profit hospital owner, Ecumena company. Nevertheless, the tension between economic and human success was an ongoing part of the 1987–1988 plots.

"Organizations Need to Change in Response to a Changing Environment"

As we noted earlier, prime time organizations generally are presented as closed systems which interact very little with their environments. As a result, these organizations are displayed as rather stable entities which are resistant to change. Indeed, prime time organizations change their personnel only when they must (e.g., if a character leaves the show), and these personnel changes almost always involve mere substitutions of persons for positions. Thus, when the attractive, dark-haired, Dr. Ben Samuels (David Birney) left St. Eligius hospital after the 1982–1983 season, he was replaced by the equally (or more) attractive, dark-haired male Dr. Robert Caldwell (Mark Harmon). Of course, the stability of the prime time work place is not surprising, given the network assumption that audiences come to identify with organizations and characters and that these audiences may be disappointed (and possibly tune out) if these organizational characters were to disappear each week and be replaced by other characters.

Unfortunately, prime time's resistance to organizational change does not help viewers learn that "real" organizations must change in order to survive. Indeed, changing markets, advances in technology, government regulations and deregulations, and changes in work force demographics are some of the organizational realities that prime time organizations simply ignore (see Emery & Trist, 1965; Starbuck, 1976; Weick, 1979). Yet, organizations require technological and marketing innovation, restructuring and redesign, layoffs and cutbacks, and other changes to deal with these and other environmental changes. Television misses the chance to illustrate how such changes can be accomplished in positive and productive manners. One notable exception has been St. Elsewhere (NBC) which, in the 1987–88 season underwent a corporate takeover and a series of cosmetic and substantive changes in the organization's philosophy, ownership administrators and leaders, and staff as a result of being sold by the city to the for-profit Ecumena corporation.

"Organizations Can Be Instruments of Domination"

As Morgan (1986) has asserted: "Though we are usually encouraged to think about organizations as rational enterprises pursuing goals that aspire to satisfy the interests of all, there is much evidence to suggest that this view is more an ideology than a reality. Organizations are often used as instruments of domination that further the selfish interests of elites at the expense of others. And there is often an element of domination in *all* organizations." (pp. 274–275). Indeed, as Morgan and others of a more critical bent have argued, organizations can be instruments of domination that exploit employees by subjecting them to physical dangers such as work hazards, occupational diseases, and industrial accidents and to mental dangers such as stress, workaholism, and social alienation. Such a position has led many to offer (radical) critiques of organizations and organizational research in an effort to point out the problems of organizational life and to emancipate employees (see Brown, 1973; Deetz, 1985; Frost, 1980; Giddens, 1979).

Although prime time does indeed offer us presentations of selfish corporate villains who exploit other individuals, *organizations* themselves are usually depicted in positive ways. As we noted earlier in this chapter, most prime time organizations are cast as families, and *happy* families at that. Thus, prime time television's negative depictions of organizational life are directed at the level of the evil individual but not at the level of the potentially evil institution. Such a presentation is limiting insofar as audiences are encouraged to blame single "bad" individuals for organizational problems which may have broader institutional sources. Thus, when the guest hotel operations manager of the St. Gregory Hotel acted in a lecherous political manner, we learn that bad guys such as he can be (and are) fired; what we do not learn is that his actions are emblematic of the larger problem of institutional sexism that pervades organizational life in America. This institutional lesson has not yet been presented on prime time television, at least not in network television series.

"Organizations Can Be Very Dull Places"

Organizations in America are not always (and sometimes not ever) exciting contexts for action. Stereotypic visions of organizational monotony, of course, include the assembly line worker or telephone operator or cashier at the supermarket, characters whom we assume lead very routine work lives. However, even glorified organizations such as police forces and hospitals have more than their share of mundane moments. Police, for example, spend most of their working hours performing routine tasks such as writing tickets, filling out forms, handling false alarms, and endlessly cruising the streets. Indeed, as Reiss (1971) has pointed out, the average shift for the police officer does not involve the arrest of even one criminal and 90% of all shift activities do not involve violence of any kind. In short, organizational America is generally a rather routine place.

However, prime time television suggests that organizations are incredibly exciting places to work. There is constant action which is overtly dramatic and usually melodramatic. To work on prime time is to never experience boredom, routine, or monotony. Even those "machine-like" military organizations that serve as backdrops against which MacGyver and the A-Team perform their nonroutine duties are depicted as cold and calculating rather than mundane and monotonous. Quite simply, organizational life on prime time is exciting, dramatic, and passionate.

We doubt that such overdramatized visions of organizational life provide dangerous lessons to viewing audiences. After all, prime time television is designed to entertain, and overt physical and interactional drama is what American audiences have come to expect as entertainment. Nonetheless, the overdramatization of certain organizations such as police forces, law firms, and private investigation agencies may lead audiences to adopt a glorified vision of these organizations. So, too, the underutilization of other contexts such as manufacturing plants and mining operations prevents prime time from showing the potential satisfactions that these jobs may indeed hold for workers. Whatever the case, it is very clear that prime time does not present viewing audiences with an appropriate sense of the excitement or mundaneness that is experienced by members of organizational America.

In summary, while television presents many important lessons about organizational life, it also ignores other important lessons about organizations. Television, in this respect, has far to go before it presents the fullest and richest lessons about organizational life the medium is capable of displaying. In the next section, we discuss some of the implications for television and organizational research and practice which may suggest how we can use prime time television to teach some of the organizational lessons currently presented, as well as how prime time television can offer even richer lessons of organizational life in America.

LEARNING THE ORGANIZATIONAL LESSONS OF PRIME TIME TELEVISION: IMPLICATIONS FOR RE-SEARCH AND PRACTICE

We conclude our examination of organizational life on prime time television with some of the implications of this study for research and practice. Specifically, we first examine some of the implications for television research and practice. We then turn our attention to the implications of this study for organizational research and practice.

Implications for Television Research and Practice

As noted throughout this book, mass communication researchers have been (and will be for some time) interested in the content and structure of television programming. Not surprisingly, this interest has led many to look at television's occupational demography, as we summarized in Chapter 2, as well as television's enactment of organizational processes (e.g., problem solving, information processing) and cultural values (e.g., honesty, equality, etc). In this vein, our book has attempted to expand this body of television research by looking at the occupational, industrial, managerial, and cultural presentations of organizational America. Yet we believe more research is needed to fill out the portrait.

First, historical analyses can be conducted to give us a richer sense of how prime time occupations, organizations, and industries have changed over the last four decades. Studies summarized in Chapter 2 indicated that the occupational and industrial demographies of prime time organizations have changed over time, but have there been corresponding shifts in the kinds of managerial styles and organizational values presented on prime time? And how have the organizational lessons which television presents to viewers shifted over the last four decades? As expanded video archives and other program materials become available to television scholars, we may be better able to answer some of these and other historical questions.

Second, more interview and observational research should be conducted to assess the extent to which television producers, directors, writers, and network executives consider the depiction of prime time organizations as they make decisions about the production and programming process. For example, how is the selection of an organizational context actually enacted by these television personnel? And, once selected, how does that organizational context reflect and shape the subsequent actions of these television personnel? Certainly, the decision to create a medical drama in a hospital such as St. Eligius (St. Elsewhere) demands certain kinds of sets, props, and costumes (e.g., patient rooms, medical machines, and nurses' uniforms) as well as certain kinds of technical knowledge (often supplied by so-called "medical consultants" to programs). But how does the organizational context shape other decisions such as the development of characters and story lines? This question is particularly interesting when television uses itself as a organizational context for prime time programs as, for example, in *The Mary Tyler Moore Show*, *Goodnight Beantown*, and, more recently, *Max Headroom*. Indeed, in these latter cases, additional ethnographic research may tell us more about how television uses itself, and thus reflects and shapes itself, in its prime time programs.

Finally, and perhaps most importantly, additional audience research must be conducted to assess the extent to which viewers actually learn these and/or other organizational lessons of prime time television. Researchers can conduct studies to examine if audiences actually attend to the organizations in the programs, if they find these organizations "realistic," how they compare fictional television and "real" organizations during and after viewing, if they like or dislike these organizations, if they identify their own organizational experiences in the context of these prime time organizations, and if prime time organizations have helped them to perform differently in their own organizations. Researchers might pay particular attention to those viewers of prime time organizations who themselves actually work in those particular organizations. Thus, we can and should learn more about what police think of *Hill Street Blues* and *Miami Vice*, what lawyers think of *L.A. Law* and *Matlock*, what doctors and nurses think of *Trapper John, M.D.* and *St. Elsewhere*, what private detectives think of *Moonlighting* and *Simon and Simon*, and so forth. Although real-life organizational members have commented on the "unrealistic" nature of their prime time organizations in newspaper articles and on television talk shows such as *Good Morning America*, their richer interpretations of these prime time organizations have received little attention in the scholarly literature.

Additionally, our book has implications for the *practice* of television as well. First, we believe that television, as practiced by the television industry (particularly network television), can be improved by the consideration of some of the issues raised by our studies. We believe network executives, producers, and programmers have done a commendable job presenting some important organizational lessons to viewing audiences but that they can and should focus on other lessons as well. As we noted above, they need to turn their (and our) dramatic eyes on *institutional* actions and issues and develop the organizational and social consequences of these actions and issues in prime time programming. Indeed, as networks offer increasingly more complex productions of organizational life, perhaps they can tackle increasingly more complex visions of those organizations. Developing the *interorganizational* aspects of the program characters' lives could assist in developing stronger, more believable characters. So, too, tackling more pressing organizational problems (especially economic ones) could lead to more interesting story lines. We are not asserting that television executives must immediately hire management consultants for programs in the same way that medical consultants have served as advisors for medical dramas such as *M*A*S*H* or that legal consultants have served as advisors for *L.A. Law*, but such a possibility should be considered. Indeed, some very rich stories could be generated by reading management and organizational casebooks. Besides, given the overwhelming success of management books such as *In Search of Excellence* (Peters & Waterman, 1982) and *The One-Minute Manager* (Blanchard & Johnson, 1983), it is clear that management is a best-seller which can generate high ratings. Peters and Waterman, get your bags ready for Hollywood (unless you are already there)!

Another sense of the practice of television involves television viewing (and uses and gratifications of television viewing) by audiences. Although skeptics will abound, we believe that audiences can in fact develop more informed readings of organizational life by watching prime time television. Parents, long considered the primary consultants to their children who watch television programs, can and should add organizational issues to their repertoires of such topics as violence and sex as they discuss the "meanings" of television programs with their children. So, too, popular and scholarly critics alike can and should examine and evaluate organizational readings of prime time programs.

Implications for Organizational Research and Practice

This book also has important implications for organizational research and practice. Perhaps most importantly, we believe that organizational researchers must spend more attention investigating the *values* of organizations and their members. As noted in Chapter 5, values are at the heart of corporate culture research but this research usually offers rather anecdotal accounts of the value structures of organizations. Such values and value structures must be examined in more systematic ways as well. Indeed, while the "buzzword" status of "corporate culture" may have passed for now, its legacy, the realization that cultural values are important aspects of organizations, will stay with us. In this respect, since television is a primary transmitter of cultural values, it makes sense that organizational researchers should examine how the values of American television have influenced or are influencing American organizations. We believe that the list of values noted in Chapter 5 is one starting point for such investigations.

Television may seem an odd place for organizational researchers to study organizational life. However, organizational researchers have begun to liberate their thinking about what constitutes the appropriate "data" for organizational analysis. Indeed, organizational researchers have examined a variety of nontraditional organizational texts including poetry, novels, movies, and other art forms. As Weick (1979) challenged: "Organizational theorists bite off too little too precisely and we've tried to encourage them to tackle bigger slices of reality. And if poetry, appreciation, and the artistry of inquiry need to be coupled with science to produce those bigger bites, so be it" (p. 234). If Newcomb (1974) is correct in his assertion that television is "the most popular art," then a closer look at television should indeed help organizational researchers produce these bigger bites of organizational life.

In terms of organizational practice, we believe prime time television programs can be used effectively in management training. Management training seminars frequently rely on video productions to dramatize key points because such dramatizations show *performances* of organizational procedures, management styles, and other aspects of organizational life. In this respect, prime time programs may have some distinct advantages over the traditional management training video. First, the production qualities of prime time are usually much better than even the slickest management training video. Second, many employees who would attend such seminars already would be familiar with (and perhaps avid fans of) many prime time programs. In fact, these employees may already identify with these organizational characters who, thus, could serve as more potent role models. Third, employees often watch prime time programs at home, though we are not familiar with too many employees who take home management training videos for viewing entertainment. Thus, if organizations spend some time to help their employees assign organizational meanings to these prime time programs, management training continues at home. Fourth, because prime time programs are familiar to both insiders and outsiders, they can be used to illustrate organizational problems and issues to those outside the immediate work environment. In sum, the true potential of television for organizational learning may be that it can help teach organizational members the appropriate (and inappropriate) values of the organization and of American society.

The idea of management training through prime time television, no doubt, sounds dangerous to those of a more critical bent who have already critiqued and castigated television for providing sometimes bland, often stereotyped, and usually safe content; for distorting the social facts of American culture; and, most importantly, for reinforcing the dominant (and often constraining) ideology of American capitalism. Such critics would certainly look even more disparagingly on management's use of television to inculcate preferred organizational and cultural values in employees.

However, as we have argued throughout this book, prime time television does not merely affirm and reinforce the status quo of organizational management but it also offers multiple (alternative and oppositional) images and visions of organizational life in America. Indeed, prime time television presents images of organizations which are notable for their differences as well as their similarities. And it is these differences in prime time portrayals of organizational life, coupled with the differences of viewing audiences who are themselves members of various organizations, which may facilitate active dialogues among managers and employees (as well as among parents and children and husbands and wives). In this way, prime time television has been, for better and for worse, one medium through which different audiences have developed their understandings of how organizations operate (and should operate) in American society.

References

Abravanel, H. (1983). Mediatory myths in the service of organizational ideology. In L.R. Pondy, P. Frost, G. Morgan, & T. Dandridge (Eds.), *Organizational symbolism* (pp. 273–294). Greenwich, CT: JAI.

Adams, W., & Schreibman, F. (Eds.). (1978). *Television network news: Issues in content research.* Washington, DC: George Washington University.

Adler, R.P. (1976). Introduction: A context for criticism. In R. Adler & D. Cater (Eds.), *Television as a cultural force* (pp. 1–17). New York: Praeger (Aspen Institute Series on Communications and Society).

Adler, R.P. (Ed.). (1981). *Understanding television: Essays on television as a social and cultural force.* New York: Praeger.

Allen, R.C. (1985). *Speaking of soap operas.* Chapel Hill, NC: University of North Carolina Press.

Allen, R.W., Madison, D.L., Porter, L.W., Renwick, P.A., & Mayes, B.T. (1979). Organizational politics: Tactics and characteristics of its actors. *California Management Review, 22,* 77–83.

Alley, R.S. (1976). Media medicine and morality. In R. Adler & D. Cater (Eds.), *Television as a cultural force* (pp. 95–110). New York: Praeger (Aspen Institute Series on Communications and Society).

Alley, R.S. (1977). *Television: Ethics for hire?* Nashville, TN: Abingdon.

Allison, G. (1971). *Essence of decision: Explaining the Cuban missile crisis.* Boston: Little, Brown.

Anderson, J.A. (1987). *Communication research: Issues and methods.* New York: McGraw-Hill.

Anderson, N. (1986). Mythological messages in "The A-Team." *English Journal, 75,* 30–34.

Ang, I. (1985). *Watching Dallas: Soap opera and the melodramatic imagination:* New York: Methuen.

Argyris, C. (1957). *Personality and organization.* New York: Harper & Row.

Arlen, M.J. (1974). *The view from Highway 1: Essays on television.* New York: Ballantine.

Aronoff, C.E. (Ed.). (1979). *Business and the media.* Santa Monica, CA: Goodyear.

Aronson, J. (1972). *Deadline for the media: Today's challenges to press, TV, and radio.* Indianapolis: Bobbs-Merrill.

Babson, R.W. (1923). *What is success?* New York: Fleming H. Revell.

Barker, D. (1985). Television production techniques as communication. *Critical Studies in Mass Communication, 2,* 234–246.

Barnard, C.I. (1938). The functions of the executive. Cambridge, MA: Harvard University Press.

Barnouw, E. (1975). *Tube of plenty: The evolution of American television.* New York: Oxford University Press.

Barry, A. (1982, April). Women in the workplace — TV style. *Across the Board, 14,* 18–21.

Bazerman, M., & Lewicki, R. (1983). *Negotiating in organizations.* Beverly Hills: Sage.

Becker, E. (1973). *The denial of death.* New York: Free Press.

Becker, S.L. (1984). Marxist approaches to media studies: The British experience. *Critical Studies in Mass Communication, 1,* 66–80.

Bednar, D.A. & Hineline, J. (1982). The management of meaning through metaphors. Paper presented at the annual meeting of the Academy of Management, New York.

Bellah, R.N., Madsen, R., Sullivan, W.M., Swidler, A., & Tipton, S.M. (1985). *Habits of the heart: Individualism and commitment in American life.* Berkeley, CA: University of California Press.

Bennett, J.R. (1981). Newspaper reporting of U.S. business crime in 1980. *Newspaper Research Journal, 3*(1), 45–53.

Benton, M., & Frazier, P.J. (1976). The agenda-setting function of the mass media at three levels of information holding. *Communication Research, 3,* 261–274.

Berger, P.L. & Luckmann, T. (1967). *The social construction of reality.* Garden City, NY: Anchor.

Bernstein, P.W. (1982). Things the B-school never taught. In P.J. Frost, V.F. Mitchell, & W.R. Nord (Eds.), *Organizational reality: Reports from the firing line* (2nd ed.), (pp. 234–238). Glenview, IL: Scott Foresman.

Bernstein, R. (1983). *Beyond objectivism and relativism: Science, hermeneutics, and praxis.* Philadelphia: University of Pennsylvania Press.

Beyer, J.M. (1982). Ideologies, values and decision making in organizations. In P. Nystrom and W. Starbuck (Eds.), *Handbook of organizational design* (Vol. 1, pp. 166–202). London: Oxford University Press.

Beyer, J.M., & Lodahl, T.M. (1976). A comparative study of patterns of influence in United States and English universities. *Administrative Science Quarterly, 21,* 104–129.

Blanchard, K., & Johnson, S. (1983). *The one minute manager.* NY: Berkeley Books.

Blau, J.R., & McKinley, W. (1979). Ideas, complexity, and innovation. *Administrative Science Quarterly, 24,* 200–219.

Blau, P.M. (1977). *Inequality and heterogeneity.* NY: Free Press.

Bormann, E.G. (1983). Symbolic convergence: Organizational communication and culture. In L.L. Putnam & M.E. Pacanowsky (Eds.) *Communication and organizations: An interpretive approach* (pp. 99–122). Beverly Hills: Sage.

Bormann, E.G., Pratt, J., & Putnam, L.L. (1978). Power, authority and sex: Male response to female leadership. *Communication Monographs, 45,* 119–155.

Breen, T. (1983, December). From hotel to 'Hotel': The reality behind the hit TV show's illusion. *Hotel & Motel Management, 198,* 1, 12–13, 31.

Brockriede, W. (1974). Rhetorical criticism as argument. *Quarterly Journal of Speech, 60,* 165–174.

Brockriede, W. (1977). Characteristics of argument and arguing. *Journal of the American Forensic Association, 13,* 129–132.

Brooks, T., & Marsh, E. (1985). *The complete directory to prime time network TV shows 1946-present.* New York: Ballantine.

Broom, G.M., & Dozier, D.M. (1986). Advancement for public relations role models. *Public Relations Review, 12,* 37–56.

Brown, L. (1972). *Television: The business behind the box.* New York: Harcourt Brace Javanovich.

Brown, R.H. (1973). Bureaucracy as praxis: Toward a political phenomenology of formal organizations. *Administrative Science Quarterly, 23,* 365–382.

Brummett, B. (1976). Some implications of 'process' or 'intersubjectivity': Postmodern rhetoric. *Philosophy and Rhetoric, 9,* 18–39.

Burke, K. (1962). *A grammar of motives.* Berkeley: University of California Press. (original work published 1945).

Burke, K. (1969). *A rhetoric of motives.* Berkeley: University of California Press. (original work published 1950).

Burke, K. (1972). *Dramatism and development.* Barre, MA: Clark University Press.

Burns, T. (1954). The directions of activity and communication in a departmental executive group. *Human Relations, 7,* 73–97.

Burns, T. (1961). Micropolitics: Mechanisms of institutional change. *Administrative Science Quarterly, 6,* 147–181.

Burns, T., & Stalker, G.M. (1961). *The management of innovation.* London: Tavistock.

Business Week. (1980, October 27). Corporate culture: The hard-to-change values that spell success or failure, pp. 148–160.

Campbell, K.K. (1972). *Critiques of contemporary rhetoric.* Belmont, CA: Wadsworth.

Cantor, M.G. (1980). *Prime-time television: Content and control.* Beverly Hills, CA: Sage.

Cantor, M.G., & Pingree, S. (1983). *The soap opera.* Beverly Hills: Sage.

Carey, A. (1967). The Hawthorne studies: A radical criticism. *American Political Science Review, 32,* 403–416.

Carlson, J.M. (1985). *Prime time law enforcement: Crime show viewing and attitudes toward the criminal justice system.* New York: Praeger.

Cassata, M., & Skill, T. (Eds.) (1983). *Life on daytime television: Tuning in American serial drama.* Norwood, NJ: Ablex.

Cater, D., & Adler, R. (Eds.). (1975). *Television as a social force: New* approaches to TV criticism. New York: Praeger (Aspen Institute Series on Communications and Society).

Cawelti, J.G. (1965). Apostles of the self-made man: Changing concepts of success in America. Chicago: University of Chicago Press.

Cawelti, J.G. (1976). Adventure, mystery and romance: Formula stories as art and popular culture. Chicago: University of Chicago Press.

Chambers, D. (1987, May 2). In her own words . . . Diane says goodbye to Cheers — as only she can. TV Guide [with Cheri Eichen & Bill Steinkellner], pp. 4–7.

Chatman, S. (1978). Story and discourse: Narrative structure in fiction and film. Ithaca, NY: Cornell University Press.

Cheney, G. (1983). The rhetoric of identification and the study of organizational communication. Quarterly Journal of Speech, 69, 143–158.

Chesebro, J.W. (1979). Communication, values, and popular television series — A four-year assessment. In H. Newcomb (Ed.), Television: The critical view (2nd. ed., pp. 16–54). New York: Oxford University Press.

Cirino, R. (1971). Don't blame the people: How the news media use bias, distortion, and censorship to manipulate public opinion. New York: Random House. (Vintage Books Edition, 1972).

Comstock, G. (1978). The impact of television on American institutions. Journal of Communication, 28, 12–28.

Comstock, G. (1980). Television in America. Beverly Hills, CA: Sage.

Comstock, G., Chaffee, S., Katzman, N., McCombs, M., & Roberts, D. (1978). Television and human behavior. New York: Columbia University Press.

Conrad, C. (1985a). Chrysanthemums and swords: A reading of contemporary organizational communication theory and research. Southern Speech Communication Journal, 50, 189–200.

Conrad, C. (1985b). Strategic organizational communication: Cultures, situations and adaptation. New York: Holt, Rinehart & Winston.

Conrad, C., & Ryan, M. (1985). Power, praxis, and self in organizational communication theory. In R.D. McPhee & P.K. Tompkins (Eds.), Organizational communication: Traditional themes and new directions (pp. 235–257). Beverly Hills, CA: Sage.

Cooley, C.H. (1889). Personal competition: Its place in the social order and effect upon individuals: With some considerations on success. Economic Studies, 4, 78–172.

Csikszentmihalyi, M., & Kubey, R. (1981). Television and the rest of life: A systematic comparison of subjective experience. Public Opinion Quarterly, 45, 317–328.

Cunningham, M. (1984). Power play. New York: Simon & Schuster.

Dandridge, T.C. (1983). Ceremony as an integration of work and play: The example of Matel. Paper presented at the Organizational Folklore Conference, Santa Monica, CA.

Dandridge, T.C. (1985). The life stages of a symbol: When symbols work and when they don't. In P.J. Frost, L. Moore, M.R. Louis, C. Lundberg,

& J. Martin (Eds.), *Organizational culture* (pp. 141–153). Beverly Hills: Sage.

Davidson, B. (1986, February 15–21). "I have to be bullheaded." *TV Guide*, pp. 26–28, 30.

Deal, T.E. & Kennedy, A.A. (1982). *Corporate cultures: The rites and rituals of corporate life*. Reading, MA: Addison-Wesley.

Deetz, S. (1985). Ethical considerations in culture research in organizations. In P.J. Frost, L.F. Moore, M.R. Louis, C.C. Lundberg, & J. Martin (Eds.), *Organizational culture* (pp. 253–270). Beverly Hills, CA: Sage.

DeFleur, M.L. (1964). Occupational roles as portrayed on television. *Public Opinion Quarterly, 28*, 57–74.

DeFleur, M.L., & DeFleur, L.B. (1967). The relative contribution of television as a learning source for children's occupational knowledge. *American Sociological Review, 32*, 777–789.

deLaurentis, T. (1979). A semiotic approach to television as ideological apparatus. In H. Newcomb (Ed.), *Television: The critical view* (2nd ed.) (pp. 107–117). New York: Oxford University Press.

Deming, C.J. (1985). *Hill Street Blues* as narrative. *Critical Studies in Mass Communication, 2*, 1–22.

Deming, C.J., & Gronbeck, B.E. (1985). *The (not quite) comprehensive bibliography of broadcast criticism*. Mimeograph distributed at the University of Iowa Symposium and Conference on Television Criticism, Iowa City, Iowa, April.

Deming, C.J., & Jenkins, M.M. (1983). Bar talk: Male and female communication in *Cheers*. Paper presented at Western Speech Communication Association, Albuquerque, NM.

Denzin, N.K. (1983). Interpretive interactionism. In G. Morgan (Ed.), *Beyond method: Strategies for social research* (pp. 129–146). Beverly Hills, CA: Sage.

Dominick, J.R. (1974). Children's viewing of crime shows and attitudes on law enforcement. *Journalism Quarterly, 51*, 5–12.

Dominick, J.R. (1981). Business coverage in network newscasts. *Journalism Quarterly, 58*, 179–185, 191.

Donohue, W. (1981). Analyzing negotiation tactics: Development of a negotiation interact system. *Human Communication Research, 7*, 273–287.

Donohue, W., Diez, M., & Stahle, R. (1983). New directions in negotiation research. In R. Bostrom (Ed.). *Communication Yearbook 7*. Beverly Hills: Sage.

Dreier, P. (1982). Capitalists vs. the media: An analysis of an ideological mobilization among business leaders. *Media, culture, and Society, 4*, 111–132.

Duncan, H.D. (1968). *Symbols in society*. New York: Oxford University Press.

Dyer, W.G. & Dyer, J.H. (1984). The M*A*S*H generation: Implications for future organizational values. *Organizational Dynamics, 13*, 66–79.

Eason, D.L. (1984). The new journalism and the image-world: Two modes of organizing experience. *Critical Studies in Mass Communication, 1,* 51–65.

Edelman, M. (1964). *The symbolic uses of politics.* Urbana, IL: University of Illinois Press.

Efron, E. (1971). *The news twisters.* Los Angeles: Nash.

Efron, E. (1979). The media and the omniscient class. In C.E. Aronoff (Ed.), *Business and the media* (pp. 3–32). Santa Monica, CA: Goodyear.

Emery, F.E. (Ed.). (1969). *Systems thinking.* Harmondsworth: Penguin.

Emery, F., & Trist, E. (1965). Socio-technical systems. In C. Churchman & M. Verhulst (Eds.), *Management science: Models and techniques* (pp. 83–97). Oxford: Pergamon.

England, G.W. (1967a). Organizational goals and expected behavior of American managers. *Academy of Management, 10,* 107–117.

England, G.W. (1967b). Personal value systems of American managers. *Academy of Management, 10,* 53–68.

England, G.W. (1975). *The manager and his values.* Cambridge, MA: Ballinger.

England, G.W., Dhingra, O., & Agarwal, N. (1974). The manager and the man: A cross-cultural study of personal values. *Organizational and Administrative Sciences, 5,* 1–97.

England, G.W., & Lee, R. (1971). Organizational goals and expected behavior among American, Japanese, and Korean managers — a comparative study. *Academy of Management Journal, 14,* 425–438.

Epstein, E.J. (1973). *News from nowhere: Television and the news.* New York: Random House.

Farace, R., Monge, P., & Russell, H. (1977). *Communicating and organizing.* Reading, MA: Addison-Wesley.

Feldman, H.D., & Aronoff, C.E. (1980). Trends in newspaper coverage of business and economics, 1968–1978. *Newspaper Research Journal, 1,* 54–65.

Feuer, J., Kerr, P., & Vahimagi, T., (Eds). (1984). *MTM: "Quality television."* London: British Film Institute.

Fiske, J. (1984). Popularity and ideology: A structuralist reading of Dr. Who. In W.D. Rowland, Jr. & B. Watkins (Eds.), *Interpreting television: Current research perspectives* (pp. 165–198). Beverly Hills: Sage.

Fiske, J. (1987). *Television culture.* London: Methuen.

Fiske, J., & Hartley, J. (1978). *Reading television.* New York: Methuen.

Ford, J.E., & Klumpp, J.F. (1985). Systematic pluralism: An inquiry into the basis of communication research. *Critical Studies in Mass Communication, 2,* 408–429.

Fortune. (1977, November). The reliability of Maytag: Edward Faltermayer, "The man who keeps those Maytag repairmen lonely," pp. 192ff.

Fortune. (1983, October 20). The lures and limits, pp. 84–90.

Franke, R. (1979). The Hawthorne studies: A re-view. *American Sociological Review, 44,* 861–867.

Frederick, W. (1960). The growing concern over business responsibility, *California Management Review*, 2, 54–61.

Frederick, W. (1983). Corporate social responsibility in the Reagan era and beyond. *California Management Review*, 25, 145–157.

Frost, P.J. (1980). Toward a radical framework for practicing organizational science. *Academy of Management Review*, 5, 501–508.

Frost, P.J., Moore, L.F., Louis, M.R., Lundberg, C.C., & Martin, J. (Ed.). (1985). *Organizational culture*. Beverly Hills: Sage.

Frye, N. (1971). *Anatomy of criticism: Four essays*. Princeton: Princeton University Press, paperback edition. (original work published 1957).

Gale, J.L., & Wexler, M.N. (1983). The image of business on Canadian-produced television. *Canadian Journal of Communication*, 9, 15–36.

Gans, H.J. (1979). *Deciding what's news: A study of "CBS Evening News," "NBC Nightly News," "Newsweek," and "Time."* New York: Pantheon.

Garnham, N. (1983). Toward a theory of cultural materialism. *Journal of Communication*, 33, 314–329.

Geertz, C. (1973). *The interpretation of cultures*. New York: Basic Books.

Geller, A.N. (1985, February). Tracking the critical success factors for hotel companies. *Cornell H.R.A. Quarterly*, 76–81.

Gentile, F., & Miller, S.M. (1961). Television and social class. *Journal of Sociology and Social Research*, 25, 259–264.

Gerbner, G. (1972). Violence in television drama: Trends and symbolic functions. In G.S. Comstock & E.A. Rubinstein (Eds.), *Television and social behavior. Vol. 1. Media content and control* (pp. 128–187). Washington, D.C.: U.S. Government Printing Office.

Gerbner, G. (1977). Television: The new state religion? *Et cetera*, 34, 145–150.

Gerbner, G., & Gross, L. (1976). Living with television: Violence profile. *Journal of Communication*, 26, 173–199.

Gerbner, G., Gross, L., Elee, M.F., Jackson-Beeck, M., Jeffries-Fox, S., & Signorielli, N. (1977). TV violence profile no. 8: The highlights. *Journal of Communication*, 27, 171–180.

Gerbner, G., Gross, L., Elee, M. F., Jeffries-Fox, S., Jackson-Beeck, M., & Signorielli, N. (1976). *Violence. Profile no. 7: Trends in network television drama and viewer conceptions of social reality: 1967–1975*. Philadelphia: Annenberg School of Communications, University of Pennsylvania.

Gerbner, G., Gross, L., Jackson-Beeck, M., Jeffries-Fox, S., & Signorielli, N. (1978). Cultural indicators: Violence profile no. 9. *Journal of Communication*, 28, 176–207.

Gerbner, G., Gross, L., Morgan, M., & Signorielli, N. (1980). The 'mainstreaming' of America: Violence profile no. 11. *Journal of Communication*, 30, 10–29.

Gerbner, G., Gross, L., Morgan, M., & Signorielli, N. (1982). Charting the mainstream: Television's contributions to political orientations. *Journal of Communication*, 32, 100–127.

Gerbner, G., Morgan, M., & Signorielli, N. (1982, February). Top job: Television doctors. *Across the Board, 14,* 8–9.

Gerbner, G., & Signorielli, N. (1979). *Aging with television: Images of television drama and conceptions of social reality: A preview of the final report of a research conducted under a grant from the Administration of Aging, Office of Human development, Department of Health, Education and Welfare.* Philadelphia: Annenberg School of Communication, University of Pennsylvania.

Giddens, A. (1979). *Central problems in social theory.* Berkeley: University of California Press.

Gitlin, T. (1983). *Inside prime time.* New York: Pantheon.

Glasser, T.L. (1985). Objectivity precludes responsibility. In R.E. Hiebert & C. Reuss (Eds.), *Impact of mass media: Current Issues* (pp. 51–59). New York: Longman.

Goethals, G.T. (1981). *The TV ritual: Worship at the video altar.* Boston: Beacon Press.

Goffman, E. (1959). *The presentation of self in everyday life.* Garden City, NY: Anchor-Doubleday.

Goldhaber, G.M. (1979). *Organizational communication* (2nd ed.) Dubuque, IA: William C. Brown.

Goodman, R.A. (1976). A system diagram of the functions of a manager. *California Management Review, 10,* 27–38.

Grant, J.H. & King, W.R. (1982). *The logic of strategic planning.* Boston: Little, Brown.

Greenberg, B.S. (Ed.). (1980). *Life on television: Content analyses of U.S. TV Drama.* Norwood, NJ: Ablex.

Greenberg, B.S., Simmons, K.W., Hogan, L., & Atkin, C.K. (1980). The demography of fictional TV characters. In B.S. Greenberg (Ed.), *Life on television: Content analyses of U.S. TV drama* (pp. 35–46). Norwood, NJ: Ablex.

Gregory, K.L. (1983). Native-view paradigms: Multiple cultures and culture conflicts in organizations. *Administrative Science Quarterly, 28,* 359–376.

Gronbeck, B.E. (1980). Dramaturgical theory and criticism: The state of the art (or science?). *Western Journal of Speech Communication, 44,* 315–330.

Gronbeck, B.E. (1983). Narrative, enactment, and television programming. *Southern Speech Communication Journal, 48,* 229–243.

Gronbeck, B.E. (1984a). *Writing television criticism.* Chicago: Science Research Associates, Modules in Mass Communication.

Gronbeck, B.E. (1984b). Audience engagement in *Family.* In M. Medhurst & T. Benson (Eds.), *Rhetorical dimensions of mass media.* Dubuque, Iowa: Kendall/Hunt.

Haberstroh, C.J., & Gerwin, D. (1972). Climate factors and the decision process. *General Systems, 17,* 129–141.

Hadas, M. (1962). Climates of criticism. In R.L. Shayon (Ed.), *The eighth art: Twenty-three views of television today.* New York: Holt, Rinehart & Winston.

Hage, J., & Dewar, R. (1973). Elite values versus organizational structure in predicting innovation. *Administrative Science Quarterly, 18,* 279–290.

Haffner, R.D. (1973, September 15). Television: The subtle persuader. *TV Guide,* pp. 25–26.

Halloran, J.D. (1983). A case for critical eclecticism. *Journal of Communication, 33,* 270–278.

Harre, R. & Secord, P.F. (1973). *The explanation of social behavior.* Totowa, NJ: Littlefield, Adams.

Hartley, J. (1982). *Understanding news.* London: Methuen.

Harvey, E. & Mills, R. (1970). Patterns of organizational adaptation: A political perspective. In M. Zald (Ed.), *Power in organizations* (pp. 181–213). Nashville: Vanderbilt University Press.

Hay, R. and Gray, E. (1974). Social responsibilities of business managers. *Academy of Management Journal, 17,* 135–143.

Head, S.W. (1954). Content analysis of television drama programs. *Quarterly of Film, Radio, and Television, 9,* 175–194.

Hellriegel, D., & Slocum, J.W. (1985). *Management.* (4th ed.) Reading, MA: Addison-Wesley.

Henning, M. & Jardim, A. (1976). *The managerial women.* New York: Pocket Books.

Himmelstein, H. (1984). *Television myth and the American mind.* New York: Praeger.

Hirsch, P.M. (1979). The role of television and popular culture in contemporary society. In H. Newcomb (Ed.), *Television: The critical view* (2nd. ed., pp. 249–279). New York: Oxford University Press.

Hirsch, P.M. & Andrews, J.A. (1983). Ambushes, shootouts, and knights of the round table: The language of corporate takeovers. In L.R. Pondy, P. Frost, G. Morgan, & T. Dandridge (Eds.), *Organizational symbolism* (pp. 145–155). Greenwich, CT: JAI Press.

Holsti, O.R. (1969). *Content analysis for the social sciences and humanities.* Reading, MA: Addison-Wesley.

House, R. (1971). A path-goal theory of leader effectiveness. *Administrative Science Quarterly, 16,* 321–338.

Hurleigh, R.F. (1979). The social responsibility of the media in reporting on corporate social responsibility. In C.E. Aronoff (Ed.), *Business and the media* (pp. 196–204). Santa Monica, CA: Goodyear.

Husband, R.L. (1985). Toward a typology of organizational leadership behavior. *Quarterly Journal of Speech, 71,* 103–118.

Intintoli, M.J. (1984). *Taking soaps seriously: The world of "Guiding Light."* New York: Praeger.

Janis, I. (1980). The influence of television on personal decision-making. In S.B. Withey & R.P. Abeles (Eds.), *Television and human behavior: Beyond violence and children* (pp. 161–190). Hillsdale, NJ: Lawrence Erlbaum Associates.

Jenkins, S. (1984). *Hill Street Blues.* In J. Feuer, P. Kerr, & T. Vahimagi

(Eds.), *MTM: "Quality television"* (pp. 183–199). London: British Film Institute.

Kalisch, P.A., Kalisch, B.J., & Scobey, M. (1983). *Images of nurses on television.* New York: Springer.

Kanter, R.M. (1977). *Men and women of the corporation.* NY: Basic Books.

Kaplan, M. (1960). *Leisure in America: A social inquiry.* New York: John Wiley & Sons.

Katz, D. & Kahn, R.L. (1966). *The social psychology of organizations.* New York: Wiley.

Katz, E., & Gurevitch, M. (1976). *The secularization of leisure: Culture and communication in Israel.* Cambridge: Harvard University Press.

Katz, E., Gurevitch, M., and Haas, H. (1973). On the use of the mass media for important things. *American Sociological Review, 38,* 164–181.

Katz, E., & Liebes, T. (1987). Decoding Dallas: Notes from a cross-cultural study. In H. Newcomb (Ed.), *Television: The critical view* (4th ed, pp. 419–432). New York: Oxford University Press. [Reprinted from *Intermedia* (1984, May), *12.* A preliminary version appears in *Media and Values* (Summer 1985), 14–16].

Keeley, J. (1971). *The left leaning antenna: Political bias in television.* New Rochelle, NY: Arlington House.

Kerr, P. (1984). The making of (the) MTM (show). In J. Feuer, P. Kerr, & T. Vahimagi (Eds.), *MTM: 'Quality television'* (pp. 61–98). London: British Film Institute.

Kluckhohn, C. (1958). Have there been any discernible shifts in American values during the past generation? In E.E. Morrison (Ed.), *The American style* (pp. 158–204). New York: Harper.

Koch, S. & Deetz, S. (1981). Metaphor analysis of social reality in organizations. *Journal of Applied Communication Research, 9,* 1–15.

Koehler, J.W., Anatol, K.W.E., and Applbaum, R.L. (1981). *Organizational communication.* (2nd ed.). New York: Holt, Rinehart & Winston.

Kotter, J.P. (1982). *The general managers.* New York: The Free Press.

Krefting, L.A., & Frost, P.J. (1985). Untangling webs, surfing waves, and wildcatting: A multiple-metaphor perspective on managing organizational culture. In P.J. Frost, L.F. Moore, M.R. Louis, C.C. Lundberg, & J. Martin (Eds.), *Organizational culture* (pp. 155–168). Beverly Hills: Sage.

Kreps, G.L. (1986). *Organizational communication.* NY: Longman.

Krippendorff, K. (1980). *Content analysis: An introduction to its methodology.* Beverly Hills, CA: Sage.

Lakoff, G., & Johnson, M. (1980). *Metaphors we live by.* Chicago: University of Chicago Press.

Lasswell, H.D. (1936). *Politics: Who gets what, when and how.* New York: McGraw-Hill.

Lawler, E.E., Porter, L.W., & Tannenbaum, A. (1968). Managers' attitudes toward interaction episodes. *Journal of Applied Psychology, 52,* 432–439.

Lawrence, J.F. (1979). The press: Too soft on business? In C.E. Aronoff (Ed.), *Business and the media* (pp. 75–86). Santa Monica, CA: Goodyear.

Lawrence, P.R., & Lorsch, J.W. (1967). *Organization and environment.* Cambridge, MA: Harvard Graduate School of Business Administration.

Levinson, R., & Link, W. (1983). *Stay tuned.* New York: Ace.

Lewin, K., Lippitt, R., & White, R. (1939). Patterns of aggressive behavior in experimentally-created 'social climates.' *Journal of Social Psychology, 10,* 271–299.

Likert, R. (1967). *The human organization.* New York: McGraw-Hill.

Lincoln, J.R., Olson, J., & Hanada, M. (1978). Cultural effects on organizational structure: The case of Japanese firms in the United States. *American Sociological Review, 43,* 829–847.

Louis, M.R. (1980). Surprise and sense making: What newcomers experience in entering unfamiliar organizational settings. *Administrative Science Quarterly, 25,* 226–251.

Mangham, I.L., & Overington, M.A. (1983). Dramatism and the theatrical metaphor. In G. Morgan (Ed.), *Beyond method: Strategies for social research* (pp. 219–233). Beverly Hills: Sage.

Marc, D. (1984). *Demographic vistas: Television in American culture.* Philadelphia: University of Pennsylvania Press.

March, J.G. (1980, September 25). How we talk and how we act. D.D. Henry Lecture, University of Illinois, Urbana.

March, J.G. (1981). Footnotes to organizational change. *Administrative Science Quarterly, 26,* 563–577.

March, J.G., & Olson, J. (Eds.). (1976). *Ambiguity and choice in organizations.* Bergen: Universitets-forlaget.

Margulies, L. (Ed). (1981, Summer). Proliferation of pressure groups in prime time symposium: Academy of television arts & sciences and the caucus for producers, writers and directors. *Emmy,* A-1-A-32.

Martinez, L. (1985, February 9–15). Harry Anderson of *Night Court. TV Guide,* pp. 10–13.

Martin, J. & Powers, M.E. (1983). Truth or corporate propaganda: The value of a good war story. In L.R. Pondy, P.J. Frost, G. Morgan, & T. Dandridge (Eds.), *Organizational symbolism* (pp. 93–108). Greenwich, CT: JAI.

Martin, J. & Siehl, C. (1983). Organizational culture and counter culture: An uneasy symbiosis. *Organizational Dynamics, 12,* 52–64.

Maslin, J. (1980, February 10). In prime time, the workplace is where the heart is. *New York Times,* Section 2, p. 1.

Mayes, B.T., & Allen, R.W. (1977). Toward a definition of organizational politics. *Academy of Management Review, 2,* 672–678.

McCain, T.A., Childberg, J., & Wakshlag, J. (1977). The effect of camera angle on source credibility and attraction. *Journal of Broadcasting, 21,* 35–46.

McCall, M.W., Kaplan, R.W., & Gerlach, M.C. (1982). Caught in the act: Decision makers at work. Technical Report no. 20. Center for Creative Leadership, Greensboro, NC

McCammond, D.B. (1985, February). The growth of ethical awareness. *Public Relations Journal*, pp. 8-9.

Maccoby, M., & Terzi, K.A. (1979). What happened to the work ethic? In W.M. Hoffman & T.J. Wyly (Eds.), *The work ethic in business: Proceedings of the third national conference on business ethics* (pp. 19-64). Cambridge, MA: Oelgeschlager, Gunn & Hain.

McCombs, M.E., & Shaw, D.L. (1972). The agenda-setting function of the mass media. *Public Opinion Quarterly, 36,* 176-187.

MacDougall, C.D. (1979). Business's friend, the media. In C.E. Aronoff (Ed.), *Business and the media* (pp. 44-54). Santa Monica, CA: Goodyear.

McFadden, C. (1985, October, 19-25). Introducing "The Golden Girls" . . . Where your age doesn't matter unless you're a cheese. *TV Guide*, pp. 6-10.

McGregor, D. (1960). *The human side of enterprise*. New York: McGraw-Hill.

McLeod, J., Durall, J., Ziemke, D., & Bybee, C. (1977). Expanding the concept of debate effects. In S. Kraus (Ed.), *The great debates: 1976: Ford vs. Carter* (pp. 348-367). Bloomington, IN: Indiana University Press.

McMillan, C.J., Hickson, D.J., Hinings, C., & Schneck, R.F. (1973). The structure of work organizations across societies. *Academy of Management Journal, 16,* 555-569.

McNeil, A. (1980). *Total television: A comprehensive guide to programming from 1948 to 1980*. NY: Penguin.

McPhee, R.D. & Tompkins, P.K. (Eds.). (1985). *Organizational communication: Traditional themes and new directions*. Beverly Hills: Sage.

The Media Institute. (1981, October). Crooks, conmen, and clowns. *Across the Board*, pp. 62-73.

Meindl, J.R., Ehrlich, S.B., & Dukerich, J.M. (1985). The romance of leadership. *Administrative Science Quarterly, 30,* 78-102.

Meyer, H.E. (1978). How the boss stays in touch with the troops. In P.J. Frost, V.F. Mitchell & W.R. Nord (Eds.), *Organizational reality* (pp. 259-263). Santa Monica, CA: Goodyear.

Meyer, J.W., & Rowan, B. (1977). Institutionalized organizations: Formal structure as myth and ceremony. *American Journal of Sociology, 83,* 340-363.

Mintzberg, H. (1973). *The nature of managerial work*. New York: Harper & Row.

Mintzberg, H. (1979). *The structuring of organizations*. Englewood Cliffs, NJ: Prentice-Hall.

Mintzberg, H. (1983). *Power in and around organizations*. Englewood Cliffs, NJ: Prentice-Hall.

Mintzberg, H., Raisinghani, D., & Theoret, A. (1976). The structure of 'unstructured' decision processes. *Administrative Science Quarterly, 21,* 246-275.

Mitroff, I.I. & Kilmannn, R. (1978). *Methodological approaches to social science*. San Francisco: Josey-Bass.

Mitroff, I.I. & Kilmann, R. (1975). The stories managers tell: A new tool for organizational problem solving. *Management Review, 64*, 18–28.

Modleski, T. (1982). *Loving with a vengeance: Mass-produced fantasies for women.* New York: Methuen.

Montgomery, K. (1981). Gay activists and the networks. *Journal of Communication, 31*, 49–57.

Moore, K.M. (1984). The role of mentors in developing leaders for academe. In W.E. Rosenbach & R.L. Taylor (Eds.), *Contemporary issues in leadership* (pp. 209–222). Boulder, CO: Westview.

Morgan, G. (Ed.). (1983). *Beyond method: Strategies for social research.* Beverly Hills: Sage.

Morgan, G. (1986). *Images of organization.* Beverly Hills: Sage.

Moscow, V., & Wasko, J. (Eds.). (1983). *The critical communications review. Vol. 1: Labor, the working class, and the media.* Norwood, NJ: Ablex.

Newcomb, H.M. (1974). *TV: The most popular art.* New York: Doubleday Anchor.

Newcomb, H.M. (Ed.) (1976). *Television: The critical view,* 1st ed. New York: Oxford University Press.

Newcomb, H.M. (Ed.). (1979a). *Television: The critical view* (2nd ed.) New York: Oxford University Press.

Newcomb, H.M. (1979b). Toward a television aesthetic. In H. Newcomb (Ed.), *Television: The critical view* (2nd. ed.) (pp. 420–436). New York: Oxford University Press.

Newcomb, H.M. (Ed.). (1982a). *Television: The critical view* (3rd. ed.). New York: Oxford University Press.

Newcomb, H.M. (1982b). Texas: A giant state of mind. In H. Newcomb (Ed.), *Television: The critical view* (3rd. ed.) (pp. 167–174). New York: Oxford University Press.

Newcomb, H.M. (1984). On the dialogic aspects of mass communication. *Critical Studies in Mass Communication, 1*, 34–50.

Newcomb, H.M., & Alley, R.S. (1983). *The producer's medium: Conversations with the creators of American TV.* New York: Oxford University Press.

Newcomb, H.M., & Hirsch, P.M. (1984). Television as a cultural forum: Implications for research. In W.D. Rowland & B. Watkins (Eds.), *Interpreting television: Current research perspectives* (pp. 58–73). Beverly Hills: Sage.

Noelle-Newmann, E. (1983). The effect of media on media effects. *Journal of Communication, 33*, 157–165.

O'Day, R. (1974). Intimidation rituals: Reactions and reform. *Journal of Applied Behavioral Science, 10*, 373–386.

O'Donnell-Trujillo, N., & Pacanowsky, M.E. (1983). The interpretation of organizational cultures. In M.S. Mander (Ed.), *Communications in transition: Issues and debates in current research* (pp. 225–241). New York: Praeger.

Orth, C.D., Wilkinson, H.E., & Benfari, R.C. (1987). The manager's role as coach and mentor. *Organizational Dynamics, 15*, 66–74.

Ortony, A. (1975). Why metaphors are necessary and not just nice. *Educational Theory*, *25*, 45–53.

Ouchi, W.A. (1981). *Theory Z: How American business can meet the Japanese challenge*. Reading, MA: Addison-Wesley.

Pacanowsky, M.E., & O'Donnell-Trujillo, N. (1982). Communication and organizational cultures. *Western Journal of Speech Communication*, *46*, 115–130.

Pacanowsky, M.E., & O'Donnell-Trujillo, N. (1983). Organizational communication as cultural performance. *Communication Monographs*, *50*, 126–147.

Papandreou, A.G. (1952). Some basic problems in the theory of the firm. In B.F. Haley (Ed.), *A survey of contemporary economics* (2nd ed.) (pp. 183–219). Homewood, IL: Irwin.

Parsons, T. (1951). *The social system*. Glencoe, IL: Free Press.

Pascale, R.T. (1978). Communication and decision making across cultures: Japanese and American comparisons. *Administrative Science Quarterly*, *23*, 91–110.

Pascale, R.T., & Athos, A.G. (1981). *The art of Japanese management: Applications for American executives*. New York: Warner.

Pavalko, R.M. (1971). *Sociology of occupations and professions*. Itasca, IL: F.E. Peacock.

Peters, T.J. (1981). Management systems: The language of organizational character and competence. *Organizational Dynamics*, *9*, 2–26.

Peters, T.J., & Waterman, R.H. (1982). *In search of excellence: Lessons from America's best-run companies*. New York: Harper & Row.

Peters, T.J., & Austin, N. (1986). *A passion for excellence*. New York: Harper & Row.

Pettigrew, A.M. (1979). On studying organizational cultures. *Administrative Science Quarterly*, *24*, 570–581.

Pfeffer, J. (1981a). Management as symbolic action: The creation and maintenance of organizational paradigms. *Research in organizational behavior*, *3*, 1–52.

Pfeffer, J. (1981b). *Power in organizations*. Marshfield, MA: Pittman.

Pfeffer, J., & Salancik, G.R. (1978). *The external control of organizations: A resource dependence perspective*. New York: Harper & Row.

Phillips, E.B. (1977). Approaches to objectivity: Journalistic vs. social science perspectives. In P.M. Hirsch, P.V. Miller, & F.G. Kline (Eds.), *Strategies for communication research* (pp. 63–78). Beverly Hills: Sage.

Phillips, D., & Hensley, J.E. (1984). When violence is rewarded or punished: The impact of mass media stories on homicide. *Journal of Communication*, *34*, 101–116.

Pilotta, J. (Ed.). (1983). *Women in organizations*. Prospect Heights, NJ: Waveland Press.

Pollan, M. (1981, October/November). The businessman on the box. *Channels*, pp. 46–50, 60.

Pondy, L.R. (1978). Leadership is a language game. In M.W. McCall & M.M.

Lombardo (Eds.), *Leadership: Where else can we go?* (pp. 88–99). Durham, NC: Duke University Press.

Pondy, L.R., Frost, P., Morgan, G., & Dandridge, T. (Eds.). (1983). *Organizational symbolism*. Greenwich, CT: JAI.

Pool, Ithiel de Sola. (1959). (Ed.) *Trends in content analysis*. Urbana: University of Illinois Press.

Porter, L.W., Allen, R.W., & Angle, H.L. (1981). The politics of upward influence in organizations. *Research in Organizational Behavior, 3,* 109–149.

Posner, B.Z., & Schmidt, W.H. (1984). Values and the American manager: An update. *California Management Review, 26,* 203–215.

Putnam, L.L. (1982). Paradigms for organizational communication research. *Western Journal of Speech Communication, 46,* 192–206.

Putnam, L.L. (1984). Bargaining as task and process: Multiple functions of interaction sequences. In R. Street & J. Capella (Eds.), *Sequence and pattern in communication behavior* (pp. 225–242). London: Edward Arnold.

Putnam, L.L., & Geist, P. (1985). Argument in bargaining: An analysis of the reasoning process. *Southern Speech Communication Journal, 50,* 225–245.

Putnam, L.L., & Pacanowsky, M.E. (Eds.). (1983). *Communication and organizations: An interpretive approach*. Beverly Hills: Sage.

Real, M.R. (1977). *Mass-mediated culture*. Englewood Cliffs, NJ: Prentice-Hall.

Redding, W.C. (1984). *The corporate manager's guide to better communication*. Glenview, IL: Scott, Foresman & CO.

Redding, W.C., & Sanborn, G.A. (Eds.). (1964). *Business and industrial communication*. New York: Harper & Row.

Reiss, A.J. (1971). *The police and the public*. New Haven: Yale University Press.

Riley, P. (1983). A structurationist account of political culture. *Administrative Science Quarterly, 28,* 414–437.

Ristau, R.A., & Wilson, K.A. (1983, June). Network negatives: TV gives business bad ratings. *Management World,* pp. 44, 46.

Robinson, J.P. (1972). Toward defining the functions of television. In E.A. Rubenstein, G.A. Comstock, & J.P. Murray (Eds.), *Television and social behavior. Vol. 4: Television in day-to-day life patterns of use*. Washington DC: Government Printing Office.

Roethlisberger, F.J., & Dickson, W.J. (1939). *Management and the worker*. Cambridge, MA: Harvard University Press.

Rogers, E.M., & Agarwala-Rogers, R. (1976). *Communication in organizations*. New York: Free Press.

Roiphe, A. (1979). Ma and Pa and John-Boy in mythic America: The Waltons. In H.M. Newcomb (Ed.), *Television: The critical view* (2nd ed.) (pp. 8–15). New York: Oxford University Press.

Rokeach, M. (1973). *The nature of human values*. New York: Free Press.

Rokeach, M. (1979). *Understanding human values: Individual and societal.* New York: Free Press.

Rollings, J. (1983). Mass communications and the American worker. In V. Mosco & J. Wasko (Eds.), *The critical communications review. Vol 1: Labor, the working class, and the media* (vol. 1, pp. 129–152). Norwood, NJ: Ablex.

Rondina, M.L., Cassata, M., & Skill, T. (1983). Placing a 'lid' on television serial drama: An analysis of the life styles, interpersonal management skills, and demography of daytime's fictional population. In M. Cassata & T. Skill (Eds.), *Life on daytime television: Tuning in American serial drama* (pp. 3–22). Norwood, NJ: Ablex.

Rosenfield, L.W. (1968). The anatomy of critical discourse. *Speech Monographs, 25,* 50–69.

Rosenfield, L.W. (1974). The experience of criticism. *Quarterly Journal of Speech, 60,* 489–496.

Rowland, W.D., Jr., & Watkins, B. (Eds.). (1984). *Interpreting television: Current research perspectives.* Beverly Hills: Sage.

Rosengren, K.E. (Ed.). (1981). *Advances in content analysis.* Beverly Hills, CA: Sage.

Rosengren, K.E., Wenner, L.A., & Palmgreen, P. (1985). *Media gratifications research: Current perspectives.* Beverly Hills, CA: Sage.

Rubin, A.M. (1983). Television uses and gratifications: The interactions of viewing patterns and motivations. *Journal of Broadcasting, 27,* 37–51.

Rubin, B. (Ed.). (1977). *Big business and the mass media.* Lexington, MA: D.P. Heath and Company.

Sathe, V. (1983). Some action implications of corporate culture: A manager's guide to action. *Organizational Dynamics, 12,* 4–23.

Saussure, F. de. (1960). *Course in general linguistics.* New York: Philosophical Library.

Sawyer, J., & Guetzkow, H. (1965). Bargaining and negotiation in international relations. In H.C. Kelman (Ed.), *International behavior: A social psychological analysis* (pp. 463–484). NY: Holt, Rinehart and Winston.

Sayles, L.R. (1964). *Managerial behavior: Administration in complex organizations.* New York: McGraw-Hill.

Schank, P., & Abelson, R.P. (1977). *Scripts, plans, and knowledge.* Hillsdale, NJ: Erlbaum.

Schatz, T. (1987). *St. Elsewhere* and the evolution of the ensemble series. In H.M. Newcomb (Ed.), *Television: The critical view* (4th ed.) (pp. 85–100). New York: Oxford University Press.

Schrag, R.L., Hudson, R.A., & Bernabo, L.M. (1981). Television's new humane collectivity. *Western Journal of Speech Communication, 45,* 1–12.

Schriesham, C., & Kerr, S. (1977). Theories and measures of leadership: A critical appraisal of current and future directions. In J. Hunt & L. Larson (Eds.), *Leadership: The cutting edge* (pp. 9–45, 51–56). Carbondale, IL: Southern Illinois University Press.

Schudson, M. (1987). The politics of Lou Grant. In H.M. Newcomb (Ed.),

Television: The critical view (4th ed.) (pp. 101–105). New York: Oxford University Press.

Schwichtenberg, C. (1987). *The Love Boat:* The packaging and selling of love, heterosexual romance, and family. In H.M. Newcomb (Ed.), *Television: The critical view* (4th ed.) (pp. 126–140). New York: Oxford University Press.

Scott, W.A. (1955). Reliability of content analysis: The case of nominal scale coding. *Public Opinion Quarterly, 19,* 321–325.

Seggar, J.F., & Wheeler, P. (1973). World of work on TV: Ethnic and sex representation in TV drama. *Journal of Broadcasting, 17,* 201–214.

Selnow, G.W. (1986). Solving problems on prime-time television. *Journal of Communication, 36,* 63–72.

Sethi, S.P. (1977). The schism between business and American news media. *Journalism Quarterly, 54,* 240–247.

Shapira, Z., & Dunbar, R.L.M. (1980). Testing Mintzberg's managerial roles classification using an in-basket simulation. *Journal of Applied Psychology, 65,* 87–95.

Shapiro, W. (1987, May 25). What's wrong: Hypocrisy, betrayal, and greed unsettle the nation's soul. *Time,* pp. 14–17.

Shaw, D. (1986, October 11). The partner lay there dead . . . Face down in a dish of beans. *TV Guide,* pp. 34–38.

Shisgall, O. (1981). *Eyes on tomorrow: The evolution of Procter & Gamble.* Chicago: J.G. Ferguson.

Siehl, C. (1985). After the founder: An opportunity to manage culture. In P.J. Frost, L.F. Moore, M.R. Louis, C.C. Lundberg, & J. Martin, *Organizational culture* (pp. 125–140). Beverly Hills: Sage.

Simon, H.A. (1945). *Administrative behavior.* New York: Macmillan.

Simons, H., & Califano, J.A., Jr. (Eds.). (1979). *The media and business.* New York: Random House, Vintage Books.

Sklar, R. (1980). *Prime-time America: Life on and behind the television screen.* New York: Oxford University Press.

Smigel, E.O. (Ed.). (1963). *Work and leisure.* New Haven, CT: College and University Press.

Smircich, L. (1983). Concepts of culture and organizational analysis. *Administrative Science Quarterly, 28,* 339–358.

Smircich, L. (1985). Is the concept of culture a paradigm for understanding organizations and ourselves? In P.J. Frost, L.F. Moore, M.R. Louis, C.C. Lundberg, & J. Martin. (pp. 55–72), *Organizational culture.* Beverly Hills: Sage.

Smith, K.K., & Simmons, V.M. (1983). A Rumpelstiltskin organization: Metaphors on metaphors in field research. *Administrative Science Quarterly, 28,* 377–392.

Smith, R.R. (1980). *Beyond the wasteland: The criticism of broadcasting* (Rev. ed.). Urbana, IL: ERIC Clearinghouse on Reading and Communication Skills and SCA.

Smythe, D.W. (1954). Reality as presented by television. *Public Opinion Quarterly, 18,* 143–156.

Starbuck, W.H. (1976). Organizations and their environments. In M.D. Dunnette (Ed.), *Handbook of industrial and organizational psychology* (pp. 1069–1123). Chicago: Rand.

Steele, E.D., & Redding, W.C. (1962). The American value system: Premises for persuasion. *Western Speech, 26,* 83–91.

Stein, B. (1979). *The view from Sunset Boulevard: America as brought to you by the people who make television.* New York: Basic Books.

Stogdill, R. (1974). *Handbook of leadership.* New York: The Free Press.

Strong, E.P. (1965). *The management of business: An introduction.* NY: Harper & Row.

Tavris, C. (1983, March). Edward T. Hall: A social scientist with a gift for solving human problems. *Geo,* 10–16. [interview]

Taylor, F. (1911). *Principles of scientific management.* New York: Harper & Row.

Terkel, S. (1975). *Working.* New York: Avon Books. [Originally published in 1972 by Pantheon Books].

Thayer, L. (1987). Rethinking leadership for public relations. *Public Relations Review, 12,* 3–12.

Theberge, L.J. (Ed.). (1981). *Crooks, conmen and clowns: Businessmen on TV entertainment.* Washington, DC: The Media Institute.

Thompson, V. (1963). *Modern organizations.* New York: Alfred A. Knopf.

Thorburn, D. (1976). Television melodrama. In R. Adler & D. Cater (Eds.), *Television as a cultural force* (pp. 77–94). New York: Praeger (Aspen Institute Program on Communications & Society.)

Timberg, B. (1982). The rhetoric of the camera in television soap opera. In H.M. Newcomb (Ed.), *Television: The critical view* (3rd ed.) (pp. 132–147). New York: Oxford.

Tompkins, P.K. (1977). Management qua communication in rocket research and development. *Communication Monographs, 44,* 1–26.

Tompkins, P.K. (1984). The functions of communication in organizations. In C.C. Arnold & J.W. Bowers (Eds.), *Handbook of Rhetorical and Communication Theory* (pp. 659–719). Newton, MA: Allyn & Bacon.

Tompkins, P.K., & Cheney, G. (1985). Communication and unobtrusive control in contemporary organizations. In R.D. McPhee & P.K. Tompkins (Eds.), *Organizational communication: Traditional themes and new directions* (pp. 179–210). Beverly Hills: Sage.

Trujillo, N. (1983). "Performing" Mintzberg's roles: The nature of managerial communication. In L.L. Putnam & M.E. Pacanowsky (Eds.), *Communication and organizations: An interpretive approach* (pp. 73–97). Beverly Hills, CA: Sage.

Trujillo, N. (1985). Organizational communication as cultural performance: Some managerial considerations. *Southern Speech Communication Journal, 50,* 201–224.

Tuchman, G. (Ed.). (1974). *The TV establishment: Programming for power and profit*. Englewood Cliffs, NJ: Prentice-Hall.

Tuchman, G. (1978). *Making news: A study in the construction of reality*. New York: Free Press.

Tuchman, G. (1983). Consciousness industries and the production of culture. *Journal of Communication, 33*, 330–341.

Turnan, K. (1985, July 6). Cheers' George Went. *TV Guide*, pp. 28–30.

Turner, S. (1977). Complex organizations as savage tribes. *Journal for the Theory of Social Behavior, 7*, 99–125.

Turner, V. (1977). Social dramas and stories about them. *Critical Inquiry, 7*, 141–168.

Turow, J. (1984a). *Media industries: The production of news and entertainment*. New York: Longman.

Turow, J. (1984b). Pressure groups and television entertainment: A framework for analysis. In W.D. Rowland & B. Watkins (Eds.), *Interpreting television: Current research perspectives* (pp. 142–164). Beverly Hills: Sage.

Turow, J. (forthcoming). *Playing doctor: Television, storytelling, and medical power*. NY: Oxford University Press.

Turow, J. & Coe, L. (1985). Curing television's ills: The portrayal of health care. *Journal of Communication, 35*, 36–51.

Tushman, M.L. (1977). A political approach to organizations: A review and rationale. *Academy of Management Review, 2*, 206–216.

Udy, S.H. (1959). *Organizations of work*. New Haven: HRAF Press.

Velasquez, M., Moberg, D.V., & Cavanaugh, G.F. (1983). Organizational statesmanship and dirty politics: Ethical guidelines for the organizational politician. *Organizational Dynamics, 12*, 65–80.

Vidmar, N., & Rokeach, M. (1974). Archie Bunker's bigotry: A study in selective perception and exposure. *Journal of Communication, 24*, 36–47.

Vroom, V., & Yetton, P. (1973). *Leadership and decision making*. Pittsburgh: University of Pittsburgh Press.

Wander, P., and Jenkins, S. (1972). Rhetoric, society, and the critical response. *Quarterly Journal of Speech, 58*, 441–450.

Weaver, D.H., McCombs, M.E., & Spellman, C. (1975). Watergate and the media: A case study of agenda-setting. *American Politics Quarterly, 3*, 458–472.

Weber, M. (1930). *The protestant ethic and the spirit of capitalism*. New York: Charles Scribner's Sons.

Weick, K.E. (1980). The management of eloquence. *Executive, 6*, 18–21.

Weick, K.E. (1979). *The social psychology of organizing*. (2nd ed.) Reading: MA: Addison-Wesley.

Williams, C.T. (1979). It's not so much, "You've come a long way baby" — as "You're gonna make it after all." In H.M. Newcomb (Ed.), *Television: The critical view* (2nd ed.) (pp. 64–73). Beverly Hills: Sage.

Williams, R. (1970). *American society: A sociological interpretation.* (3rd. ed.). New York: Alfred Knopf.

Winston, B. (1983). On counting the wrong things. In V. Mosco & J. Wasko, *The critical communications review: Labor, the working class and the media* (Vol. 1) (pp. 167–188). Norwood, NJ: Ablex.

Wood, P.H. (1976). Television as dream. In R. Adler & D. Cater (Eds.), *Television as a cultural force* (pp. 17–36). NY: Praeger.

Young, L.H. (1982). Views on management. Speech to W. Howell, International Links Club, New York. [Cited in T.J. Peters & R.H. Waterman, *In search of excellence: Lessons from America's best-run companies* (p. 156). New York: Harper & Row.

Appendix A

Sample Weeks of Television

1986 SAMPLE

NBC

The A-Team (3/11)
Blacke's Magic (3/12)
Cheers (3/13)
The Cosby Show (3/13)
Facts of Life (3/15)*
Family Ties (3/13)*
Gimme' a Break (3/15)*
Golden Girls (5/15)*
Highway to Heaven (3/12)
Hill Street Blues (3/13)
Hunter (3/11)
Knight Rider (3/14)

Miami Vice (3/14)
Night Court (3/13)
Punky Brewster (3/16)
Remington Steele (3/15)
Riptide (3/14)
St. Elsewhere (3/12)
Silver Spoons (3/16)
Stingray (3/11)
227 (5/15)*
Valerie (3/17)
You Again (3/17)

CBS

Airwolf (3/22)
Bob Newhart (3/24)*
Cagney and Lacey (3/24)*
Charlie and Company (4/25)
Crazy Like a Fox (4/5)
Dallas (3/22)
The Equalizer (4/22)
Fast Times (3/19)
Foley Square (7/23)*
Kate and Allie (3/24)*

Knot's Landing (4/17)
Magnum, P.I. (4/17)*
Mickey Spillane's Mike Hammer (4/22)*
Mr. Sunshine (7/25)*
Morningstar/Eveningstar (4/22)
Murder She Wrote (4/27)*
Scarecrow and Mrs. King (3/24)*
Simon and Simon (4/17)*
Tough Cookies (3/19)
Trapper John, M.D. (3/18)

---

* Indicates 1986 Rerun

ABC

Benson (3/8)
The Colbys (3/6)
Diff'rent Strokes (3/7)
Dynasty (3/5)
Fall Guy (3/7)
Fortune Dane (3/8)
Growing Pains (3/4)
Hardcastle & McCormick (3/10)*
He's The Mayor (3/7)

Hotel (3/5)
Love Boat (3/8)
MacGyver (3/5)
Mr. Belvedere (3/7)
Moonlighting (3/4)*
Spencer for Hire (3/4)
Webster (3/7)
Who's the Boss? (3/4)

1987 SAMPLE

NBC

The A-Team (6/7)*
Alf (3/16)
Amen (3/14)
Cheers (3/14)*
The Cosby Show (3/12)
Crime Story (3/17)
Days and Nights of Molly Dodd (5/21)
Facts of Life (3/14)*
Family Ties (3/12)
Golden Girls (3/14)

Highway to Heaven (3/11)*
L.A. Law (3/12)*
Matlock (6/2)*
Miami Vice (5/26)
Our House (3/15)
Night Court (6/10)
Rags to Riches (3/15)
St. Elsewhere (5/27)
Valerie (3/16)
227 (3/14)*

CBS

Bob Newhart (4/13)
Cagney and Lacey (6/8)*
Dallas (4/10)
Designing Women (4/13)
The Equalizer (6/10)
Falcon Crest (4/10)
Hard Copy (1/25)
Houston Knights (3/25)
Kate and Allie (6/8)*
Magnum, P.I. (3/25)

My Sister Sam (4/13)
Shellgame (6/17)*
Murder She Wrote (6/7)*
The New Mike Hammer (3/25)
Nothing is Easy (4/10)
The Popcorn Kid (4/10)
Spies (4/7)
Take 5 (4/1)
The Wizard (6/9)*

ABC

The Charmings (3/20)
Dynasty (3/18)
Growing Pains (3/17)
Gung Ho (6/13)
Harry (3/18)
Head of the Class (6/10)*
Hotel (3/18)
Jack and Mike (3/17)

MacGyver (3/23)
Moonlighting (3/17)
Perfect Strangers (3/18)*
Sidekicks (6/13)
Spencer for Hire (6/9)
Starman (3/21)
Webster (3/20)
Who's the Boss? (3/17)

---

* Indicates 1987 Rerun

Author Index

295

Subject Index